The Leavises

Recollections and
Impressions

The Leavises

Recollections and Impressions

Edited by

DENYS THOMPSON

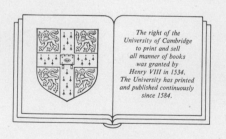

The right of the
University of Cambridge
to print and sell
all manner of books
was granted by
Henry VIII in 1534.
The University has printed
and published continuously
since 1584.

CAMBRIDGE UNIVERSITY PRESS
Cambridge
London   New York   New Rochelle
Melbourne   Sydney

Published by the Press Syndicate of the University of Cambridge
The Pitt Building, Trumpington Street, Cambridge CB2 1RP
32 East 57th Street, New York, NY 10022, USA
10 Stamford Road, Oakleigh, Melbourne 3166, Australia

© Cambridge University Press 1984

First published 1984

Printed in Great Britain by
the University Press, Cambridge

Library of Congress catalogue card number: 83–27289

British Library cataloguing in publication data
The Leavises.
1. Leavis, F. R.   2. Leavis, Q. D.
3. Critics – Great Britain – Biography
I. Thompson, Denys
820′.9   PR29.L4
ISBN 0 521 25494 9

Contents

v

Illustrations

Acknowledgements

I am grateful to Mary Pitter, Christopher Parry, Hilary Steuert, my wife and especially Michael Black for their help, and to the following for the gift or loan of photographs: Chatto and Windus, Nora Crook, Gwendolen Freeman, the Librarian of Girton College, D. W. Harding, the National Portrait Gallery, Mary Pitter and the Editor of the *Times Literary Supplement*. 'Leavis: an appreciation', by John Harvey, was first published in the May 1979 issue of *Encounter*, with whose permission it is now reprinted. Grateful acknowledgement is made also to the Master of Emmanuel College for permission to make use of material in the college archives and to reprint material that had earlier appeared in the College Magazine; to the literary executors, Professor G. Singh and Robin Leavis, for permission to reprint 'Little-boy-man' by F. R. Leavis and to quote from letters by F. R. and Q. D. Leavis; to the Editor of *The Sewanee Review* (Fall 1981), for part of an article 'Remembering Scrutiny' by L. C. Knights; and to Mrs M. T. Parsons and the Editor of *New Universities Quarterly* for 'On being F. R. Leavis's publisher', by the late Ian Parsons. Every effort has been made to secure permission to reproduce copyright material, and the publishers will rectify any omissions of which they are informed.

D.T.

Cambridge
May 1984

I

Introduction

DENYS THOMPSON

The original aim of this book was to record, while it was still possible, recollections and impressions of F. R. Leavis and his wife. However its scope has widened, though not according to a set scheme. The latter would have tried to throw light on all facets of a nearly lifelong partnership, and would have supplied slots for contributors to fill. Thus there would have been some account of Gordon Fraser's start as a publisher, a contribution from the theatre, a view from America – though that omission is perhaps unimportant, for Leavis's impact there was not deep – and a record of the years at York. In the event there has been little overlapping, contributions have dovetailed closely, and the two figures emerge more fully in the round than could at first have been expected. In fact there is assembled here the basic material for a Life. This ought to be undertaken, as a piece of the cultural history of the times. It would not be easy, so much of the story being within the man, but it could not fail to be illuminating.

There are apparent contradictions in any account of their lives, but they can be reconciled by those who knew the protagonist well. Some of the differences are due to varying emphases, selection or point of view. For example the divergent opinions on Leavis as teacher, in different periods. No one could have indefinitely sustained the quality of the teacher so warmly praised by earlier pupils. The elasticity required was in demand elsewhere, for writing, for meeting the three crises of his wife's health, and for coping with the usual family cares. Moreover it must be strongly emphasised that Leavis never had a single one of the sabbatical years that seem regularly to come the way of established academics, alone among teachers.

The main question must be: how was it that the 'once gay, good looking and hopeful' couple of the letter quoted by Professor

Bradbrook became the embittered, resentful and suspicious pair of the later years, with Leavis cast as the ogre of Downing for the gutter press to caricature? The seeds of the attitudes that came to form their public image are there in every human being, and circumstances conspired to germinate them and feed them. So far as Q.D.L. is concerned, total rejection by her family on her marriage to a gentile was an act of cruelty that left a lasting wound. That expulsion she did not forgive, and she did not relent when her parents were killed by a bomb. The poison was never purged. Given the right kind of help and the capacity to accept it, she might have overcome the infliction; as it was, it seems that she did not. That she did not receive the needed help was no fault of Leavis's, unless extreme delicacy and tact are faults. With that seeming failure to come to terms with what had happened may perhaps be linked her subsequent illnesses, cancer and heart trouble. Leavis told me that thrice doctors had taken him aside to warn him that his wife had only hours/days to live; each time she never gave in, but made good recoveries. The inability to concede rarely lapsed; it took her years, if ever, to forgive people for being the occasion of her own offensiveness. This unyieldingness may have been part of the Jewish will and power to survive. Other cultural traits were her warmth and generosity, evinced in her kindness to many and her excellence as a hostess – life-long, as Nora Crook and I can testify – and very strong family feeling.

Another aspect of the will to survive was Q.D.L.'s need for success, conceived in worldly terms. She rejected the traditions and religious sanctions of the Jews, and the gap was filled by certain philosophers and by current anthropology and sociology. It is also easy to recognise as part of her heritage the sense of belonging to a chosen people, hardening into a conviction of her own infallibility, which made it natural for her to go along with Leavis in his refusal ever to compromise. Thus she was intolerant, readily contemptuous of other people and their views, and arrogant. She would for example dismiss with disdain a request for permission to quote from her writing, rejecting as a contemptible popularisation the work for which permission was sought, and referring to her own publication as 'seminal'.

For Leavis the circumstances of his father's death (recorded by John Harvey below) and the traumatic experience of trench warfare were never distanced with the completeness achieved, say, by Robert Graves in *Goodbye to All That*. Like so many who survived physically, including his brother Ralph, Leavis was a war casualty for a long time; the scars remained. After the wonderful start of the Leavises' publishing career and his establishment as an outstanding teacher, things began to go sour. His teaching quality was never in question, as one can infer from the tributes in these pages, but the local university failed to recognise the quality of either of them – it may be that at a comparatively new Downing he was unable to benefit from strong college backing. In his writing he was fortunate in having a well-to-do pupil who started publishing as an under-graduate, and was open to his teacher's suggestions. Gordon Fraser was followed by Ian Parsons, who had joined Chatto and Windus on going down from Cambridge. With rare perception and acumen Parsons not only recognised the quality of Leavis's writing and started a partnership that continued to bear fruit even after their deaths, but also developed his firm as a leading publisher of English literature and criticism. The university however never fully re-paired its omission, unlike the state, which made him a C.H. at the very end of his life. Queenie also failed to win the academic recognition deserved by her sparkling teaching and criticism, which if sometimes wayward was always engaging. Despite some short-comings, *Fiction and the Reading Public* was a genuinely pioneer piece of research, and more than one book has chugged along in its wake.

What seems to have happened to both is that early wounds were never healed – a condition by no means unique, but one which for them weakened the strength of resistance to the infection of suspicion and hostility that poisoned both. That of course is a sim-plification; the bodily analogy should not be pressed too far; and they were both as complex as human beings can be. F.R.L. had the rare kind of intelligence of feeling that far transcends what he him-self called 'cerebral muscle'. Queenie, it must be said, had not.

Leavis's influence, especially in setting an example that led many graduates to teach, was wide and deep, as we can see from Frank

Whitehead's precise and authoritative assessment; his books were successful by any standard; he established *Scrutiny*; and tribute to his teaching and criticism was paid all over the English-speaking world. But sadly none of this gave him any deep satisfaction; the 'enemies' were credited with more importance than they deserved, while the steadfast support of friends and former pupils appeared to count for little. Of course he made enemies, as will anyone who takes a position and defends it. He regarded any concession, any meeting half-way as selling the pass, the affirmation of a basic solidarity. He did not find it possible to criticise a man's views without appearing to attack him personally, and the holding of opinions different from his own seemed somehow to be regarded as a moral lapse. However so presented, he himself was not an arrogant man; rather had he a craftsman's confidence in his own power and achievement, a craftsman who knew what he wanted to do, was assured of its importance, and proud of his skill and attainment. Unlike his wife, he was humble in disclaiming any expertise outside his own field; he would always defer to those who had. This may go some way to explain why (in Frank Whitehead's words) he 'devoted so little of his immense energy to the problems of school education'; he merely got on with what he knew he could do. A certain innate aggressiveness would cause him to over-react; innate too seems to have been the 'guarantee of disappointment' remarked by Professor Knights.

The personal recollections of the early years come first, in roughly chronological order, followed by views of Leavis as editor and author. Thirdly we have records of the later years, and more general impressions. Finally Professor Harding takes both a close look and a perspective one; his must clearly be the last word, so far as this collection is concerned.

2

Queenie at Girton

GWENDOLEN FREEMAN

'With most people at Girton who are called to mind one thinks, "Ah yes. Her great friend was So-and-So." With Queenie I cannot recall ever seeing her in company with anyone. She seemed withdrawn into the world of work.'

'Outside her own field she was extraordinarily naive.'

'I remember her being pointed out as a brilliant research student. She gave the impression of being very remote; of being hooded, with her hair curving over her glasses. Looking neither to right nor left. Always in dark colours.'

Of the three Girton students here recalling Queenie Roth, one came from her own year, one from a year junior to her and one from three years junior when Queenie was already above ordinary college life.

I myself, coming up a year after Queenie, was friendly with her for a good long time, but one picture of her stands out with extreme clarity. We were jolting up the Huntingdon Road to Girton in the college bus, all of us hungry and relaxed after a morning of Cambridge lectures and reading. Near college we passed Queenie erect and alone, strolling along the path. She was not only not hurrying to lunch. She was reading as she walked, her book held high before her eyes, which may have been short-sighted. (I never asked why she wore glasses.) It could not have been easy to read as one walked along that country path, and presumably she had been reading all the two-and-a-half miles from Cambridge.

In the October of 1926 I had joined the bewildering world of 150 students, 50 to each year, all seeming high-spirited and talented, as most of them were. Among them, however, were some solitaries, and Queenie was one. I met her fairly early as she invited me to 'jug' (the traditional evening cocoa party), but a student in my

5

own group, Freda Midgley, had known her previously. Freda remembered her meeting with Queenie in 1925:

'We were both called for interview at Girton to read English, so it was natural we should get together. Without being strongly attracted, I liked her and found her enthusiasm stimulating. I had no idea of her brilliance then, nor did I find her Jewishness later obtrusive.

'Queenie was awarded a scholarship, and I was recommended to try again the following year. This time I was successful, and, before going up, I wrote to Queenie several times for advice, which she gave generously, though about clothes she was not helpful. As a fresher I was soon aware that she was regarded with awe for her ability and for her spartan existence. I never knew anyone less interested in possessions, other than books.'

Freda adds, however, that she 'never knew the mature Queenie. We met in 1925, and, though we kept in touch for a while after her marriage, we had drifted apart by the early 1930s.'

Not such a kindly comment comes from a member of Queenie's own year. She concedes that Queenie at twenty might have been thought handsome, with 'a lovely clear magnolia type of complexion and really lovely soft brown eyes and very pretty wavy dark hair'. But she also recalls that Queenie, when she arrived at Girton, was 'full of the fact that she was top scholar though her parents had "waived the emoluments". And she talked endlessly about it. When we all met as freshers we talked to each other, but soon got sorted out into small groups of special friends, and I doubt if I ever spoke much to Queenie after those first few days. We would say a few words in passing, but I have no recollection at all of ever having a conversation with her.'

This judgement might well be echoed by others of Queenie's contemporaries. The girls taking English in her year were cheerful, friends among themselves and interested in social occasions as well as work. In my letters home I did mention one, Isobel Cumming, who joined with Queenie in inviting me to 'jug' when I first arrived, but on the whole they laughed a little at her.

The Girton to which Queenie came up in 1925 might seem quaint now, but it did provide what one former student calls 'golden days'. The red Victorian building with its tower, which could be seen for miles over the flat countryside, may seem dark and warrenlike today, but to us, when we got used to it, it became a place where we gained status and liberty. We still recall the glimpses of sunny green through corridor windows, the hard-soap smell of 'gyp-wings' where we washed up after tea-parties, the woodland walks with the fritillaries near the back gate, the pleasure of thinking ourselves grown-up and having friends.

The Victorian pioneers were still close to us. As freshers we came up two days early and were given a talk on them by the Mistress, Miss Major. Their portraits, including that of George Eliot, were on the walls. For some reason a bust of Mr Gladstone was at the end of my ground-floor corridor and was most useful as a guide when I got lost in my first days. The names of the pioneers were about too in the scholarships that helped to provide for us. We always remembered that Girton had been England's first residential college for women.

Arrangements were also rather Victorian. Our room-space was lavish; those with scholarships were each given a bedroom and connecting sitting-room. But there were still basins and ewers on wash-stands, and I remember one winter morning when the water was frozen over; so the rooms must have been cold before we lighted our fires. We had individual fires that were cleared out by the gyps cleaning our rooms. At one period I was waked at six every morning by a gyp banging about with fire-irons in the room overhead. Though timid, I was finally so desperate that I crept up to find the source of the clatter and startled the girl kneeling before the grate. That morning when I went into chapel the gyps standing in a line nudged one another, and I felt deeply embarrassed.

One of the pleasures of Girton was that we did not have to do housework. Country girls did the work, but, except for Portress at the door, who was popular, we did not pay much attention to the domestic staff. I did, however, write home that the gyps were polite and friendly, and the students gave them a Christmas party. Towards the end of my stay I grew friendly with two of them, and they became real people to me. Queenie probably was unaware that they were there.

I think that some students showed their superiority by grumbling about the food, but to me it always seemed good. Girton students' appetites were said to be legendary, and the joke was passed round – perhaps it is still current – of the porter who said, 'They heats and heats with hintervals for meals.' We brought up food from home and had supplies of tea, coffee and cocoa in our cupboards, and when we were giving parties bought 'deadlies' in Cambridge – rich little chocolate cakes costing the astonishing price of four old pennies each. Queenie, as far as I know, did not discuss food nor give many 'jugs'.

When we came up – you had to remember to say 'up' and not 'down' – you learnt the Cambridge vocabulary and at first were terrified of not conforming. You were a 'fresher' and were entertained at evening 'jugs' by older students and had to entertain them back. Your own group of friends, which you kept with variations through the three years, eating with them, sitting with them at lectures, was known sentimentally as a 'family'. Evening dinner was 'hall', and you had to learn about getting 'exeats'. You did not ask other students, 'What is your subject?' but said, 'What shop are you?' If you made a noise in the corridor at night you could be 'jumped'. The aggrieved student emerged to protest, and you had to go and apologise the next day.

One Victorian practice which I think was dropped in the late 1920s was the fire-drill. Girton had been too far out for the Cambridge fire brigade to serve it. So the students had their own brigade, who rushed along the corridors, seized curled-up hoses stacked in corners, ran along unwinding them without twisting and coupled them with others brought along by other groups. It was a useless exercise and got members of the brigade out of bed early in the morning. Queenie did not belong to the brigade when I was there, but there was a general alarm once a year which brought all students out from their rooms.

There was a short service in the chapel before breakfast each morning, with an organ student to play. Students tended to go to chapel in their first weeks and then either lose their faith or become indifferent or lazy. In any case this would not have affected Queenie as a practising Jew. She would also have been unaffected by the various Christian movements, whose leaders arranged study-groups of four or five in their rooms, where you might discuss aspects of the Bible, sin or immortality.

Elegant students who wore fur coats, had been to Paris and had many men friends in Cambridge grumbled about the chaperon rules by which you had to take a girl friend with you when you visited a man's rooms and men had to be out of Girton before hall at night. You had to ask for an exeat if you wanted to be out in the evening, and there was a certain amount of climbing-in at ground-floor windows by students who had forgotten to ask or were returning in the small hours. But for most of us, who had come up straight from school, the rules were no burden, and it was pleasant to signify your friendship by asking somebody to come with you to a man's rooms or similarly to be asked by a friend.

Some people were sorry for us because we were two-and-a-half miles out of Cambridge, on a distant site chosen for etiquette's sake in the early 1870s. We had to have bicycles, and there was a crowded cycle-shed off the main college entrance. Very few students had cars, and a white rose used to bloom in the courtyard, now a car-park, behind the tower. But none of us, as far as I know, objected to being where we were, and the open country made it possible for the college to have acres of beautiful grounds. On Violet Sunday, near the end of the Lent term, you were allowed to pick large violets by the woodland paths and pack the flowers in boxes and send them home. Honeysuckle Walk, with its ramparts of bloom coming out just before we went home in June, was noted among us, and at all seasons you could escape from the throng in the winding walks among the trees. Outside, the Huntingdon Road, bordered with fields much of the way from Cambridge, led to an unknown flat countryside which most of us liked. On autumn days we used to pick 'autumn leaves' for our rooms.

Queenie was probably too busy with her books ever to look much at the grounds. Nor do I think she took part in those comfortable Sunday-evening stocking-darning sessions in friends' rooms when we had no social engagements in Cambridge, nor in those interminable discussions between two or three friends – on literature, religion, love – which might go on into the small hours, even

9

occasionally till the sky paled in the north-east and we were almost too tired to go to bed.

We had hard and grass tennis-courts, and Queenie must have played, for a small photograph remains of her in a short white dress, very much of the period, sitting with a racquet beside her. But as far as I know she never joined the hockey, lacrosse or net-ball teams that were led by third-year enthusiasts.

Her lack of close friends did not necessarily stem from her Jewishness, though this may have made some barrier. There were several Jewish girls at Girton, including the top scholar in English in the year senior to her. Grace Cohen was also solitary, but others fitted in. Queenie herself, however, was aware of her superiority. She once said to me that Jews' minds worked much faster than other people's and that when she entered a room she knew immediately who was Jewish by the speed of the reactions. I accepted this. I had known clever Jewish girls at school.

At that period the English Tripos, as ever, was under discussion. Outsiders referred to it scornfully as 'the novel-reading Tripos', and something had to be put in to stiffen it. Up to then it had been Anglo-Saxon, and the English school at Oxford also included Anglo-Saxon. But while Oxford was ending its syllabus with the Victorians, Cambridge considered itself far superior because it studied T. S. Eliot and other moderns. It also considered that a love of literature did not necessarily coincide with an ability to read Anglo-Saxon. So the literature students were allowed in their third year to change to history or French. Queenie however, adhered to the hard Anglo-Saxon and got the high mark of a II.1 in the difficult examination. This choice may also have helped a little to cut her off from her contemporaries.

But before I got to know Queenie well we were introduced to Dr Leavis. Miss Hilda Murray, our white-haired, icy but good-hearted tutor, announced that we were to meet him for weekly essay-coaching in the annexe, a wooden hut that remained from the First World War. She thought that we should find him in-teresting, and she seemed to admire him as somebody of special talent. Actually we did find those late-afternoon coachings of our group of nine a pleasure.

Leavis used to cycle out to Girton and arrive exhausted, shirt open at the neck. Stories went round of how he had been a stretcher-bearer in the war and had been gassed. He roused our pity, and I am told that I wrote home saying he was like a fawn. He had the attractive habit of not sounding his R's, and would say, 'I wesent it vewwy stwongly', thought I don't remember what he resented. His general attitude was melancholy.

The junior student who remembers Queenie with a 'hooded look' also remembers gossip about Leavis. In her year he was said to be 'a funny little man with a rucksack who was always saying, "I am so fatigued." But after he got engaged to Queenie he said, "I shall never be fatigued again."'

One of my group at the coachings says that he, like Queenie herself, 'seemed much milder in the 1920s than afterwards'. She recalls a kinder judgement on Tennyson than he showed later. 'Tennyson was at a low ebb in our schools in those days, and, when Leavis said one afternoon that we should discuss him next week, Elizabeth burst out, "Oh Tennyson!", at which Leavis turned away a little as was his custom when he did not agree with the speaker and said, "There are good things in Tennyson."'

But Leavis did then and at his university lectures do us, I think, one disservice. In our schools, at the time of the successful ending of the women's suffrage movement, we were told that we, as women of the future, could do great deeds in the world. Now Leavis told us that the world was a sink of vulgarity. Literacy on a national scale had made the mob our dictators in taste. The Harmsworths were selling *Titbits* and *The Daily Mirror* by the million. Good writers were being swamped. Outside Cambridge stretched a desert of non-culture. The ideal time was apparently the eighteenth century, before the Industrial Revolution, when there was an aristocracy of good taste and the rest of the nation lived happily on the land, unable to read but following worthwhile handicrafts. Later, when I came across many broadsheets and pamphlets of the period, and found them far more vulgar and sensational than anything Lord Northcliffe had perpetrated, I wondered if Leavis had ever studied the period closely.

But now the corruption of taste was his theme, and there was T. S. Eliot lamenting away in *The Waste Land*. We accepted their theories that the world was corrupted and agreed that Cambridge was the only home of culture. We did not suspect that Leavis's complaints, like Eliot's, might be partly due to personal dissatisfactions. This made the prospect of our later exodus into the world a shadowy nightmare.

But years at Cambridge still stretched ahead. We learned to use the favourite word 'awareness' a great deal, though I never quite fathomed its difference from 'consciousness' which we had used before. And in our spare time we wrote verse in imitation of Eliot – which was very easy as has been proved since.

Having a scholarship, I was the representative of the Girton English students of my year and, as Queenie represented her year, we met officially now and then. One curious and flat incident occurred in my first year. Girton had a struggling English society, and Grace Cohen, as representative of her year, had the idea that we might ask E. M. Forster to speak to it. He was one of the favourites of the time with his *Passage to India*, and he was in residence at King's.

What previous arrangements Grace had made I do not know. I was only told to accompany her and Queenie to King's. Queenie and I met Grace at the gate, and we were ushered into Forster's room. We sat in a row against the wall, and he sat facing us in the middle of the room. Grace put her request that he would speak at Girton. In a soft but determined voice he said he would not. He gave no reason. Grace and Queenie tried persuasion, but it was no good. He was adamant and I think rather rude. In a short while we sheepishly filed out. At the gate of King's Grace left us, and Queenie and I returned to Girton. She was angry, saying that the idea had been entirely Grace's and Grace had made a mess of it. I was a little flattered to have one grand Girton student complaining to me about another.

A letter I wrote home in my last Michaelmas term mentioned, all too briefly, a contact between Queenie and another literary figure. I had been summoned to coffee with Miss Major, the Mistress of Girton. That evening Virginia Woolf was visiting Girton to talk to one of the societies, and Queenie came to fetch me. One of my friends told her that I was with Miss Major, and Queenie went away.

'So I didn't', I wrote, 'see Virginia after all, and apparently she read a marvellous paper and is going to print it and dedicate it to the society . . . She was very impressed with Queenie and is going to send her a pamphlet of some kind.' The talk became *A Room of One's Own*.

Slowly our acquaintance with Queenie grew. My friends criticised her for lack of dress sense, and I, echoing group gossip though I had no dress sense either, wrote home, so my sister remembers, that she regularly showed her underclothing. Two of my acquaintances concerned themselves with her clothes. One, when she heard that Queenie was going shopping in Cambridge, offered to accompany her, but was 'turned down sharply'. She appeared to believe that 'I might lead her into extravagance.'

On the other hand Queenie did ask Freda Midgley, the student who had met her in 1925, to help her to buy a new dress. 'This desire', Freda writes,

was most unusual, for clothes were merely necessary coverings for her. We went into Cambridge, and I found one of those little black dresses that were fashionable at the time. When she learnt the price Queenie was appalled and declared she could not possibly spend three guineas on herself when there were millions of starving people in the world. In vain I pointed out that it would be a good investment as it would last for years. Finally I said with truth that the dress suited her, and she capitulated.

Freda thought this may have been because of her growing feeling for Leavis.

Freda cannot remember any other remarks made by Queenie in those times of intimacy. I remember only a few. She could gossip amusingly about our lecturers, and once burst out that Shakespeare was utterly mistaken in making Othello kill Desdemona. (She was in love with Leavis at the time.) Othello, she said could not possibly have murdered a wife he loved so soon after marriage. His passion would have been too strong; she would have been essential to him.

In an early letter home I wrote that I had been to jug with Queenie and another second-year student, and they had joked about I. A. Richards and Mansfield Forbes, an eccentric lecturer.

Richards believes in studying poetry intensively, and will spend a whole term's lectures on two lines. Last year he started a wonderful experiment. He believed that the way in which different people read poetry would give it quite a different interpretation. So he and Forbes, his friend, worked together.

Richards entered the room accompanied by stamps from undergrads, and read loudly and solemnly but quite ordinarily some poem or other. Meanwhile Forbes stayed outside the door so that he shouldn't be influenced by Richard's interpretation. When Richards had done Forbes marched in accompanied by more stamps from the undergrads. He stood up on the platform and read the same poem in exactly the same ordinary voice. There were more stamps and then Richards got up and said, 'Oh Mr Forbes I never thought of that interpretation before. How wonderful it is', and the experiment ended in perfectly tumultuous stamping.

We heard Forbes was going to lecture the next day, and, though we weren't supposed to go . . . we determined to see him. Miss Roth, the girl who was talking, said he looked like a mooncalf or an archangel, and he certainly did.

Later, when she had become a research student, she told me that she had got past reading novels. She had read all that were worth reading and she did not want fiction any more. The only novelist she could possibly bear was Henry James. I think I did feel a little amused at this.

Gradually we became aware that Queenie had strong feelings for Leavis. The friend who remembers Leavis defending Tennyson also recalls a meeting with Queenie in the Girton waiting-room in Cambridge. Leavis had just published some article or review, and Queenie, turning over the pages 'with girlish excitement', said 'in a confidential happy tone, "He's writing again."'

She came closest to us in her third year because she wanted to talk about Leavis. She was in love with him but he, though he kept meeting her, gave no sign. Time was growing short as she would be leaving Cambridge in the June after she had taken her final examination. She waited, and grew desperate, and used us as confidantes.

She frequently talked about this to me, but she told me not to say a word of it to anybody else. Her health may have been affected, for one day she was very sick and I found her prostrate when I went to her room. I cleared up while she lay wanly on the bed, and she was grateful and friendly. As she had ordered, I said nothing about her secret.

But later a look or a stifled remark among my friends led to a discovery. Queenie had confided in a number of other people too and had bound them all to secrecy. One of my friends had been to a co-educational school and had men friends from the school in Cambridge. Queenie asked for advice on how to deal with men, as Lily had had more experience than she had.

In the May term of 1928 her misery was at its height. Thinking back now, I can appreciate her self-control in working for her examinations. In spite of emotional strain she got a first-class degree with special credit.

I learnt recently an odd little story of the influence of this on the future teaching of classics. The younger student who remembered Leavis as 'a funny little man' also heard a story that Queenie had 'almost no memory'. It was said that before each paper she sat up all night learning quotations, and remembered them long enough to use them the next day. 'I have told generations of students', Edith says, 'of Queenie's determination. When they complain that Latin or Greek is hard I point out how she went on to success through her will to work.' Queenie never knew that she was being held up as an example to classics classes.

Towards the end of the May term we saw less of her and her manner changed. She became brisker; looked more cheerful; was more self-absorbed and out more. Then she told me that all was well. She and 'the doctor' had talked things over during a trip on the river, and now they were engaged. Leavis was frantically chasing round to collect scholarships for her so that she could stay on at Cambridge and become a research student. Miss Murray was helping.

Now she did not want us any more. She was complacent; an incipient great lady. I was sorry that she had changed, but she was only a tiny part of our crowded lives and we did not intrude on her.

But I must have remained friendly with her, for at the end of my own time at Cambridge, when the future was casting its shadow, I asked her how I could keep my intelligence in Leavis's world of vulgarity. I did not realise, as other people seem to have done, that her knowledge outside the world of Cambridge was slight. I had the feeling that she knew everything. Her only suggestion, as far as I can remember, was that I should diligently read the three literary weeklies of the time – *The New Statesman*, *The Spectator* and *Time and Tide*. But she did invite me to call on her after her marriage if I were ever in Cambridge.

So some months later I did call, and it was a disastrous visit. Queenie seemed a stranger, and she treated me as one. There were other people there, and they made Cambridge jokes that I did not understand. Queenie showed off the arrangements of her drawing-room and made much of 'the doctor's' books. She alluded to Leavis always as 'the doctor'.

The Leavises had been on a cycling-tour and had passed through Oxford. They both mocked at the abominable long lines of red-brick suburbs in 'the other place'. The visitors laughed and agreed with their scorn of Oxford.

I think it was then that Queenie described how she had mortally offended the ladies of Cambridge drawing-rooms. She had declared that Frances Cornford, 'one of the great Darwin clan', and noted for her simple jingle about the 'fat white woman whom nobody loves', was 'no poet'. The dowagers had been aghast.

Slowly it was borne in on me that the university had a social side of which I knew nothing and that Cambridge might not be the Eden that it had seemed in my student days.

I left soon, deeply disconcerted. I never saw Queenie again.

6, Chesterton Hall Crescent, and the early years

MARY PITTER

My earliest memories of F.R.L. go back to when I was three or four years old. My grandfather had designed and built the house in Chesterton Hall Crescent, which was then among fields outside the town; and after his death as the result of a motorcycle accident, my grandmother continued to live there with F.R.L. and her other son, Ralph, and her daughter Ruth (my mother) until her marriage in 1919. My grandmother died in 1929, and in that same year F.R.L. became engaged to one of his students, Queenie Roth, and came to stay at my parents' house in Sussex. I was then eight years old and I remember vividly my first impressions of Queenie ('Auntie Queenie' as she came to be called by myself and my sisters.) She was extremely vivacious and attractive, and so enthusiastic and happy. I was fascinated by her and clearly remember thinking she was the most wonderful person I had ever seen.

After their marriage they lived first of all in a small house in a road not far from Chesterton Hall Crescent, which they called 'The Criticastery'. Later they moved to 6, Chesterton Hall Crescent (now demolished for new housing) because the house had been empty since my grandmother's death and remained unsold. In her time the kitchen and outbuildings – a large glazed roof lean-to where the washing was done and everything was stored – was very old-fashioned and inconvenient, and though I always thought the house had charm and character, the disposition of the rooms was not planned for easy running. On both the ground floor and the first floor there were long corridors from one end of the house to the other, and the amount of walking entailed was a great source of complaint from Queenie. I remember being young enough to be able to sit underneath the dining-room table and play with my grandmother's black cat while the grown-ups were having a meal, and I could see F.R.L.'s dog, Quip, lying on his rug. He was very old, smelt quite strong, and he finally had to go when Queenie took over the house. He was, by then, as she rightly observed, too unhygienic to tolerate. In his heyday apparently he had been an animal of remarkable character, and my uncle was fond of reminiscing about his intelligence and sense of humour, and how he had a fondness for ripe gooseberries and would nip them off the bush neatly with his teeth. I think he would have liked another dog but Queenie did not share this affection for animals, nor, as far as I can recall, did she share my uncle's interest in the natural world. She often accused the Leavises of lavishing more affection on animals than on human beings. So far as my mother was concerned I am afraid she was right, but F.R.L. had a genuine and deep appreciation for all natural things, plant and animal, though I never knew him to be sentimental about it. There is evidence that he had this feeling for nature from an early age. In my possession I have two copies of a magazine he produced as a boy for family consumption, which he called 'The Home made Magazine' and charged a penny-halfpenny for each copy. The copies I own were my mother's and are dated October 1907 and May 1908. In both he writes at length on a nature section. In the May number it is headed 'The garden month by month', in which there is a well-observed description of frogs waking up from their winter's sleep, and he goes on to describe what frog-spawn looks like and how it develops into tadpoles. At the time he was writing this there was a large pond in the garden, subsequently filled in, and his whole article has the ring of truth about it that comes from a first-hand observation and not facts copied from a natural-history book. The nature article in the second magazine is headed 'Nature's Page' and again it is a lively description of the life of a stickleback; it seems very probable that this was also a first-hand observation from his visits to the river bank, a mere ten minutes' walk from Chesterton Hall Crescent.

A small bibliographical note: the magazines state that they are printed and published at the Home-Made Offices, Mill Road.

Slipped into the description of his brother's and sister's gardens is some information about the workmen having finished the tiling, and that 'the joists have been laid and many windows have already been put in'. This suggests that they were already beginning to cultivate the garden while the house was being built. It is possible that it was during this period that my grandfather began to plant his orchard, which thirty years later provided the house and garden with complete seclusion and privacy from surrounding properties. I have no other record saying when F.R.L.'s parents moved to their new house, but from the evidence of the magazines it must have been some time before the end of 1907.

Queenie found the house intolerably old-fashioned and inconvenient and she soon got to work to change everything. Many items I remembered as a small child before she came to live there disappeared – the case of butterflies which hung on the wall in the downstairs passage, a quantity of Victorian bric-a-brac, including a statuette of a knight in armour on a table by the front door, and prints of birds and animals, all of which delighted me as a child in my grandmother's time. There had been in those days a fascinating summerhouse beyond the lawn, which had coloured glass, red, blue and green, in the window, and many treasures lying around inside, such as boxes of assorted sea-shells, boxes of birds' eggs, and various other natural-history collections which provided a happy hunting-ground for myself and my two sisters. I wonder whether these had been F.R.L.'s collection? Sadly, the summerhouse disappeared, as also did the pond, which used to be situated amongst a wilderness of trees and bushes.

As far as we were concerned in those early days, F.R.L. was a fairly shadowy figure. I remember him chiefly for giving us interesting books on our birthdays. Even up to the year of his death he remembered to send my mother a card for her birthday, although by that time they had not seen one another for some years.

It was after Queenie and F.R.L. were married and came to live at 6, Chesterton Hall Crescent that they became an influence which has remained all my life. In those days, before they had any family, my two sisters and I were frequent visitors and we spent some of the happiest days of our childhood with them. Queenie was wonderfully imaginative about entertaining children. She knew how to please us and stimulate our interest and spared more time for us than anybody else had in the family. Looking back now it seems incredible that she managed to entertain us so well, when at the same time she was extending hospitality to F.R.L.'s students and colleagues and doing all his typing for him as well. By this time the house had been modernised and improved, and all traces of the Victorian atmosphere I remembered in my earliest years had totally disappeared. The Victorian prints on the walls, including a sentimental picture of two cats which I loved to look at before going to sleep, and all the old wash-hand stands with their basins and ewers had gone. In place of the prints hung large reproductions of Gauguin and Van Gogh's two views of the Bridge at Arles, and the dark curtains had been replaced by lighter, more cheerful material. Gone too were the depressing maroon-coloured walls in the dining-room and down the corridor, and the rambling glazed out-house beyond the kitchen had given way to a proper brick-built scullery and larder. A modern sink replaced the old brown earthenware one, and a new, more efficient boiler was fitted. Nothing had been improved or touched for years; no wonder Queenie was so depressed by the house when she moved in, and took immediate steps to remedy matters. She had a remarkable talent for interior decoration and had a very good eye for colour and design. She took great pride in matching materials to make an agreeable colour-scheme in a room, and much care to make her surroundings tasteful and pleasant to live in. I remember her taking me to the room F.R.L. had in Downing College to show me how she had improved the appearance of the furnishings by careful choice of chair-covers and curtain materials. She even took pains to find a teapot and cups and saucers with the right colour to go with the room.

The garden remained much the same, minus the pond and summerhouse. The orchard my grandfather planted had grown to maturity and provided almost complete privacy, an amenity which F.R.L. prized as much as anything else. Whenever the weather was fit, they would both spend much time out of doors. My uncle's gardening was mostly confined to pruning the fruit trees and scything the lawn, though he did plant a few vegetables. Queenie's interest in the garden was wholly in the crops of fruit and vegetables produced, the surplus of which she bottled for winter use or made into jams and pickles. She was too occupied with other pursuits to have any time to be interested in gardening, and F.R.L. used to remark, when she asked for something out of the garden which was not in season, that she had no idea of the growing-seasons for plants or any appreciation of plant cultivation. Not that F.R.L. wanted to take any special interest in it, as he once said to a friend prescribing a more intense concentration on growing plants as a therapeutic exercise 'I have better things to do, Youngman, better things to do.' His chief interest in the garden was that it provided a peaceful and private environment in the open air. There was a balcony on the first floor at the top of the stairs where he could sit and work undisturbed facing the sun and overlooking greengage and apple trees. I have many times been playing in the orchard below and looked up to see him writing, half hidden by leafy branches. He taught me my first lesson in appreciating beauty of form. I had spent my pocket money on a packet of nasturtium seeds which depicted both double and single flowers on the front. He pointed to the double flower and remarked, 'A beautiful natural form spoiled,' and I saw at once what he meant. There was hardly a visit when he did not extend and educate my first steps in discernment and appreciation. The lessons learnt were given and received in a completely natural way, because this was all part of how he lived and what he believed.

Although my parents were musical, especially my father, looking back on my childhood I think it was F.R.L. who taught me to listen with a critical ear. He listened a great deal to records. A great favourite of his was an oboe concerto by Mozart, and I would hear him whistle airs from it all over the house. Queenie's taste in music was a little different. She was fonder of opera I believe than anything else, but she was also interested in folk songs and introduced us to Cecil Sharp's collection. She gave us copies of this as birthday presents and we continued to sing and play the songs at home. She would also sing them while doing various household tasks and I learnt many tunes by heart from her, and continued the tradition later with my own children. F.R.L. would sing too on occasions, and I particularly remember the opening lines of a wassailing song, which he sang in a gentle, melodious voice: 'My master will send us a good piece of beef, and a good piece of beef that we all may enjoy.' As I remember him singing this at the table before dinner I suppose he was about to carve a joint of beef! There was so much optimism and happiness then; I appreciated later when I was no longer a child that at the same time they were struggling to make a living, but they seemed not to be unduly burdened by it. They were happy with each other and fully occupied in their collaboration over academic work. I have so many happy memories of that period which cannot all be described here. I could go on to describe the many cycle-rides we had (they hired bicycles for us when we came to stay) and the many excursions on the river to Grantchester, the many picnics on the Gog Magog Hills, and the wonderful expeditions with Queenie to a toy shop which used to be on Peas Hill, and the visits to the Fitzwilliam Museum with both of them and walks in the Botanic Garden. Then there were the times when we were taken out to tea to friends' and colleagues' houses. Once we were taken to have tea with Miss Fanny Johnson and her sister, Alice. (They were sisters of W. E. Johnson, the celebrated logician who had supervised all the Cambridge philosophers from Russell onwards. The tea-party I describe was held in their home, Ramsay Lodge, Barton Road. The Johnsons were often at home to lecturers for the Moral Sciences Tripos, distinguished old pupils, and visiting philosophers, who after 1929 would have included Wittgenstein.) We sat in their large and elegant drawing-room, which had literally been built round their enormous concert grand piano, there being no other way of getting it in, and ate minute genteel sandwiches. I sat with my sisters as quiet as a mouse, while F.R.L. held the centre of attention conversing with Miss Fanny, a great admirer of his. My youngest sister, Sasha, was four years old and Queenie confessed years later that she had been terrified in case we broke the delicate and fragile tea-cups, which Miss Fanny told her were eighteenth-century and very valuable.

In 1935 their eldest son, Ralph, was born. My sisters and I were becoming too occupied with school to come to Cambridge very often and as time went on I was often the only one of us who went to stay. The relationship between my parents and the Leavises became more strained from this time on, and I was becoming painfully aware of divided loyalties which were to haunt me for the rest of the lives of all four of them. My father became very embittered and accused me of disloyalty for choosing so often to spend my holidays in Cambridge and not at home. Looking back, I can see how their different temperaments and life-styles clashed.

I was very fond of my parents and looked up to them, but they could not come up to the more ascetic, self-disciplined life of the Leavises and their scrupulous high code of conduct, which I took for a pattern throughout my childhood and early adolescence. It was only after growing older that I began to think that some of my uncle's condemnation of people living more indulgently than himself might perhaps be a little too ruthless. For many years he never had any alcohol in the house nor any luxuries at all. Though this was no doubt as much for economic reasons as for moral ones, it was very much part of their way of life not to indulge themselves. F.R.L. once described himself as a 'Puritan without religion', and to have been only this seems very unattractive, but of course he was not. He thought and acted from his heart as much as from his head. Perhaps one cause for the estrangement which too often occurred between him and other members of the family were blunders committed by well-intentioned people, when a little wisdom and greater understanding could have prevented much bitterness and hurt feelings.

I remember my father sending them a bottle of Cointreau as a special treat, knowing that in their early married life they were struggling financially and endeavouring to produce *Scrutiny* on a very slim budget. He innocently thought a luxury gift would have been gratefully received, but all he got as acknowledgement was a letter from F.R.L. not only not thanking him for the present but saying tersely 'Don't ever do such a thing again.' It was hurtful and unnecessary and helped to compound the bitterness my father felt. This kind of thing happened more than once, and though with greater fore-thought my father should have known better than to have sent the Leavises such a gift, it was after all only an error of judgement, and sent with good intentions, and should have been seen as such.

My father was not properly appreciated by either Queenie or F.R.L. until many years after his death, when they had both mellowed in their attitude towards him. The incident such as the mistake over the Cointreau may have been a minor one, but there were more serious misjudgements made, which caused such remorse in my uncle's mind that I believe it poisoned his later years to a greater extent than the acrimonious attitude he met with from Cambridge academics, or, as he could utter with venom, 'The Establishment'. This is not generally known, because it involves the private side of his family life, but he did on many occasions unburden himself to me. Queenie's animosity towards her Leavis in-laws was a constant nagging which F.R.L. endeavoured to placate, though his nervous disposition suffered in consequence. It must be understood, however, that she had good reason to feel exasperated and bitter. By marrying outside her Jewish tradition she had isolated herself from her family, and had hoped, and expected, to be fully integrated into her husband's family. Her eager demonstrative nature found no similar response. Though they had not meant to convey this, my relations' undemonstrative attitude was interpreted by her as unfeeling and cold. This lack of feeling, coupled with their ineptitude in so many areas where she herself excelled, made her impatient and bitter with them. Through her marriage she had hoped to have found a sister in my mother with whom she could share feminine interests in her new family. Being Jewish, this need to belong to and share a family, was very important to her, and the consequent disappointment of my mother's inability to respond was a deep blow from which she never wholly recovered. It exacerbated those traits of his Leavis upbringing she saw in F.R.L. which made her feel he had been brought up to be indifferent to sharing the domestic burden of bringing up a family, which she might not otherwise have felt had she been more supported domestically by her in-laws. She was academically important in her own right, and it must have seemed very unfair that she should have borne the brunt of running the home while at the same time having to cope with her academic and professional life. It is scarcely surprising that she needed to let off steam by railing against F.R.L.'s family, who never lifted a finger to help her.

Because I had little to do with his academic life my knowledge of my uncle is essentially domestic, and it would be impossible to talk about F.R.L. in isolation from Queenie. It seems fairly clear that Queenie's lack of extended family relations, where she could have exercised her particular matriarchal propensities, was largely responsible for the tensions she built up round her. No one in my own family could match her practical common sense, her incredible industry and ingenuity and her continual generosity to her nieces, and friends, and even to the next generation of those nieces and friends. But they could not live up to her extraordinary energy and could not reciprocate as she would have liked, and she felt this to be ungenerous and unfeeling. This lifelong experience of feeling thwarted and unsupported by my family inevitably affected F.R.L. as well, and this, added to their constant battle with academic philistinism, caused great tension, and though their wills were indomitable their nervous energy was constantly drained. His letters to me show to what extent he worried about family relationships and his sense of helplessness in the face of circumstances. There is such poignancy and such intense remorse, such testimony to a restless conscience underneath, that they make his letters deeply moving. In 1972, for example, his brother Ralph (whom I nursed at my home in Ludlow till his death in 1973) was seriously ill, and I wrote to F.R.L. to tell him. He replied in a letter of March 12: 'There is so little I can do – could ever do. If only he can be made to feel I *care*, and have always cared, that will give him some relief.' And later in the same month, again referring to his brother: 'I feel guilty in a complex way, but I cannot tell myself just how I ought to have acted instead. Life sets us insoluble problems, but we have always the responsibility to save and foster what we can.' It is tragic that he is known so much for being unbending in his judgements and so destructive and hurtful but that he is not known enough for the very real warmth and sympathy which was an essential part of his personality.

During the war I contrived to visit Cambridge as often as I could, and Queenie's and F.R.L.'s generosity and concern for my welfare in a time when it was difficult enough for everyone was touching and much appreciated. I once cycled over from Bury St

Edmunds to spend a weekend with them, still suffering a little from the shock of working on a forestry camp with some rough and noisy Lancashire mill girls. I was greatly strengthened and helped by F.R.L. and given much useful advice on how to deal with a new and a rather frightening situation. With two young children they had plenty to worry about over possible air raids and the difficulties of food-rationing, though later on during the war they received food-parcels from America, sent by grateful students concerned for their welfare.

During my wartime visits we contrived to cycle out into the country for relaxation whenever possible. The roads were safer for cycling in those days, and Ralph on his small bicycle accompanied the rest of the family, and Kate sat on a seat on her father's bicycle. F.R.L. was very fond of the country round Cambridge and knew a great deal about its geography and history. He gave me fascinating descriptions of East Anglian villages he had known as a boy, and how he used to go skating in the winter on the flooded fens between Cambridge and Ely with his family. His father was renowned for being an accomplished skater. The family were also taken out on regular outings in a pony and trap. F.R.L. derived enormous pleasure from walking or riding in the country, and many of my remembered pleasures are of being out with him and his family and sharing his appreciation of all that was to be seen and enjoyed along the way.

Apart from the anxieties about the war, another worry was looming up when Queenie discovered she had cancer of the breast. She said nothing about it for some time, as her youngest child was hardly walking yet and she felt no one could take her place at that particular time. After she had the operation, complications set in, when she was receiving radium treatment, and a burn on the sternum refused to heal. There followed on this a long protracted period when she had to have further operations and skin grafts in the burns unit of Norwich hospital. F.R.L. visited her constantly, though the strain of the journey to and from Cambridge was long-drawn-out and exhausting. It was many months before Queenie had fully recovered, and it was only her indomitable courage and tenacious will which pulled her through this painful experience.

It was now that she needed F.R.L.'s assistance with some of the work in the house, and it was his particular contribution to do the washing-up, though not always with a good grace. When I was staying there I offered to take over this particular job but he never allowed me. 'It is my job', he would say grimly, putting on an apron, and proceed to wash up in tight-lipped silence. Sometimes domestic tensions would bring him to breaking-point, and he would jump up in a rage, and rush out, slamming the door behind him. I once heard him rage out of the front door, and say, as he accidentally kicked over half a dozen milk-bottles, scattering them in all directions, 'Damn! damn! damn!', not loudly, but with venom. Then, a moment or two later, he suddenly burst into laughter at the absurdity of the situation. He had only two expletives to the best of my knowledge, and they were 'blast' and 'damn'. He could give both words a more explosive punch than anyone else I know, and his repetition of 'Damn him! damn him!' about somebody he was angry with had to be heard to get the full force of a word now rarely used with the power of an uttered curse. Not only heard either; his flashing eyes and clenched fist lent an incredible force to his malediction. He had a very mobile face, which registered dramatically the mood he was in. I have seen him silent and smouldering with anger, and I have seen him utterly charming. One did not readily forget the warm handshake, and winning smile of welcome on entering his house, and to me he always extended kindness and a sense of truly belonging to the family. He had his small vanities of course. It used to be a joke in my family that F.R.L. and his brother, Ralph, took a special pride in certain physical attributes. Ralph used to boast of his unusually small feet and F.R.L. of his broad shoulders and narrow hips. He was very athletic and could leap over a five-barred gate well into middle age. Queenie used to tease him about boasting of his fine physique and he would mildly defend himself on the grounds that 'all men must be allowed their small vanities'. His physical actions when necessary could be remarkably quick. I remember once, on a walk with him and his family, his small daughter, Kate, aged about three, suddenly darted out into the road in front of an on-coming car. Before we had time to take it all in, F.R.L. had leapt after her, seized her in his arms, and dashed safely to the further side, all in a matter of seconds. The incident left us momentarily speechless. Such presence of mind has left an indelible memory on me to this day. My own reactions, mental and physical, were always slower than either F.R.L. or Queenie, who were so quick – especially Queenie. Until he grew older and more frail, my memories of my uncle are that he was always extremely energetic and thoroughly enjoyed physical activity. I have seen him scythe the grass at Chesterton Hall Crescent utterly absorbed in the bodily rhythm of swinging the scythe, sweeping it level and low in a semi-circular progress in front of him, his shirt open at the neck almost to the waist, revealing a deeply bronzed chest. As a child I was fascinated to stand and watch him admiringly, and quite rightly, as I discovered later during the war, having watched countrymen scything, that he was as professional at using a scythe as any of them.

My whole life has been nourished and enlarged by his influence, and Queenie's also. They were an integral part of my own family background. Sometimes this was painful, mostly it was wonderfully enriching, always it was a relationship I have been glad and privileged to have had.

F.R.L. in his bath at Mill Road, Cambridge

F.R.L. with his sister Ruth (centre) and his brother Ralph (right)

F.R.L. before the First World War

Queenie Roth and Grace Cohen at Girton, 1925–6

Queenie Roth at Girton, about 1928

The engaged couple, with F.R.L.'s sister Ruth, his niece Mary
and his brother Ralph, summer 1929

F.R.L. with his niece Mary and Rumpus, in the early 1930s

Drawing of F.R.L. by Richard Austin

F.R.L. in 1943 or 1944

F.R.L. at Downing:
not a photograph he liked

F.R.L. in 1969

Q.D.L. in 1979

Q.D.L. and F.R.L., about 1977

4

'Nor Shall My Sword': the Leavises' mythology

M. C. BRADBROOK

A year before her death, Queenie Leavis wrote to a contemporary, Ena Mitchell, who had been talking of early days to a mutual friend:

... you had delighted him with your reminiscences of myself and my husband in our earlier days here. I will be greatly obliged if you could find time to write them down ... It would make my task [of writing a biography of F.R.L.] easier and also more convincing and interesting if I could give first hand records other than my own. It would also give great pleasure to my children who can remember us only as grey haired and worn down with battling for survival in a hostile environment – in fact I can hardly remember myself that we (F.R.L. and I) were once gay, good looking and hopeful.

The nuances in lives outwardly consistent may be hinted by looking at the Four Leavises; the young pair of 1929-36; the old campaigners of the sixties and seventies.

For my first two years at Girton College, 1927-9, I lived next to Queenie Roth's double set, A7, and was taught by F. R. Leavis, whom she married in the summer of 1929 when she was twenty-two, he thirty-four. He cycled up Castle Hill on Wednesday afternoons to the old army hut where classes were held in Practical Criticism and modern literature. Leavis had taken his Ph.D. on the rise of journalism, culminating in *The Tatler* and *The Spectator*; he had read history before turning to English, and the impress of G. M. Trevelyan was plain. He had been initiated into social history before it became widely studied; to the section of the Tripos papers known as 'Life and Thought' he brought a persuasive mingling of relevant views and interpretative selection of literary example. His method

29

was the *explication de texte*, particularly by reading. Some of my contemporaries say they can still hear his voice, inevitably, when they turn to certain poems. For me, a few poems of Hardy – 'Neutral Tones', 'The Ghost', 'After a Journey', 'The Voice' – are impressed on my mind in this way.

George Steiner gave an eloquent account of the effects of Leavis's lecturing (*Encounter*, XVIII 5 (May 1962), 37–45); unfortunately, no recordings appear to have been taken.

Leavis, pre-eminently a teacher by the direct method, was both orator and actor. His writings, which put the contemporary Cambridge approach into general circulation, emerged from circles of Socratic debate, each led by a master – the most eminent circle being the philosophic one of G. E. Moore. I remember at the end of a rather brashly confident paper at the Moral Science Club, Moore reflectively tapping his pipe out and saying meditatively: 'Oh . . . so you think so . . . do you?' It was mercilessly final, by reason of the tone of voice. Leavis was also master of this art. I remember his opening a paper at the Union Society 'Are you with me or against me?', but talking about the 'reverent openness' with which literature should be approached till it sounded like Julian of Norwich on prayer. But one of his students told of the sallies delivered in the late thirties against other members of the English Faculty – 'Listen to the Henn – cackling' as Tom Henn's deep tones resounded from a nearby lecture room; or, preparing to mount his bicycle, a Parthian shot, leg cocked over the bar – 'Ah, yes, Willey; a Methodist . . .' then, foot on the pedal, 'cowardly and deceitful' (i.e. a wee sly 'un). And away he rode, on his high old-fashioned boneshaker. Later, I became a target myself.

The nervous electric vitality that Leavis radiated, his cocksparrow alertness, even to our unpractised eyes covered a defensive wariness. He had the air of being at once exhilarated and threatened. Our master in the twenties, I. A. Richards, enjoyed the same power to move in opposite directions at the same time, as he foresaw the impact of psychology on the analysis of reading, and yet the doom-laden consequences of 'mass civilisation'. He suggested to Queenie Leavis the topic for her doctoral thesis, *Fiction and the Reading Public*, which he also supervised.

Richards had been trained in philosophy and psychology; their conjunction with literary criticism was something quite new and to my generation, surrounded as we were with new and complex works – poetry by Eliot, novels by Joyce – it gave us the means to approach texts that were to us oracular but obscure. Leavis was engaged in replacing the annalist histories of Saintsbury and Elton – today quite forgotten – by interpretative 'lines of development'. Richards himself had little concern for literary history, and Leavis's 'dating exercises' though developed from Richards's method, were not of his devising. Some of them were taken from other critics whom Leavis admired. 'Surprised by joy', one of Manny Forbes's most powerful readings, was compared by Leavis with Wordsworth's sonnet on Westminster Bridge; the comparison of Morris's 'Nymphs' Song to Hylas' with Marvell's 'The Nymph Complaining . . .' came from Eliot. Leavis's unmistakable tones can be heard in one of the contributions (8.5) to *Practical Criticism*, on D. H. Lawrence's 'Piano' (p. 113).

The second part of *How to Teach Reading, a Primer for Ezra Pound* (1932) reveals Leavis's strength and weakness, in the analysis of passages from *Macbeth* – and in the specification of essential critical tools, which at this time included the works of Richards, Empson, Eliot as critic, Grierson's preface to *Metaphysical Poetry from Donne to Butler*, Mark van Doren's *John Dryden* and a set of his own 'exercises'.

The intervening three years since I had been taught by Leavis and witnessed Queenie's Spartan and secluded Girton life had been years of extreme activity; they had laid the ground for the myth the Leavises created and the myth they generated.

I have written elsewhere in 'Queenie Leavis: the Dynamics of Rejection' about the effects upon her of her Jewish family's casting her off when she married a gentile.[1] Her father was a 'draper and hosier' at 79, Silver Street, Edmonton – a rabbi said that as an undergraduate he used to take her out and give her a cup of tea because she seemed not able to afford it. She must have been spending every penny on books. In 1925 Queenie, like others, had joined a little college 'family' of which one member, Helge Krabbe, a Dane, recalls her silences at the evening coffee-drinking, with the occasional interjection: 'You're not really intellectual – are you?', or: 'You're rather a noisy lot, aren't you?' Another contemporary, Dr Heap, remembered her as 'brainy, self-possessed, very confident, and reclusive'. She boasted of having gained her scholarship before her eighteenth birthday. One of my own 'family' recalls being accosted: 'Do you know who I am? . . . I am Queenie Roth, and I got a star first in my Tripos.' She also boasted that she had worked through every Tripos paper from its inception.

Her ejection from her family is painfully reflected in her holding her weekly At Homes on Friday evening. Their ritual mourning for a lost daughter had its grim counterpart when a bomb wiped out the family home in 1940, killing both parents. Queenie let it be known that she wanted no gestures of mourning from friends.

Leavis's exit from his college, described by him as unceremonious,[2] came soon after his marriage; his probationary Faculty lectureship, gained in 1927, also expired. Before his marriage Leavis had developed a close friendship with Stanley Bennett, who directed studies at Emmanuel, and his wife Joan, née Frankau, a Girtonian from a more liberal Jewish family than Queenie's.

I have previously touched on this. It was believed at Girton that Queenie had accused Joan of taking material from Leavis's lectures – their periods were similar. If Joan had been attacked, Stanley would have grown quite implacable. So he certainly remained. But neither party talked. (Joan's probationary lectureship also expired shortly.)

The break with the Richardses came at about the same time. It was part of Leavis's version of events that hostility to a lectureship for him came from Tillyard, but that Sir Arthur Quiller-Couch, the professor who had been his supervisor, was friendly and well-disposed.

The charge against Tillyard is open to question, for 'Q's real deputy at this time was the Chairman of the Faculty, his closest friend, H. F. Stewart.[3] 'Q' and Tillyard were both members of Jesus College, both ardent Liberals (Asquith secured the chair for 'Q'), both officers of the celebrated Jesus society, the Roosters. Ivor Richards later told me that 'Q' thought Leavis should move, and asked Ivor to put to him the idea of going to Leeds; which Ivor did, to his own undoing. It is simply one version against another here. 'Q' carried weight in Leeds.

I am inclined to suspect that Tillyard was elevated as 'my enemy' and 'the arch-political boss' (covertly and obliquely identified in a letter to the *Times Literary Supplement* of 18 December 1975) because Tillyard with Leavis had been a member of the Perse School; this family were academic leaders of the musical life of the university, whilst Leavis's father kept a piano shop. Perhaps a touch of Town *v*. Gown persisted. Basically, Leavis was very sure of himself, at the same time that he felt, with another part of himself, very insecure. He reminded me of the child who makes an attack and then darts off with cries of 'Fegs me!' or 'Barley!' His style was evasive, full of hints, whereas Queenie was always a Bold Slasher; his was the more feminine, hers the more masculine style. But as her teacher he had shaped her mind, and whilst she acted as assistant editor for *Scrutiny*, she also seems to have acted as his research assistant and collaborator in some of his books, as her later testimonies assert. The collaboration is shown in the relations of *Fiction and the Reading Public* (1932) to Leavis's first pamphlet, *Mass Civilisation and Minority Culture* (1930). Their talents were complementary; neither would have been able to achieve so much without the other. The price was, later, psychological collusion.

Leavis's style was nervy, jumpy; he affected certain military words. The verbs 'report', 'register', 'salute' seem to ingest the hated army system. His series of 'tips' for dealing with exams was like the common soldier's reaction to the 'system'. In the First World War, where he was a stretcher-bearer, his conscience had forbidden him to fight, but also forbidden him to take any leave. He came back to 'dislodge' the Puritan Milton he had carried in his pocket. Within the territory of their first home, The Criticastery, Leavis (you might say) was the legislative, Queenie the executive; the judiciary was a joint affair. The only poetry I ever remember to have discussed with Queenie was Crabbe's; the 'woodcut' simplicity of his line, his resemblance to Hardy.

Something of those early years has been recorded by Tillyard, Willey, Joan Bennett and Empson.[4] Poetry-games, later codified by Leavis, were all fresh and new. It is difficult now to remember how innocent we were. Queenie's study of the novel, on sociological lines already sketched by Richards in *Principles of Literary Criticism* (pp. 32, 36, 58, 60-1) was the first of its kind to rely on a questionnaire. It has been recently objected that she circulated only authors and not readers[5] – but Mass Observation was only just beginning, with the investigations of a younger Cambridge figure, Charles Madge. Consumer research, the whole field of applied sociology, was absolutely unknown; hers was genuinely pioneer work. In later years, Queenie felt that successors, like Richard Hoggart, gave her no recognition; a fierce claim to discoveries is natural enough, but too often what feels like plagiarism is merely the zeitgeist. No other woman entered the group. Queenie ruled domestically; later, inevitably, the age-gap between her and Leavis meant her powers were extended.

Scrutiny put into general circulation the views absorbed from Forbes and Richards, giving them currency and a pedagogic slanting. A complete dedication to this one purpose was disguised by Leavis's edgy, tentative style, based on the elliptical ironies of the early T. S. Eliot and on Henry James. Polemically it permitted sneer-words like 'odd' or 'unwholesome' or 'flank-rubbing', where invective is passed off as judgement. Queenie remained direct, pungent and ruthless. As a verse by one of her friends recorded, she had selected the five modern novelists worth taking seriously:

> Of modern novelists there are but five
> To the discriminating; one, ah woe! is
> Dead – D. H. Lawrence; those who are alive
> Are Forster, Joyce, V.Woolf and T. F. Powys.

These later were to be reduced to two – Lawrence and Powys.

The Leavises' first child was born in 1934, by which time their active supporters in the Faculty were also reduced to two – Hilda Murray and Brian Downs, both teaching in subjects remote from the Leavises' central concerns – she was a medievalist, he later became Professor of Scandinavian Studies. This was partly due to demands that others should 'choose' between friendship with the Leavises and friendship with those from whom they were alienated (the Bennetts and the Richardses); and partly that, while hostile reviews, such as that which F. L. Lucas gave to Queenie's book, were taken as an affront, their own abrasive attacks were considered disinterested blows in a righteous cause. 'I am a freedom fighter, you are a terrorist, they are common criminals.'

Even if it might have been possible for opponents, like legal advocates, to remain good friends out of court, a Messianic fervour made this impossible. The Minority, the Chosen Remnant, has always seemed to me Judaic rather than – as Donald Davie and others suggest – Puritanical; but the likeness to a religious sect has been remarked by many. Cambridge was their Zion to the Children of the Promise, but the holy places were usurped and prophaned by heathen. The sword should not sleep in the hand. Leavis claimed to be descended from Huguenots; in later days, when talking to me, he once suddenly exclaimed 'My Gascon blood!' and forthwith assumed an intensified foreign intonation, which persisted for the rest of our talk. He belonged to the old Fabian agnostic school of the Rationalist Press, vegetarianism, sandalled feet, the garden-city ethos; his temperament was religious, but his upbringing cut him off. For him, as for Matthew Arnold, lyric poetry distilled and replaced the reductive systems of theology and philosophy. Yet he was 'disturbed' by Eliot's *Four Quartets* (after Blake 'dislodged' Lawrence).

During the late thirties, I was much preoccupied with personal affairs and college teaching; I spent the war in London ('Doing something useful?' asked Queenie on one of my brief visits to Cambridge). I returned to find the Leavises hardened in their attitudes. 'Q' had died in 1944 aged 81 (he held the chair for life under the old statutes) and in 1946 Basil Willey was elected. This had the unfortunate effect of leaving the Faculty still without leadership; for Willey's personal modesty was disastrously transferred to the affairs of the Faculty; there was no one else to make central representations. The drastic understaffing and underpromotion during Willey's eighteen years, following 'Q's long *fainéant* tenure, meant that Tillyard (who remained a lecturer to the end of his days) Bennett and Henn, the senior dons, represented us to central administration. Leavis, who by then had published a good deal, might have cherished some secret hopes of the chair; at this time he was not even a full lecturer.[6] Soon he was promoted and also obtained some kind of grant from the Rockefeller Foundation for secretarial assistance; Queenie, who contributed less and less to *Scrutiny*, had no official position and I do not know that she ever sought one until near the time of Leavis's retirement.

I obtained my first, temporary Faculty appointment in 1945 – Leavis told my brother it was unfair I should have time to write books whilst Queenie had babies! He was much incensed by an article I wrote on the criticism of T. S. Eliot which he took as entirely personal to himself – it was not. I saw a little more of the impingement of Leavis's Downing *imperium in imperio* upon Faculty affairs. His friendly relations with the tutor, Cuttle, who brought him to Downing in 1932, allowed him control of the undergraduate entry; there were research fellows – Cox and Walton, then Shapiro and Strickland – to act as lieutenants. The ethos of the Downing group was suited to the early years of the Butler Education Act, the arrival of the meritocracy. Leavis gave extra classes and as strongly dissuaded his pupils from attending lectures as he claimed the Faculty members were directing their pupils to boycott him. He discussed the Faculty even with freshmen at other colleges where he taught.

Confidence in this alternative Faculty of his was eventually to lead to the paradoxical situation that whilst he maintained English as the central discipline, the true humane centre, he could not anywhere see such an English School in being (the theme of the later *Nor Shall My Sword* (1972)). The mood of the immediate post-war years has been recently summed up by Donald Davie, who as pupil of Tom Henn, was certainly allowed access to Leavis: it was that of the 'prig' as defined by the *O.E.D.* – Precisian.

Those [i.e. 1946–50] were the years when *Scrutiny* was my bible and F. R. Leavis my prophet . . . Every issue of the magazine made me a present of perhaps a dozen authors or books or whole periods and genres of literature which I not only *need* not read, but *should not*. To be spared so much of literature, and at the same time earn moral credit by the exemption – no wonder that I loved *Scrutiny*, and Leavis's *Revaluation* and his *New Bearings in English Verse*! . . . and indeed at some stage of his education every student needs, and even deserves to be presented with a rigorously narrow canon of approved reading such as Leavis, not altogether fairly, was widely held to be providing. An immersion in *Scrutiny*, even an infatuation with it, is no bad thing, if only one can be sure that the student will in due course pull out of it, or pass beyond it. (*These the Companions* (1982), pp. 77–8).

As Leavis's influence grew, his creative powers declined; at fifty he began to be imprisoned in his own image. He was beginning to write Retrospects; that to *New Bearings* is dated 1950. His 'literature of the present' seemed to stop at the date when *Scrutiny* was founded; his books were quarried from *Scrutiny*. Meanwhile his methods had gone out into schools, and into the remoter parts of the Commonwealth – India, South Africa, Sydney and even West Africa became centres of what began to be termed Leavisite teaching. In the United States he had long enjoyed a high esteem, strengthened by the New Criticism that arrived in the late forties.

Yet the Leavises did not often travel beyond the Norfolk coast; in spite of their belief in the reprobate nature of the Faculty, nothing could tempt them from Cambridge. Queenie at this time used to cut me dead in the street. Tom Henn, as Chairman or Secretary of the Faculty Board, kept mountainous files of letters of complaint and denunciation. Tillyard's colleague, A. P. Rossiter, shared some of Leavis's views, but I don't think they were associated. The need to reject and to be rejected remained. In a very painful incident, Tom Henn asserted (as later he told me) that Leavis had set in the Tripos the same passages that he used in his sheets of Practical Criticism in teaching his own men. Leavis replied simply that these were the *best* passages. For some years he was not invited to examine, which must have added to his sense of injury. He was a good and conscientious examiner, but with no sense of what the normal human frame could endure. Once, when he was Chairman and they had been sitting all day without any of the refreshments customarily provided, the diminutive Enid Welsford arose and with a cry of 'I want my dinner!' led a party out of Downing to the nearby University Arms. Leavis on the other hand confided to me that when he was marking, the butler of Downing used to bring him glasses of port, which he drank out of dutiful regard for the butler. He was of course a total abstainer otherwise.

Leavis now commanded the press, and after *Scrutiny* ceased in 1953, was ready to use the *Times Literary Supplement*, or any other organ of the reprobate, to publicise his views; the Faculty fastened seat-belts. (Yet one day, when I was talking with him of the Second World War, the name of Woodbine Willie suddenly surfaced; remembering it from childhood, I thought: Unfasten seat-belt!)

Although at this time the number of undergraduates expanded to about 800 at the peak, English was still largely a college-based subject, centring on King's, Pembroke, St Catharine's, Emmanuel, Jesus, Christ's and the two women's colleges, with Downing as the most important new centre. In a Cambridge where central power constantly grew, the syllabus remained so wide that it was possible to select one's own. Leavis's influence extended strongly into one or two other colleges, especially Newnham and Clare; yet in the world of the U.G.C., of the A.U.T., of I.A.U.P.E., he continued to play the 'outlaw', the outsider. The press reflected the legend.

'If you want to get a First' he said, prowling round the room in his open-necked shirt, 'you might be well advised not to use in your papers any key words or phrases that are known to be associated with my own critical approach. Words like the "texture" of a poem for example. Highly suspect word, texture.'

The advice worked like a charm. And that was more than thirty years ago. (*The Sunday Telegraph* (10 October 1965)).

This puts the advice in 1935 or earlier; at the time it was printed, the painful series of outbursts that marked Leavis's retirement were making stories for the columnists.

His last decade at Downing had been marked by a break with his friend Cuttle: he was not on speaking terms with the gentle Keith Guthrie, the Master; the question of appointing his successor provoked the storm after which he resigned his honorary fellowship. He was savage to L. C. Knights, who succeeded to the King Edward VII chair on Basil Willey's retirement, two years after his own; and to his followers, who had founded the *Cambridge Quarterly*, from which he dissociated himself.[7] He had objected to the course taken by the Faculty to train research students in the use of sources, the methods and library techniques required in modern research; and the idea that they should be allowed to research on Joyce or Pound.[8] Although retired, the Faculty elected him to sit on the Faculty Board till he reached seventy. I was Chairman during this time, and scanned the agenda closely to prepare any questions that I thought he might wish to investigate. Then he would go to sleep; whilst on what I had thought a quite innocuous agenda, he might

wax caustic and eloquent for hours. He would disown at one meeting what he had said on the previous occasion. '*Who* said that?'
(indignantly). 'You did, Dr Leavis', the impeccable Faculty Secretary would reply, consulting her shorthand. All the difficulties of
the Leavis Lectureship Fund, which eventually went to York, the
harassed queries from Downing, were intensified by the snooping
of the London dailies, the students' well organised set of 'stringers'
in search of copy; while their own journal *Varsity* carried banner
headlines every week. Leavis's invective was as rhetorical as ever;
'Snow is a – no, I can't say that; he *thinks* he is a novelist.' His
tactics were intuitive and superb; his influence remained un-
diminished throughout the sixties. *Scrutiny* was reissued; after York,
he visited Bangor, Bristol and Harvard. My impression is that he
aged mentally with some speed; but he always rose to an occasion.
In a spirited exchange with John Holloway (*The Cambridge Review*
(October–November 1964)) he charged John with the tactics he
was himself employing.

In later years Leavis became less interested in his authors than
in his campaigns. It is not difficult to pick holes in the Leavises'
'lines of development'; their genealogies were very important to
them – e.g. the 'line from the Metaphysicals to Pope' ('Not
stopping at Dryden' the students would whisper). Queenie persisted in thinking *Jules et Jim* could and must be related to *Wuthering
Heights*, though this novel was declared unknown to the author of
Jules et Jim. Then we had 'the novel as dramatic poem'. The
alternative maps they drew were in the service of the general
enterprise.

Samuel Beckett has said: 'A myth is not about something: it is
that something itself.' The myth encapsulated the ardent young
challengers of the thirties in rituals – even liturgies – for the self-
pitying experts in siege mentality of the seventies. In an essay
published posthumously in *The Critic as Anti-philosopher* (1982)
Leavis bragged that in fifty years his views on Gerard Manley
Hopkins had not changed, yet he completely changed his judgement of Dickens, of the later as against the earlier Henry James, as
of Eliot and Richards. Wittgenstein began to feature in the myth-
ology of early days – but only after he was dead.

Alma mater Cantabrigia being a good but hard mother – colleges can be kind – a love–hate relationship is common enough (it was evinced in the volume *My Cambridge* by other members of the Faculty). In the Retrospect to *Scrutiny* (1963), Leavis claimed to represent Cambridge in spite of Cambridge:

Only at Cambridge could the idea of *Scrutiny* have taken shape . . . Cambridge then figures for us civilization's anti-Marxist recognition of its own nature and needs . . . We were in fact that Cambridge . . . *Scrutiny* not only survived the hostility of institutional power; it became – who now questions it? – the clear triumphant justification to the world of Cambridge as a humane centre.[9]

In the language of *Scrutiny*:

Yes: but . . .?

'Institutionalised academic power' is not a constant.

In 1926 the English Tripos emerged in its present form along with wider reforms; – university lectureships, Faculty Boards and other bodies created by a Royal Commission. In English, the new system, lacking prototypes, worked through the power-nodes of half a dozen strong colleges, including for the first time the women's colleges. University office followed college patronage. Less than half the first set of lecturers had read English; all were older than Leavis, all directed studies and nearly all held fellowships. In place of research degrees ('Mainly for scientists') the *Register* records, for every one, university scholarships or prizes; the recognised local warrant. Tillyard and Bennett, each six years senior to Leavis, without fellowships till 1934 and 1933, learnt administration, but Tillyard reverted to being a college man; Bennett's real passion, as Chairman of the Press Syndicate, college librarian, pillar of the Bibliographical Society, was books as objects.

The year 1927 saw Leavis the eldest (except for a woman) of six probationary Faculty lecturers, most being Directors of Studies or fellows; all had read English. College office put T. R. Henn B.A. on the Faculty voting-list in 1926; in 1924, perhaps Dr Stewart had helped L. J. Potts B.A. to migrate from Trinity to Queens' with a fellowship. In 1934 university initiative prevailed when Willey, who had lived as precariously as Leavis, gained a lectureship created for the new Moralists' paper. Migrating to a fellowship at

Pembroke, he soon succeeded Attwater on the Appointments Committee.

Leavis's move to Downing had made him Director of Studies; by 1936, when his university lectureship was secured, Downing offered major scholarships and research fellowships in English. The shock of finding his juniors, Henn and Potts, promoted ahead of him in 1928,[10] must have intensified when in 1936 two much younger men, Rylands and Sykes Davies, filled vacated posts. For the academic politicians it was more a matter of getting their own man in than keeping him out. His publications did not tip the balance, as they had for Willey; and his Ph.D. counted for little (he scorned the M.A. and appeared on all lists as B.A., Ph.D.). Tillyard would back Willey, one of his first pupils; he lacked college support from Peterhouse.

Downing became ·a power-node outside the system; Leavis revived the pre-1926 practice of the colleges by giving open, unofficial lectures there – but unpaid, of course and unadvertised. A pattern was set; years stamped it in. In 1926 Leavis had been unlucky because the 'war gap' left him to lag behind men only one or two years older, like Richards, Downs and Lucas. Queenie's college work was blocked since the women's colleges expected residence. Yet Joan Bennett, who waited till 1952 for a fellowship, lectured publicly from 1927, and when Leavis's name was dropped from the lecture list in 1932, she continued to survey the seventeenth century, regarded by the Leavises as his territory. His second book, *Revaluation* (1936), made this clear.

Financial upgrading in 1946-7 did not prevent Leavis from remaining the self-proclaimed Statutory Outlaw. The source of his energy, and now of his reputation, was to be 'disturbing'; he never solved the problem of being both disturbing and co-operative. Moral fervour and ethical protest, privileges of the Opposition, are checked by accountability. His model was to prove congenial to later and lesser men.

After 1945, government grants strengthened the central channels; colleges lost economic autonomy; yet each retained its own style, cherished its graduates. College teachers, queuing for university office, formed a new class, in which Leavis's attitude became institutionalised in turn. When, in 1964, he broke his connection with Downing, all the new accompaniments of student revolt and boycott attended; yet I believe he very much disliked the 'demos' of 1968. His personal network remained, based on the loyalty and affection he so widely inspired; he became a one-man Appointments Board. Later confrontations, met by the Faculty with steady stonewalling, culminated in an attempt to set up a university lectureship over which he should retain the power of veto – thus reflecting the pangs of thirty years before.

Leavis lived almost entirely for and in great literature; his late troubled return to *Four Quartets* is proof of that. But he also wanted to be addressed as Professor and to be offered 'the biggest lecture hall in Harvard'. He was the most engaging mixture of the Prophet Elijah and Peter Pan.

Notes

1 This sketch from *The Cambridge Review* (20 November 1981) is reprinted in my *Collected Papers*, vol. II (1982). Queenie's brother was President of the Cambridge Hebrew Congregation when she came up in 1925; on her marriage, her family were said to have gone into ritual mourning.

2 See the account by John Harvey on p. 171.

3 The Rev. Dr H. F. Stewart, who lectured in French, helped in the founding of the English Faculty; an excellent administrator, he deputised for 'Q', who regarded him as his closest friend. He was Chairman of the Faculty 1930–2, and again 1935–6, and therefore *ex officio* on the Appointments Committee; he may have objected to Leavis's use of 'Q's *Oxford Book of English Verse*, in lectures, as a quarry of bad poetry.

4 E. M. W. Tillyard, *The Muse Unchained* (1958); Basil Willey, *Cambridge and other Memories* (1968); Joan Bennett, William Empson in *I. A. Richards: Essays on his Honour*, ed. Brower, Vendler and Hollander (1973). See also F. Brittain, *Arthur Quiller-Couch* (1948). Hugh Carey has written a life of Manny Forbes (C.U.P. in press).

5 John Carey, 'Queenie Leavis, a help or hindrance to her husband?' *The Listener* (7 October 1982). This muted but basically antagonistic talk drew a series of characteristically intemperate replies.

6 The value of a lectureship, £300 p.a. was supplemented by £150 for any one not a fellow of a college. If he were, this sum would be surplus; the *Reporter* of 20 May 1936 carried simultaneously the appointment to Miss Murray's lectureship in medieval literature and the offer of a part-time lectureship at £150 – awarded to Leavis in the *Reporter* of 20 October with retrospective effect from 1 October. His lectures were announced in the January list. In 1928, when two lectureships had been advertised, three

had been given, the third, Miss Welsford's, being part-time. This method of recruitment did not persist. Joan Bennett, last of the original group of six probationers, was promoted after Leavis. His upgrading to full lecturer is shewn in the accounts for 1946–7, when his salary jumped from £200 to £350, nearly maximum. The General Board would disburse; that year's Chairman in English was Potts.

7 L. C. Knights was publicly attacked in *The Times Literary Supplement* (3 March 1972). *The Cambridge Quarterly* had previously suffered there, when Leavis declared his first contribution would be his last (7 February 1966). The Leavis Lecturer also received harsh treatment.

8 See an article by Leavis, *The Times Literary Supplement* (26 July 1963) 'Research in English', which shows no recognition of the difference in educational patterns between the 1930s and the 1960s, the growing complexity of bibliographical aids available, or the effects of the growth of modern studies in all universities.

9 In a series of gathered articles, *Selections from Scrutiny* (2 vols, 1968), Queenie defined her Cambridge as being primarily that of Leslie Stephen, who became a cult figure. Chadwick, about whom she wrote anonymously, was rather surprisingly another. In our youth, she told me that all the Old English necessary could be learnt in a fortnight!

As a proponent of the 'organic community', from behind her palisades she threatened the Director of the Dunn Nutritional Laboratory with a lawsuit because she alleged his dog disturbed her.

10 In 1928 three probationary lecturers were upgraded to university posts – Henn, Potts, Miss Welsford; the probationary lectureships of Willey, Mrs Bennett and Leavis seem to have terminated in 1932, but lectures of the first two continued in the official lecture list (paid at piece rates?) whilst Leavis was dropped between October 1932 and January 1937. The later adjustment of the anomaly of his part-time lectureship (see note 6) might have been delayed only by negligence; review would not be automatic. Any one with confidence in the system, after three years would have approached his Chairman with a request to the General Board; Leavis was perhaps deterred till 1945 by what he felt as earlier discriminations against him. Miss Welsford, part-time since 1928, was upgraded with Leavis; and the category disappeared.

5

Teacher and friend

DENYS THOMPSON

After Part I of Classics my tutor, Martin Charlesworth, sent me
to F. R. Leavis as supervisor for the full English Tripos; this was
in 1928. He was an outstanding teacher, sensitive, stimulating and
always kind and gentle. One learned to read with the fullest
possible response, and to value literature as something constantly
reaching into life; his 'I don't believe in any "literary values"' is
often quoted. He set an example not only of response to writing,
but also of complete disinterestedness and unswerving devotion
to the task he set himself. I was fortunate to be a pupil of his, and
later a friend. By chance half a sheet of a poor essay on Pope that
I wrote for him has survived as a book-marker, with his comments:

An intelligent essay but never inward enough. It is clear that you have not
been able to get to grips with Pope.

What you say about him in the comparison with Tennyson isn't literary
criticism. You illustrate there the difficulty (appalling for a critic) of remembering *that poetry is written with words and that a work of art must be considered
as a work of art*, when you are judging it . . .

For relation between the work of art and the personality of the artist see
'Sacred Wood'.

– a criticism that I found firm without being harsh, full, encouraging
and constructive. The other side of the scrap records some of
Leavis's observations on the poet, as we thumbed through the
Everyman volume; filled out they would make an admirable
introduction to the author.

Even in those days myths were gathering about him. For instance:
he was a long-distance runner of Olympic standard, but his noble
Victorian father disapproved of competitive sport, so he could never
prove his mettle. His experiences as a stretcher-bearer in the war
having shattered his nerves, he did not sleep well, so one night

he got up and ran to Ely and back. As I have suggested above he was a casualty of that war, like his brother, who could not face running the family piano business, nearly opposite the building now occupied by Tesco. In 1929 he became engaged to Queenie Dorothy Roth, a pupil of his, when she proposed to him. At first they lived in a little spec. builder's house in Leys Road, named by Queenie 'The Criticastery' – 'the home of would-be critics'. Thence they soon moved to the house, formerly his parents', in Chesterton Hall Crescent, which Queenie transformed into a most pleasant home, where I stayed several times in the early 1930s. These visits I count among the happiest hours of my life, and I was delighted when for a holiday they accepted my mother's offer of a cottage in Swaledale. It was primitive, and we called it 'Bob Cottage' because the rent was 1 s. (5 pence) a week. There Frank saw the vestiges of a self-sufficient community, while Queenie sensed the life that she was later to describe in the 'Fresh Approach to *Wuthering Heights*'.

They were a happy couple, well, relaxed and cheerful, despite the jealousy and frightened hostility of the university establishment. Theirs was a welcoming house, with Queenie's amusing chatter and loyal support for Frank at every turn; she would spark off ideas and suggestions, and if they were extravagant Frank would remonstrate in the mildest possible fashion. He had great charm, and was unconscious of it. He adjusted perfectly to people, prince or pauper, on meeting them, and radiated a sweetness audible even in his regular question, 'Shall I make the coffee?' The severe Puritanism described by Mrs Pitter was doubtless there, but I never noticed it. They enjoyed life and encouraged others to do the same. The photograph (no. 9) of a rather later period is strongly reminiscent of Frank as I saw him then, strong, idealistic, hopeful for the future; that is how I like to recall him.

They had good reason to be gratified with their start as writers. Queenie's brilliant *Fiction and the Reading Public* appeared in 1932, and two years earlier Gordon Fraser, while still an undergraduate, started his publishing career with the six Minority Press pamphlets. Frank wrote two of these, and a little later contributed *How to Teach Reading: a Primer for Ezra Pound*; and since he had so great

45

an influence on it, something should be recorded about the Minority Press. The pamphlets were:

F. R. Leavis: *Mass Civilisation and Minority Culture*
T. F. Powys: *Uriah on the Hill*
William Hunter: *The Novels and Stories of T. F. Powys*
John Middleton Murry: *D. H. Lawrence (Two Essays)*
R. P. Blackmur: *Dirty Hands or The True-Born Censor*
F. R. Leavis: *D. H. Lawrence*

They were very well (by today's standards even beautifully) produced by Heffers, with a clean fount, really black ink and excellent paper. Their gray textured sewn wrappers bore Fraser's emblem, designed by the architect Raymond McGrath: a big formalised sprouting bean seed, symbol of life and power and growth. I don't know who suggested to Fraser that he should start publishing – it was the sort of idea that Queenie might throw off between the washing of a cup and saucer – but what made him different from most small 'presses' was the adequacy of his father's financial backing. I believe the latter had a large stake in a Leeds firm that made excellent copper tubes. Gordon Fraser himself was a good-natured, easy-going young man, not particularly able, but with a mind of his own. With capital to hand he was able to lengthen his list, and there soon followed Fielding's *Shamela* (introduced by Brian W. Downs), L. C. Knights' *How Many Children Had Lady Macbeth?*, W. A. Edwards' *Comedy* and Norman Angell's *The Press and the Organisation of Society*. However the Minority Press was not the only outlet. In 1932 L. C. Knights and Donald Culver launched *Scrutiny*, and Chatto published *New Bearings in English Poetry*. *Towards Standards of Criticism* (Wishart) and *Culture and Environment* followed in 1933. They were heady times, especially for those who felt that their teaching in school had received direction and powerful support. One gained from the Leavises a world picture that may have had its gloomy aspects (as Gwendolen Freeman observes), but was one which not only made sense but offered signs of hope and plenty of scope for action. Time spent with them was exhilarating.

As well as doing much typing and other work for her husband, Queenie ran the house smoothly, efficiently and without fuss. Thus

Frank was enabled to start a productive life of writing. She was a good, natural cook; I recall that the quality of her soups prompted me to give them a large Victorian ladle. She was an admirable hostess with a gift for making guests feel at home. Like Frank she was kind and encouraging to his pupils and was helpful with advice, which sometimes reflected her reading; her views on marriage for example tended to come from Bertrand Russell's current publication. She was open-handed and generous – she gave me some Hardy novels that had belonged to Frank. She was generous too in her appreciation of support in her work; *Fiction and the Reading Public* acknowledges assistance from William Hunter and myself, though I knew little of the book till it was in print, and supplied no material. She was an avid and rapid reader, and fluent in speech and writing; a teaching-period on Jane Austen, for instance, would consist of an uninterruptible monologue of excellent material. She dressed neatly, perhaps smartly later on, always in clothes of markedly fine quality, and she held herself well to the last. She had the kind of general ability that would have made her a good linguist or mathematician; as a literary critic she needed orientating hints, which she would take up in a most intelligent way.

Thus in those early days her writing benefited from the direction and standards that were imparted first by I. A. Richards and then by Frank. *Fiction and the Reading Public* was the work of a highly able, quickly moving mind, rapidly assimilating material and adapting the methods of American sociology to her own research, but the foundation of a valuable book lay in a few sentences of Richards' *Principles of Literary Criticism*. Again, of two women novelists in the thirties, clearly of roughly equal standing, Queenie would rate one very highly because she had met and liked her, while dismissing the other as run-of-the-mill. With the years however her judgement became surer and more independent, as one can tell from her reading of *Wuthering Heights*, though even here I think she drew on an earlier and unmentioned essay in *Scrutiny*. Especially of women novelists her assessments were idiosyncratic.

In her later years Queenie stated that she had assisted Frank with some of his books, but I cannot fully accept her claim because in one case (specified to Professor Ford) she was quite wrong.

After some discussion based on my experience of teaching the children of well-to-do parents, who needed defence against the entertainment industry quite as much as the offspring of poorer people, Frank and I agreed to produce a book for sixth forms. I stayed with them while he wrote *Culture and Environment*, utilising as well as his own material a good deal supplied by Queenie and myself. Otherwise my main contribution was to act as schools adviser and to offer the title. It took him only about a week to get the book into shape. He and I had great fun with parts of it, while Queenie maintained a cheerful flow of advice and chatter.

When the book was ready we offered it to Dents, who were then a leading educational publisher in the field of English. They refused it, in baffled and indignant terms – clearly it had got beneath someone's skin – and it was promptly accepted by Chatto and Windus. The first venture of its kind, it sold well and is said to have been influential. It remained in print, unaltered, for about forty years and was then reissued in America. I once raised with Frank the question of revision and sent some extensive drafts; they elicited no comment and I dropped the idea. Today the book requires replacing rather than revising. The need is greater, since not only children but also some of their teachers receive their essential, emotional education from surroundings shaped by the technological environment. Notions of what constitutes pretty girls and handsome men, and ideas of the good life are still handed out by advertising, TV and other influences. The case for *Culture and Environment* is trenchantly updated in the first of the *Lectures in America*, which invites us to feel 'shame, concern and apprehension at the way our civilisation has let [people] down – left them to enjoy a "high standard of living" in a vacuum of disinheritance'.

A pleasant characteristic of Leavis in those days was the way in which he checked any tendency to excess in his supporters by a mild and amused irony. It was effective, and it could have been applied to the whole-hog admirers of later years. But like some other people with a strong element of basic innocence, Frank in his early days was an uneven judge of character and did not always recognise adulation as such. He was tolerant of human frailty, and his natural courtesy extended to taking a polite interest even in pursuits remote from his own tastes.

My own happy and trusting relationship with the Leavises ended abruptly in 1935. Queenie was a lively and prolific correspondent, always interesting. When I mentioned in a letter that I was engaged to one of Frank's former pupils, though not the one Queenie had in mind for me, the response was a letter of perhaps a thousand words in her small, spidery, legible hand, criticising my intended wife in abusive terms. There was not much temptation to reply in kind, though it was an affectionate regard for Frank that stayed my pen rather than any reflection on the futility of combat. So my reply, though conceding nothing, tried to give Queenie the opportunity for some sort of withdrawal. I wasted my time, because there soon came two closely-filled sides of a quarto sheet in which I was now the target. She can have hardly have thought that she would achieve anything by such writing; it is just that she always thought she was right and could not contain herself. The attitude led later to displays of self-righteousness. She was incapable of seeing herself as others saw her, and this defect of imagination closed her mind to the likely consequences of her action. Another aspect of this failing was her curiously patchy understanding of children; she would be kind to them, yes, and that was good. But she could write the most extraordinary letters to a child; she would 'communicate' with a five-year-old as if she were addressing an adult. The pattern of behaviour towards me is recorded here only because it was to be repeated with other former pupils about to marry. Arrogance precluded her learning from experience – or if she did learn, she never admitted it. So not surprisingly she appeared a conceited young woman. She remarked one day to Jessie Harding that she never broke a cup, because if she dropped one she always caught it on the way down. With all this there went high expectations and large demands on life. Had she profited more from her reading she would have realised that she was an example of hubris if ever there was one. In the event nemesis inflicted some cruel disappointments, and I doubt if she ever grew in humility.

In those letters to me she associated Frank with her views and claimed to quote him, but he could not have agreed fully with her;

he was not the sort of person to interfere with one's private life, and it was probably for peace and quiet that he assented. There are letters of his, not vetted by Queenie, that belie her forthright condemnations. Not long before, probably in 1934, he had stayed with my future wife and me in a cottage on the Norfolk coast, and I recall clearly his apparent happiness. He enjoyed the swimming, sunning and walks; he was an excellent companion. Moreover during those few days his appetite for holiday food, including fish just out of the sea, was remarkably good.

After Queenie's outbursts no contact was possible, though I hoped that one day she might retract. However she was never one to apologise, and she never withdrew, though the least reflection would have opened her eyes to the damage she might be causing. Later I heard that she was ill with cancer, and got into touch. Normally very healthy, she resisted with vitality and a capacity for endurance when she was attacked by illnesses that one cannot help labelling psychosomatic. But things were never the same, despite a usually smooth surface. I saw something of them, both at their house in Newton Road, and then in Bulstrode Gardens, where they lived for the rest of their lives. They generously lent it to my wife and me for a visit in 1965. There were ups and downs in my relationship with Frank, and I find his few surviving letters intolerable reading, so painful are they. There were misunderstandings, apprehensiveness, near-charges of disloyalty, so much worry over nothings. At one time I was 'an enigma', at another a 'moral coward' – this when I took the part of an old friend with whom Frank was quarrelling – and finally, to a third party, 'a man you can trust'. There was often a high moral tone in letters that made the receiver feel a leper, till the leper placed the self-righteousness.

When I came to live in Cambridge some maladroitness of mine offended Queenie, and I never revisited them. I did see Frank occasionally. One evening my wife and I gave him a lift from the station, and he talked non-stop, about family matters. Another day I met him outside Churchill College, and again he was voluble; he inveighed for forty minutes against some of those he regarded as foes – I forget who they were. He must have been in his mid-seventies when with a return of the pride he used to take in his athleticism, he told me that he had given up long-distance running as a form of exercise because it took up too much time, and had resorted to sprinting instead.

It was very sad to see him in old age, looking not so much old or ill as miserable and harassed. Some of this was due to tension at home. Queenie's drive for success would cause her to nag him ruthlessly to demand higher fees or to seek a fee he had not thought of asking for. Once in these late years some undergraduates asked me what they could offer him in return for a talk he had given to a society, and I suggested a Cardew bowl filled with English apples and English walnuts. This is but one example of the gratitude felt and recorded by generations of students, which despite the worsening of the times, should have made for a happy old age. He would at times condemn the respect in which he was held as coming from worthless sources, whereas he could have looked back on an achievement to be proud of – a succession of powerful books, teaching that deserved the many tributes it received, and an influence in schools and universities that was only slightly marred by the extravagances of hard-line devotees. He became less than generous towards people who supported him in a way he should have recognised, and this was a pity, because instead of feeling isolated he should have been conscious of their aid and sympathy. (A minor example was *The Use of English*, a quarterly for teachers that had an excellent circulation after being taken over by Boris Ford for the Bureau of Current Affairs; it owed a good deal to Frank, but I cannot recall that he acknowledged its existence or offered encouragement to those who ran it.) Moreover he was the victim of delusions about the loyalty of friends, some of whom found themselves rejected without a jot of reason. I wish that one to whom I owe so much could have enjoyed life more.

When Frank fell seriously ill, we wrote to Queenie offering the help that I believe she needed. She sent a long, insulting refusal, so that when he died I did not write.

6

Charisma?

RAYMOND O'MALLEY

The chairman of an appointing committee in 1959 asked me 'a good question'. 'I never have understood', he said, 'how Leavis affected his early pupils so deeply. Was it charisma?'

For me, the answer is 'no'. The first impact was considerable, but for a different reason; and moreover its effect, despite some hard knocks, has not essentially changed through contacts spread over much of a lifetime. ''Tis in grain, sir, and will endure wind and weather', as Olivia says of her complexion.

The 'different reason' was that for me Leavis met a profound though unformulated need. To explain this, I must beg leave to speak for a moment of my own affairs.

For my generation, the First World War and the Great Depression formed the warp of all living. Early memories include tense crowds round casualty lists, conscripts learning the best use of the bayonet, hunger marches, and the General Strike. Add to this that my home town was preoccupied with pleasure and money and my school struggled bravely but in no clear direction.

Naturally the move to Cambridge in 1928 was something of a revelation. A university exists to be disinterested, and to make contact with what is not ephemeral; even the buildings of Cambridge reflect a worthy view of human needs. My mentors there earned my immediate respect: they cared about their pupils and they cared about fact. A whole range of insights might be gained, as was evident, from study under their guidance. And yet . . .

Somehow, insights were not quite the point. In retrospect I know that what I hoped to meet was not insights, but insight. I needed to believe that somewhere there existed a scale, a grid, a sheet of mental graph-paper, that could register both Wordsworth and the hunger marches. It was not in the least a call for 'relevance',

52

which is absurd, nor a longing for the comforts of communism or similar religions. It was just the need to encounter pledged intelligence. But I could not have put it thus at the time; simply, I was uneasy.

A trifling incident comes to my mind. Dr Tillyard gave a tea-party at Merton House for newcomers reading English. Talk turned to conscientious objection. 'Farm-work', said our host, 'is over-rated; it's mostly shovelling shit'. Fresh from our school uniforms, we all shivered in delight: this was emancipation indeed. And yet – a small corner of me was uneasy. Could one honestly be so flippant about farming? Agreed, a passing quip, quoted here without context, must not be taken solemnly; and yet the note seemed slightly out of tune. Now that we live with battery hens and crop-spraying aircraft, it is easier to see what was wrong.

A friend and I were discussing the unease, at the stage where we were still sampling lecturers. He asked: 'Have you tried this young chap Leavis yet? They say he's good.' Leavis was duly 'tried', and that first lecture was for me a turning-point. I wish I could describe the lecture, or other comparable lectures that followed, but after fifty years that is difficult. It is all the more difficult since I have no notes other than book-references and the like. At his lectures my mind (I found) was too widely occupied for note-taking to be possible. (Leavis used to say that the good lectures are those at which you *can't* take notes, and I think he was right.) It is only by way of comparison with later events that I can hope to indicate the 'feel' of the early lectures. Just occasionally over the decades I have been present when other lecturers have shown the same intellectual zest, the same seriousness, the same width of concern, and the same ability to work towards large views from demonstrable evidence; always the experience carries me back almost disconcertingly to the Cambridge of 1928 – even when the lecturer makes no show of charisma. By chance there was an instance this summer, and I must again ask leave to seem to diverge for a moment. Mr Hans Keller was speaking to an audience which had, the previous evening, listened to a performance of two string quartets, the one by Haydn and the other by Ravel. Everyone who had been listening (Mr Keller innocently began) must have noticed three technical differences between the quartets: the Haydn gives 'listening' silences to all the instruments in turn; it makes no use of mutes; and it has no tremolando. In point of fact few of his hearers, I suspect, had made conscious note of the three differences, but they can be checked from the score by any competent listener. Taken together, they begin to have a significance not previously perceived; and from this starting-point Mr Keller built a structure that led gradually to the pre-eminence of Beethoven. To me the delight of the occasion consisted in perceiving live intelligence working on live material – and that is what always impressed me about Leavis's best lectures in the early days. I have often thought that Mr Keller is the Leavis of music; once, when I told him this, he accepted the compliment – but said he would rather be seen as Leavis without the aggression.

At the first opportunity I asked Leavis to be my supervisor; Trinity had not yet any English fellows of its own, and depended on outside help of this kind. Leavis warned me: 'They say, you know, that I don't prepare my pupils for the Tripos examination.' My tutor, J. R. M. Butler, was cautious: 'They say, you know, that he doesn't prepare his pupils for the Tripos examination.' However, he consented, and made arrangements. (The allegation meant that he took a very different view of 'preparation'. The eventual class-lists gave answer enough to the question whether the preparation was effective.)

For the rest of my time in Cambridge I had the privilege of an hour of Leavis's undivided attention every week. Whenever possible we sat on the balcony of his house or in the garden. The supervisions were in equal measure tactful and unpredictable; I do not recall that they were ever dull. However thoroughly I had prepared my material, discussion brought out implications, layers, references, ironies, simple meanings, that I had missed or misunderstood; his special capacity was always that of bringing out what is 'there'. Discussion was discussion; there was no hint of the later tendency to monologue. He listened. In particular, he always searched for the sense behind a student's seeming nonsense. There was one such occasion when I had been asked to study in advance a piece from G. M. Hopkins. Hopkins was not yet widely known, and to me was quite unknown. I was absorbed, but puzzled. When invited to name a possible source, I could think of no one except Donne, and I knew that to be an impossibility. The mistake could have been a mere embarrassment, but became the occasion for an especially helpful study of 'the intolerable wrestle / With words and meanings' conducted by two men so far apart and so close together. There was nearly always this sense of discovery, for teacher as for taught, in the supervisions; when I departed with a tough reading-programme for the coming week, the prospect of effort was anything but a discouragement. Curiously, when I have occasion now to walk the pavement of Chesterton Hall Crescent, a hint of the youthful elation comes back to me. Perhaps that sounds like an effect of charisma. I think the truth is that I was beginning to see, after the provincial town and the rather aimless schooling, a possibility of meaning that continues still. Charisma can produce only something resembling the projection of a colour-slide on a white wall; genuine study looks through a window, where the objects seen have a hidden side and hidden relationships that can be explored indefinitely. Some of Leavis's specific evaluations I have, of course, turned away from, but the core of his teaching seems to me as valid now as then. In (for what it is worth) the teaching that has occupied my own lifetime, there have been, I think, three main awarenesses that I have hoped to pass on from him.

The first and simplest is the importance of working outwards from particular and verifiable perceptions.

The second is the need to develop a perception of what is *there* and waiting to be perceived in any given material of importance. Take for instance the opening paragraph of *Mansfield Park*. Once you begin to notice words like 'contemptible', it becomes something very different from the anodyne passage it pretends to be. A surprising number of readers, even adult readers, wholly overlook the trenchancy.

The third concerns an awareness of the nature of language. It is a kind of awareness that has little in common with formal linguistics; it generates no statistics and no salaries. But it compels every discussion of literature to become, equally, a discussion of the language used in it; it is pervasive, and it is all-important in the response to literature. A marked characteristic of Leavis's supervisions was that at all important points you found yourself equally involved in the two, language and literature. He would sometimes mention language as the best example there is of the nature of tradition. Every word, phrase, intonation, structure, nuance, is the product of trial and error conducted (and still being conducted) through generations; it embodies the tested experience of millions of men and women, most of them forgotten, and it places that experience at the service of anyone equipped to respond. The 'intolerable wrestle' is both general and private. Shakespeare's daffodils that 'take / The winds of March with beauty' are uniquely his own, but compounded of elements that were there and waiting.

Naturally, a friendship between Leavis and many of his pupils developed and continued into later years. The Leavises light-heartedly named their first small house 'The Criticastery'. I remember feeling sorry for them because, in those days of the Bauhaus, it had a battlemented porch. (Equally, my present house has one and I rarely notice it – so fast do the waters flow.) Soon they moved into the larger house which was to be their home through the period when I knew them best. They took a pride in entertainment, and many interesting visitors called. Once, when T. S. Eliot had been to tea, a very young member of the family said: 'Now I have seen Mr Eliot, and all I want is to see Mr Shakespeare.' Quaint as it may be, the remark captures the sense of actuality that permeated much of the conversation, and of the teaching, that went on in the house; the past seemed to be still happening, and the struggles of Donne, Hopkins, Eliot – and Shakespeare – seemed equally of the present, and crucial. Despite the harassments of getting out *Scrutiny*, the feeling of the house was cordial. An Oxford journalist–professor has lately given a *Macbeth*-like view of the couple, with Leavis infirm of purpose and his wife as the fiendlike queen who dominated him from the formative years of their marriage. At that time Leavis most commonly addressed his wife as 'my child', a term that well accords with the protective concern which, I believe, never left him. In later years, he wore himself out in trying to protect her against herself, but few people would want to talk of such matters in print. It has also been suggested that Mrs Leavis was the author or part-author of various writings attributed to her husband. Near the end of her life she herself put about this claim, but it was after a thirty-year struggle with deadly illnesses during which only her amazing tenacity kept her alive, and at a period when she made various other distressing assertions. I do not myself believe that the claim has much significance beyond what has always been obvious. At one period their study served also as a guest-room, with the consequence that visitors might at times see them simultaneously at work. Mrs Leavis's pen would flow smoothly and fast; Leavis would discard draft after draft. The effect is evident in their contrasted rhythms of thought and wording. Undoubtedly many of their beliefs grew out of prolonged interchange of ideas and perceptions, but to say this is to say nothing. How could it be otherwise?

I have said that many of Leavis's pupils became and long remained his personal friends. Certainly I for my part valued our relationship, and see many indications that the feeling was reciprocal. Mrs Leavis and my first wife were especially close friends, as became especially evident at the time of my wife's death. There were later periods of closeness too, I believe, but there were also periods of estrangement that I cannot wholly explain; they are a painful memory.

Leavis is said to have been prejudiced. If it is freedom from prejudice that marks off the 'run-of-the-mill critic from Leavis, my impulse is to give three cheers for prejudice. He did have various prejudices; they cohered and together constituted (or sprang from) an attitude to life. 'People say I am a Puritan. I *am* a Puritan!' This is true, but not in any sense that implies a distrust of the life of the senses: I have, for example, never witnessed anyone else drinking tea with such gusto, cupping his hands for the warmth, and gasping with pleasure at each sip. Rather, it was an aversion to the pretence and dishonesty common in the world of popular literature and in some areas of reviewing – 'You scratch my back and I'll scratch yours.' He would have no truck with this (nor, incidentally, with broadcasting, which he considered a medium of non-communication). One weekend paper seemingly took fright. After some directory-thumbing, it gave its front page to uncovering

The Hidden Network of the Leavisites. We were found, sinister fact, to be ensconced and 'influential' in schools, colleges and universities in several continents. It would have been odd had we been found selling cosmetics. *Of course* we were in teaching. The one such body in which 'Leavisites' are not appointed is the English Faculty at Cambridge. – Leavis's real or supposed prejudices within literature would need more space for discussion than this short note allows, but no doubt they will be considered elsewhere in this book.

Leavis is also said to have been aggressive. Certainly there were some massive detonations. I do not know how different his life might have been without his experiences in the First World War. What especially wore him down, added to direct suffering, was vicarious suffering – the need to witness, without possibility of protest, agonised deaths attributable to stupidity-in-office. His struggle towards recovery occupied much of the post-war decade and was never completed; but, at least in my hearing, he rarely mentioned the war except to praise 'the fundamental decency of the English Tommy'.

It was when the Leavises felt that (in the language of the building trade) a demolition job needed to be done that the loudest noises occurred. Loudest of all, I suppose, was the Richmond Lecture and the ensuing controversy, in which his over-kill violence damaged his own reputation. And yet, it seems to me, the job had to be done, and who else would do it? Snow's doctrine proposed, or was thought to propose, that studies based on quantity may claim equal cultural status with studies based on quality. The news came as manna to tens of thousands of bewildered young people seeking entry into higher education; no longer need they worry about Moore and Tippett and Eliot and the like. But the manna was pure plastic, and someone had to say so. Snow was being presented as the bridge between the two cultures. Scientists must judge the science, but the novels are there for all to read. And it was rumoured that Snow might arrive in Cambridge to be Master of a college. Yes, some demolition there had to be. I could wish that the thing had been done with greater dignity, but I cannot wish it undone.

On a smaller scale was Mrs Leavis's account of Dorothy Sayers in the *Scrutiny* of December 1937. Some readers felt that the objective was hardly worth the powder; but here again it will be conceded that the job needed to be done: the creator of Lord Peter, the archetypal day-dream of immature women, was being taken seriously as a literary academic. Who else undertook the task?

More typically, however, and perhaps more successfully, Leavis's literary and moral placings made little fuss. His irony did not always 'work' – indeed, I often felt embarrassed on his behalf when he exercised it; but at its best it was unanswerable. In the *Scrutiny* of June 1951 he reviewed R. F. Harrod's book *The Life of John Maynard Keynes*. Leavis quotes a passage from Harrod describing why Keynes devoted his powers to financial speculation: he *must* be independent, he *must* have money to entertain dancers and buy his friends' pictures. Says Harrod: 'He was determined not to relapse into salaried drudgery.' The irony of Leavis's resuming sentence is so quiet that it might be overlooked, but, coming from him it is devastating: 'The rejected "salaried drudgery" was university teaching.'

If Leavis was aggressive, his outbursts were comparatively few, and were spaced out over a lifetime devoted to ends that I wholly respect. My account has been, I know, partial, in more senses than one. It is partial in that some truths have been necessarily omitted out of regard for people still living. It is partial also because I am aware of a debt, both personal and intellectual, to both the Leavises. My present opinions, after so long, no doubt show the mark of their teaching – I even believe that the idea of commercial television is intrinsically corrupt, the final *trahison des clercs*. My qualified admiration for the work of the Leavises must therefore expect to carry little weight. But one verifiable fact may be pointed to. At a time when various other – salaried – lecturers now largely forgotten were directing attention to writers now largely forgotten, Leavis, unsalaried, along with I. A. Richards, was writing the syllabus for university and sixth-form literary studies today. Such is not the working of charisma.

7

F. R. Leavis: a memoir

SEBASTIAN MOORE

It is a rare and awesome thing to have had one's life touched by a genius. The chances against it are astronomical. Yet this luck, or grace, has been mine.

It is only much later in life that it becomes possible to establish a scale to measure the different depths in oneself to which various influential persons have penetrated. Towards one end of that scale, there is that region of the spirit where one can be profoundly and forever changed. For me, Leavis alone of all my teachers penetrated that region. And because I know that his impression was not what they call subjective, but on the contrary was the unifying of so many elements in experience that hardly ever come together, I feel confident in calling it the influence that only genius exerts. To study under him at Cambridge in those early days was the kind of educational experience the possibility of which now seems more and more remote.

It was an integral part of this unusual depth of influence, of course, that one was not alone in it. There were disciples – a term that nowadays is not used without mockery, except in New Testament studies, where appreciation has been driven out by technique. There was that special friendship which grows among a few people undergoing the same kind of awakening and enlightenment.

What was it that he was doing for us? What was he bringing together that the whole modern educational system seemed to put asunder? He associated literature with the hunger for ultimate meaning without which we would not be human. He came upon a world where the enjoyment of literature was confined to an 'aesthetic' sphere, while the human quest for meaning was thought to be taken care of by theologians and, in a more innocent time, by philosophers. He came into that world and said a resounding No to its division of labour and consequent emasculation of the spirit. Really to hear Shakespeare's words is to be troubled and excited in these deepest reaches of the spirit where damnation, purgation and salvation are appropriate concepts. And the test of great writing is, precisely, that it echoes in those forgotten reaches. I remember Leavis once referring to 'that almost indecent way Shakespeare has of telling you things about yourself that you didn't know you knew.' No one else was speaking like this. I met a younger Englishman at a theological conference at Boston two summers ago who, when I mentioned Leavis, said 'He was the last prophet we had in England.' And immediately we understood each other. We had both felt that oneness between some word-orderings and 'the word' which, once felt, sends shock waves of change right through the system.

I came to Leavis as a Christian and a monk. Thus I had some familiarity with a tradition that had for two millennia cultivated the soul's deepest desire, mapped out in various ways the *itinerarium mentis in Deum*. It had done this far more creatively in earlier than in modern times, so that the spiritual tradition had perforce become 'fugitive and cloistered'. Yet there was a teacher who, while remaining staunchly agnostic, allowed one's spiritual life to breathe in that world of great literature so long claimed for itself by a modernity impatient of the monkish. Yes, he really made us monks and priests feel we belonged, with all our priestliness, to the world we lived in. If this is called education, then another word will have to be found for what generally goes by that name.

I refer to 'us monks and priests', because Leavis had a large Roman clerical following. He used to say impishly that this was only because he had put Hopkins on the map, thus promoting 'one of ours' to the top rank of English poets. There was more to it than that. The soul craves for a unified vision of the world: and people like monks and priests, for whom that unified world exists *in principle*, experience a certain frustration at the failure of this believed-in unity to flesh itself out in the world we live in. Thus we perhaps more easily 'smell out' someone who offers a remedy to this spiritual schizophrenia. That was his appeal for us. And he exercised this appeal very properly in being the first critic of any note to discover that an obscure Victorian Jesuit had, in his attempt to spell out his dialogue with the infinite, achieved that combination of emotional honesty with technical sophistication that is the mark of high poetry. Who else paid attention to Hopkins in the early thirties? And Leavis pointed to the very thing that was most remarkable in a religious poet: the presence of a single integrity that dictated the confession of feelings and the ordering of words. Anyone conversant with religious writing as I am – and I include my own of course – knows with what fatal ease the hallowed phrase imposes itself, to the obfuscation of any real communication of feeling. As Eliot says: 'The religious poet says what he believes. The devotional poet says what he wants to believe.'

This was an important part of Leavis's unity of vision: emotional honesty showing itself in the way a phrase is turned. I remember him saying in a lecture, *à propos* of a sonnet of Christina Rossetti, 'She thinks she feels like that; but she doesn't feel like that.' (When a colleague to whom I quoted this commented 'What a sexist remark!' I groaned inwardly – what a long way we have come from that precision of thought and feeling.) He always would quote with approval Eliot's statement about Blake:

Blake's poetry has the unpleasantness of great poetry. Nothing that can be called morbid or abnormal or perverse, none of the things which exemplify the sickness of an epoch or a fashion, have this quality; only those things which, by some extraordinary labour of simplification, exhibit the essential sickness or strength of the human soul. *And this honesty never exists without great technical accomplishment.* [Emphasis mine – and Leavis's]

Another poetic giant received at Leavis's hands his first serious critical appraisal: T. S. Eliot. Only recently I was re-reading the chapter on *The Waste Land* in *New Bearings*, alongside the contemptuous sallies with which the accredited critics greeted that poem. Leavis was the only voice calling us to become *conscious* of living in this time and *then*, and *thus*, to read *The Waste Land*. It was the poetry of an age 'too conscious of too much', he said. Again, as a theologian, I am amazed at how early Eliot and his interpreter were grasping that new relationship of the psyche to its myths which is the most challenging and work-demanding problem for theology in our time.

I have to report another very recent experience that has brought home to me Leavis's prophetic character. Teaching the theology of salvation to American college students – not 'theological students', for we have a 'theology requirement' – I have come to realise that one of the most important signs of our 'fallen' condition is the under-development, in each sex, of a latent capacity to feel as the other sex feels. I am getting so used now to finding that 'Eliot was already there', that I thought of Tiresias. Leavis's comment on Eliot's note to this part of the poem is worth quoting. The note runs, it will be remembered:

Tiresias, although a mere spectator and not indeed a 'character', is yet the most important personage in the poem, uniting all the rest. Just as the one-eyed merchant, seller of currants, melts into the Phoenician Sailor, and the latter is not wholly distinct from Ferdinand, Prince of Naples, so all the women are one woman, and the two sexes meet in Tiresias. What Tiresias *sees*, in fact, is the substance of the poem.

Leavis comments:

If Mr Eliot's readers have a right to a grievance, it is that he has not given this note more salience; for it provides the clue to 'The Waste Land'. It indicates plainly enough what the poem is: an effort to focus an inclusive human consciousness. The effort, in ways suggested above, is characteristic of the age; and in an age of psychoanalysis, an age that has produced the last section of *Ulysses*, Tiresias – 'venus huic erat utraque nota' – presents himself as the appropriate impersonation. A cultivated modern is (or feels himself to be) intimately aware of the experience of the opposite sex.[1]

Whatever one thinks of the notes to *The Waste Land*, or of the above comment, the whole point is Leavis's realisation that it is the quality of consciousness, and the capacity to be more conscious, that matters today; that the great poet is one who can make us much more conscious; and that the great critic is one who finds 'salient' in the poet's work this transformative power. It is with a religious awe, a sense of making *anamnesis*, that I recall that Leavis did this to me and my religious contemporaries. Quite simply, he made life itself more exciting than it would otherwise have been. I love him for that.

It was he who gave me Eliot, whose poetry has stayed with me these forty-odd years, always reappearing in new places uncovered by a continuous theological probing of human experience. Without an interpreter of the calibre and charisma of Leavis, I do not think I would have been able to open my mind to the revolution in feeling that Eliot achieves and calls for. I mean that an altogether new willingness to listen to a poem with unremitting patience was required to experience what Eliot was doing with language and therefore with consciousness itself. Leavis instilled that contemplative stance, and made it seem obviously the only way to listen to real poetry. His repeated axiom, that 'there is only one right reading' for a poem is easily dismissed as dogmatism: but it envisages – what its critics showed little care for – a *consensus*, among hearers, *in* the poem, and thus a real fruitfulness of the word in the community. Nor did he believe that the elusive 'one right reading' could ever be approached without much dialogue, which he used to describe as 'saying to someone "this is what I seem to hear. What do you think about that?"' It's the same thing that runs through all his work among us: he cared. He was the educator, the nurturing one, the pastor *par excellence*.

It was in this stance of initiator to a fuller consciousness through the word, that he gave – *tradidit*! – Eliot to us. I remember how at my first supervision he handed to me the *Selected Essays*. That was something of an act of 'tradition' – a word as dear to him as it was to Eliot. I am not ashamed to compare what is still by far the most exciting educational experience I remember to something very much older, simpler, and shaped by a functional reverence – the experience, in fact, of discipleship. We are too clever and distracted for it these days. We can only take it in the phoney aura of the guru.

Shortly after the appearance of 'Little Gidding', Leavis said to me: 'The only poetic development comparable to that of Eliot from *The Waste Land* to "Little Gidding" is Shakespeare's.' I know that later he was to become sharply opposed to Eliot's poetic statement. He said to me, about fifteen years ago: 'I say No to Eliot, No to his alternatives of "pyx or pyre".' I have to say something about this change in attitude, which is fully expressed in the long chapter on Eliot in his penultimate book, *The Living Principle*. That essay begins with a strong reaffirmation of Eliot's greatness as a poet. But he finds in the *Quartets* many places where Eliot's wonderful creativity – a word that appears very frequently in the essay – lapses, and the verse goes limp. These are the places where the transcendent mystery is directly affirmed as a loving presence. Briefly, every so often Eliot chucks up the sponge and surrenders to the God of his daily Christian worship. There is no real feeling in these passages – indeed, religious surrender is made to do duty precisely for a certain inability to feel that is Eliot's sickness, evidenced in his notorious attitude to women and to sexuality. Yeeees! Eliot *is* very vulnerable just there. It has often been observed, however, that there are two types of mystic: one whose sense for the transcendent is born of emotional wounding and deprivation (Auden finds this in Dag Hammarskjold), another for whom it is born of emotional fulfilment. Eliot himself has noted both ways:

> This is the one way, and the other
> Is the same, not in movement
> But in abstention from movement; while the world moves
> In appetency, on its metalled ways
> Of time past and time future.[2]

Also, in Leavis's text a powerful assumption is at work. It is a dual assumption: that a vigorous civilisation always has a religious dimension, and that our civilisation is altogether lacking in vigour. It follows that our civilisation is incapable of producing significant religious poetry – and this is shown by the fact that *even Eliot* fails to do so – a backhanded recognition of Eliot's poetic stature! But the assumption is itself so charged with Leavis's highly individual attitude to religion that one must wonder whether it is not the *basis* for saying that Eliot's religious poetry is a failure, as well as being *corroborated* by this failure taken as independently ascertained fact. There seems to be an *argumentum in circulo* here.

This may be accountable for as follows. Leavis's religious attitude is avowedly indebted to Blake. Religiousness is the full expression of our creativity; and creativity, he believes, has no place in it for surrender to another and altogether higher power. But is this so? One might ask what religiousness, so esteemed by Leavis as an essential dimension of civilisation, *is* if not the confession of dependence on another and higher power, to which 'surrender' is appropriate and indeed enjoined by all the world religions. I don't think Leavis ever really asked that question. And he may just be projecting his own failure to face its implications onto Eliot at precisely those points where Eliot is saying 'Yes' to that very question. Where Eliot said 'Yes' – at, I believe, deep personal cost; it did cost him 'not less than everything' – Leavis said an emphatic 'No' to Eliot.

Of course this is speculation. I would prefer to emphasise that Leavis does raise the vital religious question of our time: that of a real synthesis, in feeling and image, of creativity with religious surrender, such that the latter would appear as the consummation of creativity rather than its relinquishing in favour of a higher power. It was, in fact, only recently that I realised that I had always operated out of two centres: a monk, the creature of God, and a modern, self-creating, and that now these two centres coalesce, and there is only one centre. It is, of course, to the great mystical tradition that we must look for this identity between creative self-constitution and surrender. As Bernard Lonergan – my other teacher – puts it: The infinite is mediated to the mystic through the immediacy with which he knows his or her own movement to the unknown. (I find myself wondering: Why is the top-level stuff so marvellous today, the lower levels so distracted and dreary?) And this 'movement to the unknown' is the most creative and self-constituting thing we ever do:

> We must be still and still moving
> Into another intensity
> For a further union, a deeper communion
> Through the dark cold and the empty desolation,
> The wave cry, the wind cry, the vast waters
> Of the petrel and the porpoise. In my end is my beginning.[3]

The point I am making is that it has taken me much labour to get within feeling distance of this unity, and that Leavis it was who gave the essential programme for this labour, as it was he who stumbled on its essential problematic, the issue of creativity and worship.

The problematic lurks, of course, at the heart of Leavis's crucial insight into the inseparability of great diction from the essential

movement of the soul. I shall never forget the abysmal disappointment, not to say sense of bathos, that awaited me in Rome whither
I repaired for theological studies immediately after my years at
Cambridge. In my naivete I somehow assumed that I would there
meet people who would do with a psalm or the 'Vexilla Regis'
what Leavis did with 'Put up your bright swords, for the dew will
rust them.' Nor was I entirely off beam in my complaint, as I subsequently learned when I read Northrop Frye's statement that the
most devastating failure in scripture study today is the total lack of
aesthetic, evaluative response. I recall an incident at, I think, M.I.T.
in the States. An honorary doctorate was to be awarded to some
eminent scripture scholar, and the President – whose speciality may
have been computers – asked for some representative works in that
field, so that he could make an appropriate speech. When the time
came, he opened by describing this preparatory activity and said,
of the scriptures, 'Surely these books deserve better treatment.
They are *good* books!' What Leavis called 'the higher navvying'
flourishes especially in the field of scripture scholarship. The Word
of God, which, for the believer, is *the* word, lacks that breathing-
room in the spirit which Leavis, with a lone voice, claimed for the
word. 'Our last prophet' – yes, perhaps: our last *believer* in the
word.

There were, of course, serious weaknesses in the Leavis 'movement', especially at the undergraduate level. The stringent demands
made of literature by Leavis involved the exclusion, from the
'canon', of whole tracts of poetry, prose and criticism traditionally
hallowed in the English School. Shelley, Tennyson – and, for
heavens' sake, Milton! – most of Dickens, Thackeray, Trollope . . .
the list continued. Bradley (with his footnote 'How many children
had Lady Macbeth?') was the Aunt Sally of Shakespeare criticism.
As a powerful strategy for giving more time and concentration to
certain areas and thus facilitating a revolution in consciousness, the
purge was justified. But for our young minds, the combination of
being let off an immense amount of reading with expressing lofty
disdain for the neglected authors, was too much. However, those
who outgrew this dogmatic exclusivism were able subsequently to
get more out of the neglected authors than if they had encountered

them as the classics of an Establishment. I well remember my dear friend Hilary Steuert, who was responsible for my reading English under Leavis, saying to me on one of our many walks: 'You know, I've been reading Bradley (a slight lowering of the voice for this terrible confession), and he's damned good!'

Leavis was one of those very rare 'men who opened my eyes'. There has been one other such teacher in my life: the Canadian Jesuit Bernard Lonergan. I have long felt that there must be a profound connection between these two crucial influences. Apart from the fact that Leavis, towards the end of his life, was becoming increasingly enthusiastic about Michael Polanyi, whose thought is very close to Lonergan's, I suggest the following. One of Lonergan's most transformative ideas was, that there are other *conversions* besides the religious. There is an *intellectual* conversion, which he described as follows:

The appropriation of one's own rational self-consciousness is not an end in itself but rather a beginning, for unless one breaks the duality in one's knowing, one doubts that understanding correctly is knowing. Under the pressure of that doubt, either one will sink into the bog of a knowing that is without understanding, or else one will cling to understanding but sacrifice knowing on the altar of an immanentism, an idealism, a relativism. From the horns of that dilemma one escapes only through the discovery (and one has not made it yet if one has no clear memory of its startling strangeness) that there are two quite different realisms, that there is an incoherent realism, half animal and half human, that poses as a half-way house between materialism and idealism and, on the other hand, that there is an intelligent and reasonable realism between which and materialism the half-way house is idealism.[4]

Then there is moral conversion, the feeling drawn to a good that is not simply the advantageous. Now some of us whom Lonergan has taught and changed have become convinced – and Lonergan has strongly agreed – that there is still another conversion: of feeling perhaps, of imagination, of psyche, of our mythic or symbolising consciousness. To such a conversion, surely Leavis was pointing: and he was alone in this. To hear Shakespeare or Yeats or Eliot in the 'conscious' way that he demanded is to be reborn. The old, the customary, Heidegger's *Alltäglichkeit*, dies in one, and new life springs up in its place.

God knows we need this conversion today, when a murderous defence policy is insinuating itself through a systematic murder of the language, in phrases such as 'acceptable losses', 'surgical strikes', 'fratricide' (for the collision of two warheads, causing boundless devastation). The spirit of F. R. Leavis is not absent from E. P. Thompson's admirable opening chapter of *Protest and Survive*.

I cannot doubt the part played by Leavis in whatever life-renewal I may have experienced, or in my hope of an ultimate salvation for humankind.

Notes

1 *New Bearings in English Poetry* (1950), p. 92.
2 'Burnt Norton' III.
3 'East Coker' V.
4 Bernard Lonergan S.J., *Insight: A Study of Human Understanding* (1957), XXVIII.

8

Scrutiny and F. R. L.: a personal memoir[1]

L. C. KNIGHTS

When I met him Leavis was still a probationary lecturer – Cambridge's term, then, for an assistant lecturer – in English; when that appointment ran out in 1932 he was not to receive an official university appointment for another four years. He was an active and influential supervisor, and – a late starter because of the First World War and its aftermath – he was preparing to write. His trenchant and timely *Mass Civilisation and Minority Culture* came out in 1930 as the first of Gordon Fraser's Minority Pamphlets. That, together with *New Bearings in English Poetry* (1932) and Q. D. Leavis's *Fiction and the Reading Public* (1932), suggests what we talked about – or listened to Leavis talking about with a vigour and pungency that I hadn't heard previously – at the Friday tea-parties.

At one of these, when the talk fell, as it often did, on the low state of literary journalism, someone – I forget who – said that if only we had some money we could muster sufficient talent to launch a new critical journal. I turned to a young American, Donald Culver, and said half-jokingly: 'You are an American, so you must be rich. There's an obvious use for your money.' He said he wasn't rich: he was living on an allowance. Later I called at a fellow student's rooms on some business to do with the English Research Society and found Culver and two others, E. H. McCormick (who was later to be known for his work on the painter Frances Hodgkins and New Zealand cultural history) and – was it? – Iqbal Singh. They were talking about the possibility of starting a journal to be called the *Phoenix*, in honour of D. H. Lawrence, and I joined in. A prospectus seemed called for to clarify our minds, and we tentatively agreed to collaborate. The *Phoenix* failed to fly, and I was the only one to hammer out something to put before the public. I. A. Richards introduced Culver and me to Michael Roberts, who, he thought, had a similar scheme in mind; but Roberts – looking, as Culver said, like a disappointed eagle – didn't respond, and the meeting was remarkable only for its embarrassment. Meanwhile I had, of course, reported back to Leavis, who wanted to promote the venture without, at first, taking editorial responsibility. We spent some time discussing a name for the new periodical before Leavis came up with *Scrutiny*, borrowed from the series of 'Scrutinies' in Edgell Rickword's *Calendar*: it suggested the severely discriminating eye and had a sufficiently rasping sound.

Leavis has described better than I can the inner thrust of the literary/educational campaign that in his mind he already saw taking shape. I can only report on what I know. Culver and I found a small printer, S. G. Marshall in Round Church Street, whose main business so far had been to print auction advertisements and the like, who was willing to take on the magazine at a price we felt we could afford. Mr Marshall proved to have a remarkable eye for typeface and layout. He and Culver between them produced an attractive cover, plain, elegant, and severe, that was to become familiar over twenty years. As a glorified office boy (also, of course, an editor) I had plenty of work to do. Subscriptions, which I had solicited in a small prospectus, began to come in – some from such eminences as Virginia Woolf and T. S. Eliot – and I began to discover the mysteries of marketing a literary product. Leavis has often remarked that we had no editorial underpropping. We had not indeed! Correspondence with potential contributors, potential subscribers, advertisers, and book shops was all carried on by a few people with normal work-loads outside the journal. I myself was much engaged with the research necessary for my Ph.D. thesis (later to become *Drama and Society in the Age of Jonson*) and combined *Scrutiny* business with trips to the reading-room of the British Museum. On one such occasion I called at a well-known London book-seller and glanced round the shelves to see if they stocked *Scrutiny*. An assistant asked if he could help me, and I said I was looking to see what periodicals they had. 'We don't have a periodicals section, Sir, but if you want a particular journal we shall be happy to get it for you.' I explained that I wanted to know if they would take a few copies of a new critical quarterly. The assistant's tone changed. 'Oh,' he said, 'I didn't know you were travellin'. If you're *travellin'* you go downstairs.' I went downstairs.

There were also more important matters than the market. I called on, or wrote to, a number of people, some of them established 'names', who we thought might be willing to contribute – Joseph Needham, Michael Oakeshott, W. H. Auden, Herbert Butterfield, G. Lowes Dickinson, and I. A. Richards. Auden, unfortunately, was the only one I didn't meet personally. All received me kindly, with real interest in the project, and promised to write something for an early number, as indeed they did. I have an especially vivid memory of Lowes Dickinson, whom I saw in his rooms at King's, looking like a benign Chinese sage. In due course I received one of his famous typewritten letters – rather like the one reproduced in Forster's *Life* of him – that it needed a cryptographer to decipher. To my regret it has now disappeared from the files.

To return to *Scrutiny*. Culver and I enjoyed ourselves enormously making up from galley-proofs the 'dummy' for the first number, which duly appeared on my birthday, 15 May 1932. Subscriptions were coming in (10 shillings for four numbers, post free), and there was a brisk sale in book shops. Even W. H. Smith, who had agreed to show a few copies on Cambridge station, kept sending to my parents' house – our 'office' – for more. What the *Manchester Guardian* called 'that fierce and uncompromising quarterly, *Scrutiny*' had an unexpectedly good press. Even the hands we had bitten made encouraging signals. W. J. Turner, in an article 'Education and Music' in the *New Statesman and Nation*, took the opportunity to remark: '*Scrutiny* is the most intelligent literary periodical I know of, and I hasten to recommend it before it is extinct, because it is much too good to live long.' In an advertising leaflet of 1934 we were able to quote from a clutch of favourable reviews in the *Listener*, the *Spectator*, the *Evening Telegraph* ('the best periodical of its kind in the country'), and others. There were encouraging noises from France and the United States. The *Times Literary Supplement*, the target of some of our early criticism, came up with a serious appraisal – 'a discerning review' we called it in the leaflet –

admitting the strength of our *raison d'être* ('The forces calculated to disintegrate taste are today armed with an apparatus of propaganda which has no adequate parallel in the past'), and, rightly, giving special attention to some of Leavis's editorials: 'Whatever the extent of one's agreement or disagreement with Mr Leavis, the case which he argues deserves attention . . . The editors are conscious of [*Scrutiny*'s] present limitations; but what they have published so far is enough to show that it is in responsible hands, and that it well deserves the support needed for its development.'

This was all very gratifying; but the immediate problem was to get sufficient support to keep going. The 500 copies of the first number promptly sold out, and we were able to pay the printer (some £50, as I remember). An additional 250 copies also sold, and we raised the subsequent print-runs, though never beyond 1400. Since we had no capital and no patron, *Scrutiny* depended entirely on its subscribers – and on contributors who were willing to write without pay: most of them could have done with a fee, however small. Naturally the editors 'made' nothing; later Leavis put in some of his own money, and there was one – I believe substantial – gift from a private donor; but throughout its twenty years *Scrutiny* was a – sometimes desperate – example of free enterprise. With the third number Leavis formally joined the editorial board, which was further strengthened by Denys Thompson, whose work on English in education was to prove influential. Harding became an editor in 1934, Wilfrid Mellers in 1942, and H. A. Mason (when both Harding and Mellers had withdrawn from the board, though they continued to write for the journal) in 1948. From 1935, when, apart from vacation visits to my parents' home, I left Cambridge for good (as I then thought), Leavis was not only the driving force; he was the only editor on the spot, and therefore – in spite of much correspondence with his collaborators – the one on whom, together with his wife, the main burden of unavoidable business fell. It is amazing that, since he was also teaching, he continued to write and publish so much of the criticism for which he will be remembered. From 1947 ,when I had the problems of a university department on my hands, as well as for a time those of an arts Faculty, I played a rapidly decreasing part in editorial business and policy-making. At one time I thought the only honest thing to do was to resign, but Leavis – was it just kindness, or did he really think, as he said, that I was still useful? – persuaded me to stay on: I was pleased enough to see my name still on the contents page. I suppose that as a merely nominal editor I had no reason for surprise when, in the autumn of 1953, it was from a third person that I learned of the decision to abandon publication. But I was hurt by this failure of communication. Of course Leavis was *the* editor of *Scrutiny*: he inspired it and, though it was very far indeed from being simply the organ of his critical opinions, as the silly name 'Leavisite' suggests, he set the dominant tone. *Scrutiny* without Leavis was literally inconceivable; but I like to think that without me, and without the help of Donald Culver, it would not have come into existence when it did; that is to say, times and circumstances being what they were, perhaps not at all.

Since this is a personal history, this is not the place, nor is it my business, to attempt an assessment of what *Scrutiny* achieved. But there are one or two matters on which I should like to put the record straight, and there is a problem I should like to formulate. The first is concerned with the past; the second is still important.

The charge, often made, that *Scrutiny* was more concerned with demolition – a 'methodical and uncompromising destruction of reputations' (John Hayward's phrase in 1948) – than with positive appreciation can be answered by pointing to the large number of essays and reviews that offered new insights, new opportunities for enjoyment: Leavis on Pope, Keats, George Eliot, Henry James; Harding on Jane Austen, Rosenberg, L. H. Myers, Eliot's 'middle-period' poetry; John Speirs on Burns and the ballads; James Smith on metaphysical poetry and Shakespeare's comedies; Q. D. Leavis on Edith Wharton and Santayana, as well as her astringent reviews; Derek Traversi on *Piers Plowman*, long before that poem was recognised as 'literature' rather than 'language'; Martin Turnell bringing to life for English readers French classics, well known or neglected. Selection is invidious, and a full list would be a long one, as anyone can see for himself simply by leafing through the twenty volumes of the Cambridge University Press reprint.

Nor was *Scrutiny* 'merely' a journal of literary criticism, even though the kind of attention it gave to politics and public affairs had not much immediate appeal in the thirties. In Leavis's editorial in the third number, 'Under Which King, Bezonian?', he vigorously, and to my mind unanswerably, explained why *Scrutiny* rejected the demand to 'show its colours' and to take a stand either with the Marxists or with the Conservatives and Anglo-Catholics, and why, in bringing to bear incisive imaginative thought on particular books and particular issues, it was not betraying but serving its 'social' function. Readers of a later age may need to be reminded of how hard it was at that time *not* to 'line up': Marxism in particular was not only fashionable among intellectuals – it appealed to genuine and generous ideals of social justice, and it offered a sense of certainty and purpose in a chaotic and crumbling world; its appeal was strengthened by the slump, Mussolini's Abyssinian adventure, and the rise of Hitler. 'The more seriously one is concerned for literature', Leavis remarked, 'the less possible does one find it to be concerned for that alone' – the wider concern being shown in 'the free play of thought on the underlying issues'. It was hoped of course to give meaning to that last phrase in dealing with particular issues: without detailed application it would remain a mere declaration of good intentions. And *Scrutiny*, especially in the first half of its life, consistently gave space not only to literary criticism but to articles on politics, political and social thought, the 'sociology of literature', education, and philosophical thought as it affected non-specialist thinking. Since *Scrutiny* had no programme in the commonly accepted sense, not even a shared *Weltanschauung*, it saw its function in these fields as a task of clarification.

The problem – referred to earlier – remains. It can be put most simply in words from the *Calendar's* declaration of aims: it is how 'to speak plainly without offence'. To speak plainly is often to speak severely: in literary criticism it is, when confronted with shoddy or second-rate writing, to say as clearly as possible where it falls short, even if it is widely acclaimed. There is always the possibility of mistake – that is a risk one takes; but the honest attempt to maintain standards of criticism is the only way of honouring what is really authentic and ensuring the widest possible recognition for what it essentially is – something beyond our everyday selves toward which, sometimes with immediate and delighted recognition, but sometimes with reluctance, we have to grow. To write in this spirit about the work of the past merely runs the risk of disturbing inertia. In relation to current writing the task is more difficult. None of us enjoys reading unfavourable reviews of our books, especially when we suspect there is some truth in them. A book dismissed as second-rate or as failing to live up to its own implicit claims is not just a bit of the external world: there is an author behind it, and if you prick him he bleeds.

Naturally *Scrutiny* was not much concerned with books existing at a sub-literary level, of the kind that Q. D. Leavis had examined in *Fiction and the Reading Public*. But it could not avoid dealing with work with some esteem in literary circles that seemed to demand a more astringent attention. It was here that *Scrutiny* got its reputation for a joyless destructiveness – a charge coming with more force inasmuch as none of the regulars were poets or novelists. I'm not sure how much, in any general view, this last matters. The critic has his *métier*, and even if poets and artists get their most helpful criticism from friends and fellow artists, every writer presumably needs the sense that he is writing for an audience capable of intelligent discriminations – the kind of public for which Henry James sighed in vain, the novelist, as he again and again remarked, being dependent – dependent in intimate ways affecting his creativity – 'on some responsive reach of critical perception' among his readers; whereas in the Anglo-American world curiosity about what the artist was really trying to achieve 'never emerged from the limp state.'[2] *Scrutiny* didn't presume to give advice to writers: it did aspire to make the general level of critical opinion less limp and more challenging.

'The function we envisage', Leavis said editorially (ii.4), 'is essentially co-operative . . . The critic puts his judgements in the clearest and most unevadable form in order to invite response; to forward that exchange without which there can be no hope of centrality. Centrality is the product of reciprocal pressures, and a healthy criticism is the play of these.' Centrality, more or less as Leavis defined it – the reciprocal play of intelligent interests – is something that is necessary for a civilisation, a culture, in any recognisable sense of the term. But putting on one side the necessary qualifications – in what ways does centrality need to be balanced by diversity if it is not to tend toward a body of received opinion of the kind that *Scrutiny* very properly attacked? – it is doubtful how far it can be achieved by conscious effort or a deliberate programme. The 'essentially co-operative function' of criticism is a different matter and can be endorsed without qualification. The interesting question is why *Scrutiny* in some ways failed to achieve this, or achieved it only among a circle that, if not as limited as those who disliked it asserted, was not as wide as success in the enterprise demanded. I do not think that the fault lay entirely with the unpropitious times – the rise of a mass reading public, the politics of literary reviewing, or the effects of a disruptive war. There was somthing in both programme and method that militated against the ends proposed.

At a time when there is in England *no* journal of literature and ideas to set a serious standard, the question is worth pursuing. To foster standards in literature or any other non-specialist field of the mind – to prevent them from slithering into a spineless relativism – it is necessary, as Leavis continually insisted, 'to put one's judgements' in the clearest and most unevadable form'. As Harding put it, in reviewing a book by John Macmurray (VIII.4), 'Reciprocal challenging is as much a part of genuine social life as is reciprocal sanctioning.' ('In stressing the need to love your enemies', he added, Macmurray 'says nothing of the equal need to resist your friends'.) It depends of course on how the challenging ('to invite response') is done. For me the clue is in another remark of Harding's, when, discussing the differences between dominative and integrative behaviour, he said: 'To leave his associates genuinely free to disagree with him without discomfort is not characteristic of the self-assertive person.' To leave others free to disagree without discomfort: to keep that in mind as an ideal is not to peep out timidly to see which way the wind is blowing before committing oneself; but it is to make sure that the challenging is done in such a way as not to inhibit the possibility of change, on both sides. It is largely a question of tone and manner, of unconscious assumptions and

attitudes. Conor Cruise O'Brien, speaking of what he regarded
as Simone Weil's excessive trust in intelligence and her distrust
(*not* dislike) of friendship, has written:

Does the love of good depend on the light of the intelligence? It hardly
seems so; we can all think of rather stupid people who are kind and honest,
and of quite intelligent people who are mean and treacherous. Might not
friendship conceivably be a more likely channel for the love of good than
intelligence? And might not the impairment of friendship by the demands
of intelligence be a greater evil than the impairment of the expression of
intelligence by the demands of friendship?

And a little later in the same article (in the *New York Review of
Books* (May 12 1977)) he quotes Burke: 'Falsehood and delusion
are allowed in no case whatsoever, but as in the exercise of all the
virtues there is an economy of truth. *It is a sort of temperance by
which a man speaks truth with measure that he may tell it the longer*'
(italics mine). This is part of O'Brien's extended discussion of the
place of the dedicated intellectual in politics, and there is perhaps
a too-sharp division between the claims of intelligence and friendship. But in the insistence on such intangibles as a readiness for
friendship – a readiness, where possible, to say 'we' - as on the
value of what Burke calls 'measure', even in the principled defence
of truth, there is something which those who strive to promote
cultural values, even in an insidiously hostile world, cannot afford
to forget. After all, as Montaigne reminds us, one's mind 'is always
in apprenticeship and on trial'.

In writing this I am partly trying to clear up my own mind
about the man who, whatever the support he got from a varying
body of collaborators, was, as I have said, essentially *the* editor of
Scrutiny. The notices that followed Leavis's death either emphasised
his greatness as a critic and his especial relevance to the age, or
selected for animadversion those scarecrow features that have for
decades been presented in the press and elsewhere; his prickliness,
polemic, and continuing vehemence against figures that he saw as
embodiments of all that he hated in the modern world. None did
justice to his complexity.

I have spoken of my own debt to him, both personal and intellectual, and it is a fact that very many able men and women felt

that it was their great good fortune to be taught by him at Cambridge. His influence, through his writings, his pupils, and his pupils' pupils, has been worldwide. It should have been entirely salutary. If it was not, it was for reasons that concern all of us who teach literature or write criticism. Among those who admired him he was, I think, a too powerful and pervasive force. The critic, he used to say, puts his judgements in the form 'This is so, is it not?'; and he certainly hoped to provoke a 'response' to his 'challenge'. But he did not realise the moral weight that he commanded – especially in relation to young minds fresh from school – that made 'No, it is not' virtually impossible as a response to his question. Whether he wished it or not – and consciously he didn't – his judgements and attitudes were taken over by others without his talents and without his range of supporting reading. They became a kind of orthodoxy within the prevailing orthodoxy (whatever that might be), especially among those – and I was one – who liked to feel that they were an embattled minority or a saving remnant. It was one thing for Leavis to use all his polemical skill against those he saw as representing mere establishment values or the 'technologico-Benthamite' trends that were, and are, destroying all that he valued in English culture; it was another thing when his battle cries became shibboleths. There were very few of the central *Scrutiny* group who, like Harding and James Smith, had strength of mind and personality to remain genuinely independent even while admiring him. He was himself a widely read man; his dismissive judgements had to be taken seriously because he had long pondered his texts. ('They say I don't know my Milton', he said. 'I had a pocket Milton with me all through the First World War, and it's well thumbed. He's the only English poet whose verse rhythms will stand up to heavy gunfire.') But few of those who came under his influence had either the range or the acuteness of judgement to accept the stimulus he offered and yet follow their own individual bent. He was a great liberator from received opinion; but like other liberators he did not always leave his followers free. In opposition to his own professed and genuine beliefs about teaching, there was an unconscious 'gesture of interference'. Some silly things have been said about the *Scrutiny* pantheon, as though there were some kind of formal interdict against authors outside 'the great tradition'. But pupils did pick up too easily dismissive judgements, and Leavis would have been an even greater teacher if he had more explicitly encouraged them to read whatever they felt drawn to. 'Practical Criticism' too, which he demonstrated so well in class or discussion, though it quickened many minds, did so at the expense of wide, ranging, and absorbed reading, without which Practical Criticism is inclined to become the deployment of a limited skill, as it often seems to have done today.

The *Times Literary Supplement*, reviewing at length the 1963 twenty-volume reprint, spoke of Leavis's 'splendid passion, reminiscent, at times, of the best passages of Milton's pamphleteering'. He was indeed passionate in his belief that literature *mattered*, and in his insistence on the importance of the university: in the general decay of standards the university was the only effective place for mobilising the kind of intelligence that could really affect the quality of ordinary living - with the study of English literature, reaching out as it was bound to do to other literatures and other-disciplines, as a central generative and critical force. As he often said, he wanted co-operation: he needed allies; but not responding, easily to what Richard Sennett has called 'the challenge of other ness', instead of allies he got disciples. The result was that even when his attacks on this or that milieu – Bloomsbury or whatever – were justified, he lost sight of the individuals who, more or less loosely, composed the adversary groups, and so only provided the disciples with derogatory brand-names.

I have often wondered what would really have satisfied him. When *Scrutiny* was reprinted by the Cambridge University Press I wrote to congratulate him, adding that he must be glad to see his work at last getting the recognition it deserved. He replied tartly 'Recognition from whom?', and he listed disparagingly a number of people who had praised the work. It was of course Cambridge where he most wanted recognition and authority. But I doubt whether an English faculty well stocked with men and women he had taught would have come anywhere near his ideal English school. There was an inner contradiction that both fuelled his energies and frustrated them. It was as though he was driven by some force with a built-in guarantee of disappointment. And his exasperation was turned outward on what became a monotonously repeated list of institutionally sanctioned adversary groups, as it was against a succession of former pupils and collaborators whom he saw, unjustly, as having compromised with the world. At the University of York, where after his formal retirement he held a visiting professorship for some years, he is said to have been genial and relaxed. But in relationships where he was more closely involved his attitude was that of a man who would not accept much less than total endorsement. He would not recognise that most of us are of mixed abilities and interests, that even the best of causes are unlikely to be promoted by men in uniform, and that to welcome radical diversity is not necessarily to compromise on essential aims. His later writings on T. S. Eliot – whom he had so much admired and whom he continued to regard as the greatest poet of our time – are sad reading: not because they challenge some basic assumptions behind the poetry, but because they give the impression of something like animus against a man who in his greatest poem – and certainly with no less courage than Leavis's own – refused to simplify his sense either of what life can offer or of what we can do with such creative potential as we have.

Notes

1 This contribution consists of selected parts of an article, 'Remembering *Scrutiny*', that appeared in *The Sewanee Review* (Fall 1981).
2 Phrases quoted come from the preface to the stories collected in *The Lesson of the Master*. Readers of the prefaces and letters will know how often the complaint appears – and this from a writer whose intense self-criticism might have been expected to make him independent of public taste, except of course where his livelihood was concerned.

9

On being F. R. Leavis's publisher[1]

IAN PARSONS

I cannot now recall precisely when I first met Leavis, but it was certainly more than forty years ago. And equally certainly it was not while I was still at Cambridge, for contrary to what has sometimes been suggested I was never a pupil of his. I wish I had been. True I attended his lectures, and enjoyed them, but I was far too timid to solicit his acquaintance by going up on the rostrum at their conclusion, as many of my bolder contemporaries did. No, it must have been a year or more after the publication, in 1932, of *New Bearings in English Poetry*, and therefore some five years after I had joined Chatto and Windus, that I first got to know its author.

To this day I am not quite sure why Leavis sent his manuscript to me, though it may have been that he was drawn to Chatto's because we had published some of J. H. C. Grierson's critical works, were the publishers of T. F. Powys, whom he admired, or possibly because the previous year we had published Empson's *Seven Types of Ambiguity*. Empson had been at Winchester with me, and when he came up to Cambridge a year after me we saw quite a bit of each other. I acted in one of his plays, and a considerable number of his poems first appeared in *The Cambridge Review*, of which I was editor for the Summer Term of 1928. But whatever the reason for the arrival of *New Bearings* in St Martin's Lane, I vividly remember the exictement with which I and others read it, and there was never any question but that the firm wanted to publish it. Its success was immediate, and the book soon became so widely known that – except possibly for a short time during the Second World War, owing to lack of paper – it has never been out of print from that day to this.

I have spent a large part of my working life publishing books of literary criticism, by a diversity of authors both British and American. A surprising amount of that time has been spent trying to persuade them not to use lit. crit. jargon, not to write above the likely level of their readers' intelligence, not to throw together the texts of a discarded series of lectures in the mistaken belief that what is acceptable when spoken in the class-room will be readable when printed in a book, and last but not least, to check their quotations. The latter need may seem odd when one is talking of academic authors, who are liable to possess libraries of their own and certain to have access to those of the institutions in which they work. But that is not the point. They misquote, and do so almost invariably, not because they are without the means of verification but because they are so familiar with their models that they rely on their memories – usually with disastrous results.

None of the above problems arose with Leavis's manuscripts. Years of practising what he had preached, that teaching English was a collaborative process involving the free interchange of ideas and the mutual testing of critical judgements, absolved him from any risk of patronising his readers or talking above their heads. And you cannot write Leavis's kind of criticism, which is analytical and moral rather than ameliorating and biographical, without using language very precisely. If you are subjecting an author's words to close scrutiny, are dissecting and analysing a work in a way that involves cogent comparisons, you cannot afford to indulge in sloppy sentences or verbal clichés. Equally, the words scrutinised must be the right words, not a garbled version of them.

I am well aware that in saying this I am flying in the face of Leavis's erstwhile opponents, who for many years kept up a chorus of complaint that he wrote deplorable English and repeatedly used portentous phrases like 'the infallible centrality of judgement' or 'the essential creativity of life', which they found virtually meaningless. To this I can only say that I am speaking as a publisher, and that as Leavis's publisher the number of times I've had occasion, over the last forty years, to ask him to clarify a passage could be counted on the fingers of two hands. You may say that this merely denotes the limitations of my own judgement; I would reply that surely there is a distinction to be drawn between complexity and obscurity, just as there is between jargon – the debased common coin of a discipline or trade – and the inventive use of language to describe a new concept. Certainly Leavis's prose style is often complex, sometimes involuted: it had to be if it was to reflect accurately the complex nature of his thought. As for the phrases that Leavis has coined, he has used them so insistently in contexts that clearly define their meaning that, far from being portentous or vapid, they strike me as outcrops of a strictly personal critical vocabulary. So it never entered my head to attempt to induce Leavis to write more simply: an attempt that I would have thought as presumptuous as it was ill-conceived. Not that he was ever anything but willing to consider specific textual emendations. In my experience it is always the less distinguished author who is apt to adopt an intransigent *quod scripsi, scripsi* attitude to a publisher's editorial suggestions.

But surely, someone will say, being Leavis's publisher must have been a peculiarly exacting and uncomfortable business? With so pugnacious an author there must have been endless rows, and you must have become involved, however reluctantly, in the classic literary battles which have punctuated his career? Nothing could be further from the truth. Powerful personalities always attract myths, and a popular myth about Leavis portrays him as some kind of cantankerous ogre, crouched in his Cambridge cave, snarling and ready to bite anybody who approaches. Well, I have been publishing F.R.L.'s books since 1932, have only recently published the fourteenth of them, and hope later this month to receive the manuscript of another major work. I would have thought that spoke for itself. No publisher is obliged to go on publishing an author with whom he finds it difficult to deal, just as no author is obliged to remain with a publisher in whom he has lost confidence – option clause or no option clause. There have been occasional disagreements, of course; in so long an association how could there not have been? But our very few disputes have been conducted with complete frankness on both sides, and resolved without rancour.

As for battles, Leavis has always been entirely capable of fighting his own; and since I firmly believe that publishers nearly always do more harm than good by joining in the fray (they are self-evidently *parti-pris*, and literary editors invariably give the reviewer the last

word) there have only been three occasions when I've felt com-
pelled to break my rule - none of them. I should add, at Leavis's
suggestion. The first was during the brouhaha in *The Spectator*
following that paper's publication of the Richmond Lecture, when
numerous irate correspondents delivered themselves of such widely
inaccurate statements about Leavis's status and readership that I
thought a few facts – such as that Cambridge University Press
were about to re-issue the whole of *Scrutiny* – and some sales statistics might clear the air. The second was when equally misleading
statements were made by a Cambridge don in a learned periodical,
purporting to show that Eliot was a best-seller from the word go,
and that anyway Leavis's critical method was derived from Empson.
Here again, a few relevant figures and dates were enough to explode
both propositions. The last occasion concerned the vitriolic notice
of *Letters in Criticism* in the *T.L.S.* (a salutary reminder that,
despite the flowing tide of approbation in Leavis's eightieth year,
there are still sharks about) in which the anonymous reviewer
complained that, on top of all the author's sins, his publisher's
blurb made quite unjustifiable claims for the book's contents. It so
happened that I had written the blurb myself, with some care; and
I hope, and think, I was able to show that it was the reviewer
rather than myself who was guilty of misrepresentation.

Such brief excursions, self-inflicted at that, are a small part of a
publisher's relationship with an author. Far more important is the
continuing year-to-year relationship, and here Leavis has been the
very opposite of a back-seat driver. Much too busy doing his own
work, teaching and writing, he has been content to leave us to do
ours, and has never once badgered us about sales or breathed down
our necks about publicity, as so many authors do. For that, and for
the books that have come to us, as well as for the personal kindness
and consideration that he has shown me, I am glad to have this
opportunity of expressing my gratitude.

Note

1 This article was written in 1975.

10

The long pursuit

MICHAEL BLACK

Scrutiny ceased publication in 1953, and was reissued by the Cambridge University Press in 1963 as a uniform set of 20 bound volumes, the final volume containing a Retrospect by Leavis and an index. The Press also published a two-volume selection from *Scrutiny* chosen and edited by Leavis, in 1968.

Since I looked after these publications at the Press, I came to know Leavis through them. I was at that time an Assistant Secretary to the Syndics. I had not been taught by Leavis at the University, had not even met him. But as a boy in a small and remote country grammar-school sixth form, making my first attempts to understand the poetry I was reading for the Higher School Certificate, I had come on the copy of *Revaluation* which a Cambridge-educated headmaster had put in the school library. It helped me to see what might be said and gave me words to use (his, of course, at that stage). I went up to Cambridge to read English immediately after the war. Like generations of Cambridge men and women I went to Leavis's lectures on Practical Criticism. At that period he always had a big audience; and you had to sit in the front rows if you wanted to hear him, for he lectured in an unraised conversational voice, without tricks or oratory. He looked like a ruffled bird, in his black gown, and the very imitable voice was hung upon, for various reasons. We all 'did' him, trying to catch the characteristic phrases, the little gasp or sniff before a sardonic joke, the pondering tone. It was much later that I realised what a superb reader of poetry he was, especially of Eliot (I believe some tapes survive). It was the rhythm which he had mastered, not as a matter of single phrases or lines, but as a key to the whole evolving sequence of meanings. Nobody else could read like that; yet the voice was the one we imitated, slightly nasal, seemingly flat.

By 1945 he was almost the only survivor of the founding figures of Cambridge English, and was coming into his period of critical dominance. We knew it, and rather revelled in it. Not that it was uncontested: I had a sobering glimpse of the bitterness of that struggle when, quite unexpectedly, I was sent for one evening, just before Hall, by E. M. W. Tillyard, the Master of my College. As Senior Tutor he had admitted me as an Exhibitioner, and perhaps saw me as one of his bright young men going wrong. I had no warning what it was about. It seems he had read one of my essays; pink, and trembling with rage, he told me at length that if I went on like *that* I would come to no good. I had no answer: white, and trembling with shock I went into Hall and ate my dinner in silence. I don't remember what I had written: certainly something callow and derivative. And it was true that many of my weekly essays were written with the Faculty Library's copy of the relevant volume of *Scrutiny* on the desk beside me. I got to know the contents of the early volumes quite well, and I was one of many. Cambridge supervisors must have sighed as they recognised this week's permutation of the word from Downing; and some must have been angry, like Tillyard. But it was not the reaction of a good teacher.

His outburst shook me out of an innocence. Before I took Part II, I took the trouble to discover who the examiners were – not a thing I would have done before. I became a subscriber to *Scrutiny* when I went down, and I bought and read (and reread) Leavis's books as they came out, and reviewed the later ones. I began to see what he was about; it became my settled conviction that he was the greatest critic in the language, and like others I felt that as long as he was alive there was some comfort, whatever else happened.

It must have been Leavis himself who approached the Press about the reissue of *Scrutiny*. He called formally on R. J. L. Kingsford, then Secretary to the Syndics. Kingsford was a modest and open-minded man, transparently honourable, and a great gentleman. Leavis admired the type, and the two were impressed with each other. Leavis in his formal role could be a persuasive advocate: in fact he had great social address. Kingsford was persuaded that there was a serious case for the reissue, even though it was quite unprecedented as a publishing venture. He turned to Boris Ford, then responsible for the Press's schoolbook publishing, and to me as interested in English, though still very junior. We had no hesitation, of course, and recommended publication. I was not present at the Syndicate meeting at which the proposal was accepted. Nor was the then Chairman of the Syndicate, Stanley Bennett, who was in the U.S.A. on sabbatical leave, I think. This was perhaps a fortunate chance; when Bennett returned I remember him being genially rueful, perhaps thinking that he had been spared one embarrassment at the cost of a slighter one – that his friends might ask him how *that* had happened during his chairmanship.

It was my job to administer the publication, which was quite a lengthy and complicated business. The agreement was that Leavis and Mrs Leavis should share a royalty as editors. My first task was to locate all the contributors, give them a list of their contributions, and ask for formal permission to reprint, offering a fee which was to be a first charge on the royalty. I discovered then what a wide range of contributors there had been – in the early years, at any rate. All of them agreed except W. H. Auden, who thought that *Scrutiny* had been a bad influence, did not think his own contributions 'were any good', and withheld permission. This might have threatened the whole venture, but Kingsford suggested that when we had permission from everyone else we should tell Auden and ask him to reconsider. He did so, not wishing to be the dog in the manger; but he made it a condition that a note should be printed saying that republication was 'with his consent but against his will'. I failed to remember to do this, and Auden presumably forgot that he had asked for it, which was discreet of both of us.

We printed the reissue by photolithography in the U.S.A., and bound it there as well. We ordered 2500 sets, on the argument that half might be sold in the U.S.A., and half in the rest of the world. In the event the printers supplied a lot of 'overs', so we had initial stock of nearly 3000 sets. The price, initially, was £2 a volume or £35 a set. In the event we sold rather fewer in the U.S.A., than we expected, but more elsewhere: Japan in particular took a large number of sets. The reissue went out of print in the mid-1970s. By commercial standards the publication was a success, and for some years it supplied the Leavises with a substantial proportion of their royalty-income. I assume that our reissue led Faber to reprint *The Criterion* and Frank Cass to reissue *The Calendar of Modern Letters.*

When the reissue was accepted, we had suggested to Leavis that in due course there should be a two-volume selection for those who could not afford the whole set; and he agreed. But when the time came to think about the contents he found himself in a difficult position. He had decided that he did not want to duplicate what was already available in book form; and by now both he and the other major contributors had published books collecting their *Scrutiny* articles. There was much left, but a high proportion of it was by himself and Mrs Leavis. This was a chance to do justice to her, and his material was important, but he felt sensitive nonetheless. It was my function to persuade him to suppress this feeling, and now my familiarity with the contents came in handy. He gave me a generous acknowledgement in the preface for my help, and I was very grateful for it, indeed proud of it; while knowing also that he was in a sense displacing on to me any residual criticism that there was more by the Leavises than by anyone else.

When he had put it together, his own doubts were partly overcome: indeed he said in a letter to me

I've tackled the fitting in, etc., and now suddenly (immodestly perhaps) see the whole thing as very impressive – irresistible – *ktēma es aei* – a classic, etc.

The trouble is that FR and QDL preponderate so unconscionably. No, not really unconsc.: *we* did the work, wrote more than anyone else, gave our lives to it (*not* for money or the world's love), and have left there so much unreprinted.

That brief Preface is a delicate job.

. . . If anything has to go it must surely be something of mine – *Under Which King?* I think.

At any rate, I hasten to put the upshot in front of you.

I was very anxious that the piece he mentions here ('Under which King, Bezonian?', an editorial written in 1932, one of the most intelligent texts of the literary politics of the 1930s) should go in; so I pressed him again. I was also very keen to include the exchange with F. W. Bateson on 'The Function of Criticism', first published in 1953, and giving one of the best statements of Leavis's critical position (though less well known than the exchange with Wellek). But this last item produced another small complication; Bateson, when asked for his permission to reprint, wanted the opportunity to have the last word. It was a mistake: he should have been content to have occasioned a valuable debate, in which the issues were well brought out. However his new piece did not change the ground of the discussion, merely asserting that he thought he was right. I urged Leavis to let it go in, and with the equivalent of a shrug he did.

These two publications opened a relationship with Leavis which I greatly valued – inevitably, since he was the greatest man I ever met or shall meet. There were also opportunities to extend the relationship, though I was careful not to poach on Chatto's territory. (I once in a clumsy moment pointed out that I had not done so: 'You wouldn't have succeeded', he said bleakly.) It was my idea, I think, that Leavis should be invited to compile a Cambridge Book of English Verse. I remembered from the days of his lectures how he would occasionally produce a really bad Victorian poem from the old Oxford Book, and exclaim with amused affection about Quiller-Couch's standards and taste. So it was a natural challenge to ask him to do better. After some pondering he wrote in September 1964:

My conviction is only reinforced by the intervening opportunity to revert to the matter of the anthology, and to reflect on it. I'm all in favour of the Oxford Book's being ousted by something better, but still can't believe that a massive, would-be inclusive anthology is a good thing – could be, I mean. All my considerings of the critical problems that would be involved in deciding what was properly anthologizable and what was not leave me there. The temptation to ensure that what I know *ought* to go in, given an anthology, and probably won't, has kept me reflecting. But any bent towards yielding has been inexorably checked by the confirmed realisation that the undertaking would be a major one, and that I'm now nearly a septuagenarian, and am so much distracted by my responsibilities on what I may call the Robbins front that the unwritten books most important to me don't get on except slowly.

An important initiative from his side had come in 1962. The Press had published in 1959 C. P. Snow's Rede Lecture, *The Two*

Cultures. It had had an extraordinary reception. Normally we would only sell 1000 or 1500 copies of such lectures, and over some years. Snow's lecture had reprinted and reprinted, and I stopped counting at 100,000 copies. It had also been expensively excerpted in magazines, and rumour had it that the President of the U.S.A. thought it an important statement, which ought to influence national educational policy. Leavis has recorded that when it first came out he picked it up in the showroom of the Press, saw what it was, and declined to put down his money. But when he began to find it quoted at him in scholarship examinations as received wisdom, he felt it time that it was unreceived as unwisdom; and he chose to make Snow's lecture the subject of the Richmond Lecture, also given at Cambridge. The Richmond Lecture was actually a domestic occasion at Downing College, but guests were invited, and I was one. I went not knowing what to expect, and was surprised to find the hall packed tight with people, some of them perched in the window-embrasures. There was a tension of great excitement.

Lectures are an absurd way of communicating. Only an athletic listener can carry away a long argument of any subtlety: I can't. I don't know what other listeners made of it. We were all aware that an onslaught had been delivered; and I listened glumly as at least one bully-boy among Leavis's hard-line supporters sitting up on the window-sill laughed triumphantly at the mockery of Snow (very skilled, since Leavis was determined to make a mock of Snow). I went off in a daze, only knowing that it had been a great occasion – of some sort.

Among the audience was the Cambridge Correspondent of *The Times*. I presume he had been invited in the knowledge that he was that, and that he would think the lecture should be reported. He did so, naturally enough, and the domestic occasion became a national one. The terms of the report meant that the text needed to be made available, and quite shortly *The Spectator* printed the whole lecture. This was good, since the outraged could now discover what they were being outraged by; it was bad in that *The Spectator* adorned the text with little caricatures of Snow, as if his worst offence were to wear pebble-lensed glasses and to have dewlaps. That hardly looked like an argument, so outrage was compounded, and there followed in *The Spectator* all those letters which said that Leavis was a nasty man, and had been nasty to a nice man. It was a classic case of the English tendency to turn an intellectual issue into a social friction, so confirming one of Leavis's grievances. It was often urged against him that he had a paranoid feeling that the literary establishment of metropolitan London was a conspiracy. But that was not the point, which was that where you have a herd, you don't *need* a conspiracy. Hence some of his thematic imagery, about 'flank-rubbing', or 'swimming, shoal-supported, with the tide'. He discovered, at recurrent cost, that where things are run as if they were a club, the worst offence is not to be genial to the other members, and to find that you have to tell the truth.

There was a sad inevitability about his whole long struggle, epitomised in the Snow affair. The sequence of events was not predictable, but once it had unfurled, one was tempted to be wise after the event. How else could it have gone? What was ignored in the row was what Leavis actually said. Even when the whole text was printed an angry reader would at first see it as a gratuitous attack. My experience always was that I had to read Leavis three times. The first time left me asking 'what has he said?' The second time I asked 'is that all?' The third time I said 'now I see'. That difficulty is the obvious mark of an original mind, and it ought to be expected; but most people hadn't the patience, and I have not read much criticism of Leavis which starts from the position of comprehension, of elementary homework done. That too was one of his problems: he was always ahead of people. He was also supremely courteous in that, writing or speaking at his own level, he paid his audience the compliment of assuming they were with him. They weren't, and were mostly not willing to make the effort.

So it was with deep gloom that I heard that Leavis had approached the Press, proposing that it should publish the Richmond Lecture. I attended the Syndicate meeting at which the proposal was discussed. There was a long debate, and at one moment I thought the decision was going to be yes, but then the feeling tacked the other way because of a fear that the lecture might be libellous. Judgements in English libel cases are unpredictable enough, and there was enough in the lecture to make it a reasonable fear. One Syndic asked 'Do you mean that it is suggested that Snow is not a very good scientist?' and a cool Cambridge scientific voice replied 'Oh, he won't sue on *that* count', and there was a roar of laughter. But the answer was no, though another Syndic as he made for the tea and Fitzbillies' famous almond ring said to a fourth 'I think we are going to regret that decision'. I had to convey the decision to Leavis.

I usually find myself expressing polite regret on these occasions; but for the only time in my professional life I used the formula so as to convey that I thought the decision was regrettable because wrong. As on later occasions I tried, naively I now see, to convey to Leavis that he had what is banally called a 'communication problem', and that his audience needed some help if it was to catch up with him. There were things in the Snow lecture which, merely asserted, struck the simple reader as unfounded. He replied on 1 May 1962:

> Many thanks for your two notes. I've been too driven to reply before.
>
> Of course, we neither of us [FRL and QDL] expected any other decision from the Syndics. Merely, I have a deep piety towards Cambridge, and should have liked the imprint of the Press to have been on the anti-Snow lecture as well as on Snow's. And I know from my American correspondence (voluminous) that America takes note. It isn't pro-Snow!
>
> There could be no question of enlarging the Lecture – tampering. It was addressed to the occasion: its point and edge and 'attack' are inseparable from their functional quality. There would be no point in my trying to 'explain' to the classics (who are the resisters). If one had to concede that the Lecture didn't explain itself, then there would be no point in trying to do educational work with less than a volume – or a set of volumes. And then no point . . .
>
> I've looked at the lecture again and am bound to say that I've done better than I should have thought possible.

The reprint of *Scrutiny* was going forward meanwhile, and with this experience to digest I found myself being asked to brief our American Branch about it. Leavis was then – still is – a cipher to most American readers. At that moment he would have seemed to most an obscure academic who had caught attention by making a waspish attack on the Olympian Snow; or at best very parochially English, a small Cambridge eminence. So I wrote a long brief for my American colleagues, and then saw I had material for an article. I developed it, and it was published in 1964 in two parts in *The Use of English*, which Denys Thompson had founded and was still editing. The article was called 'The Third Realm', and the title was drawn from the crucial passage in the Richmond Lecture in which Leavis develops the notion of an intellectual meeting-ground which is neither the public knowledge of scientific fact nor the private realm of the subjective apprehension of one person, but is created when one person approaches another with a report of his experience, implicitly saying 'this is so, is it not?' Typically, the other person replies with a qualification, saying 'Yes, but . . .' The ensuing exchange will bring in other people, and so in time there is built up something 'conventional' in the strict etymological sense: an agreed estimate of cultural values. But Snow had proposed of his scientific culture that its members, 'without thinking about it, respond alike. That is what a culture means'. In other words, they were members of a herd. Reflecting on the wrongness of that formulation, Leavis proposed his own.

'The Third Realm' was deliberately proposed as a metaphor, implying that figures of speech were necessary in this discussion, which had better be kept naturally a-logical and unpinned-down. Leavis's occasional and opportunistic development of the idea was also deliberately confined to an aside here or an interpolation there in his proper business of the discussion of this or that specific text. This tactic seemed an implicit denial that he had what theorists could point to as an epistemology, or indeed a method. Yet he did have an epistemology, and more than the framework of a method could be inferred or deduced. But paradoxically its consistency rested on the surrender of certain criteria or procedures which logic might require, just because he saw that logical procedures and requirements were totally inappropriate; so that any critical theory founded on them must be defective by the standards it had incorrectly invoked. His general position was, to use his own adverb, cannily staked out and defended, and it escaped the limitations inherent in what is now looked back on as the New Criticism. For instance, his whole approach to literature had a strong historical and social basis, the one adumbrated in Mrs Leavis's *Fiction and the*

94

Reading Public and elsewhere in Leavis's own writings; and his constant perception that literature, since it was about life and about the creation of human values, by definition had a moral dimension, also separates him from the mere aestheticism of most New Critics and most writers on aesthetics. So far as he was proposing a contiguity with philosophy, it is with ethics, an area where logicians and analytical philosophers have found it hard to use their favourite procedures or to invoke their normal criteria without exploding the subject.

I tried to bring this out in my article, or to start to, having realised that it was wasting his time to urge him to perform the activity of explaining himself. There seemed a modest role for a commentator. After some time I plucked up the courage to show him the article. 'I am very far from deploring it', he said, and I was very far from discontented with that.

I see from the letters that he wrote me from time to time – usually on business, but he often dropped a friendly word on other matters – that he regularly maintained what he called his 'anti-philosopher' stance, which was a paradoxical ploy, or a provocation to think what philosophy is and why he was doing something else. Of a former contributor to *Scrutiny*, recently dead,[1] he said '— was apt to be maddeningly philosophical and, in his interpretations, fantastically allegorical'. He was opposing the imposition both of the *parti pris*, and of the inappropriate consistency which went with it; but also the tendency not to let each work of literature operate according to its own unique principles. The systematic pushing of a basic position into merely logical extensions was alien to him; yet the consistency of his own position was agilely maintained over a wide front, and people sometimes said to him, as I did, 'Come now, you are some kind of philosopher yourself.' He got a mischievous amusement out of this, I think, as when he wrote to me in June 1974 a comment on his forthcoming *The Living Principle*:

It's anti-philosopher – merely more explicitly so than my work of the last 40 + years; *needs* to be, now that Philosophy Depts tell me that I don't do myself justice: I am a philosopher. (A friend of Sir Karl Popper's wrote to me from the London Sch. of Ecs, sending me *his* last book by way of justifying the bracketing of me with *him*.)

But he had the last word:

I can't help wondering whether I haven't given you a false impression of my book, and whether your conviction will survive a perusal. If it does, I shall take that as a confirmation that my method of trying to enforce my intention has justified itself. It's the intention, with the accordant 'logic' (or dialectic) that seems to me, in my innocence or non-modesty, not to be a philosopher's: it's too inescapably intent on practice – expository in that way.
I'm not saying that no philosopher is of any use.

In part, Leavis was necessarily against the conception of language of the typical Anglo-Saxon positivist or analytical philosopher (of some time ago, it must be said); but there is also an inescapable tension between his approach and that of any logician. He saw the language of the original writer as operating by other than logical modes, and having nothing to do with 'truth', or 'proof'. It is a reduction of language if the logician's (in itself necessary and valid) analysis of it is taken as anything but a specialist account of one range of uses. His moral stance was anti-analytic for related reasons: for him the philosopher's 'empty choosing will' must be a reductive fiction. But I have borrowed that phrase from a philosopher who is also a novelist: who knows therefore that the human case that the novelist (Tolstoy, say) poses is in its specificity and complexity quite unlike the simplistic case that in the past Anglo-Saxon philosophers would pose as examples. But one now sees philosophers taking an interest in literature which is more like Leavis's. And Leavis said he had only known two people to whom the word 'genius' could be applied, and one was Wittgenstein.

Apart from my letters from Leavis, which I have kept, I have the fading memory of visits and conversations. He would sometimes consult me about business matters. With great courtesy and formality he would telephone to make an appointment because I was, he considered, a busy man. I would show reciprocal regard by going downstairs to the showroom to meet him and later conducting him back downstairs. He was increasingly lonely, and increasingly driven by the thought of what he had to do in the time left to him. 'I would like a brief colloquy' he said on the telephone, but it turned into a long monologue, and there were obsessive elements in it towards the end of his life. I watched his small brown left hand on my desk, as the fingers played on it an unceasing accompaniment. He once stood in my office having dropped in on the way to the hospital where Mrs Leavis was critically ill. He must have been cycling there. He wore a black oilskin cape, and had half a dozen eggs in one hand and a half-pound of butter in the other. It was raining hard, and a drop of rain glistened on the end of his nose. He conveyed without words the intensity of his anguished preoccupation: he ought to have looked comic, and he looked awe-inspiring.

That desperate corner was turned, and I remember also, before and after, some relaxed anecdotal moments. I listened, to pick up here and there a sidelight on literary history. About the relationship with Eliot, for instance. 'There was something wrong with him down here', he once said, ostensively striking himself well below the belt. He told me, as he told others, of the occasion when Eliot, staying at Magdalene in the early 1940s, had crossed the road to Chesterton Hall Crescent where the Leavises lived, and spent a long evening pouring himself out, while the pile of cigarette ash in the grate grew and grew. And when he left (in a Jamesian narrative style, where the intense significance is conveyed, but not defined, and the reader has to fill in the meaning) 'My wife said to me "You know what he *wants*, don't you?" and I said "Of *course* . . . !"' After these oral italics and suspension points[2] it would have been crude to say 'Well, what *did* he want?' but I gathered that he had been wanting a friendship which would take the edge off criticism. I find this poignant, but Leavis did not. Eliot had gone with the herd, and had treated him badly. Eliot had felt guilt, though, and I am convinced that Leavis saw himself as one component of the 'familiar compound ghost', with 'brown baked features' (extraordinarily apt words) who calls the 'I' of 'Little Gidding' to such strict account. Indeed he finally said so in print.

I remember with embarrassment that, meaning well enough, but being obtuse, I asked him how it was possible for him to maintain his 'deep piety' towards Cambridge, after having been so shabbily treated for so long. How could he have such faith in the idea of the University? Any University would be staffed by human beings.

His face changed: perhaps it fell. I don't know whether I had said something which he was used to hearing, or the opposite. He replied that one did have to have the sense that in the end one belonged to, was working for, a community, with a common end in view. It was, as he said of other things, a necessary faith.

Lighter moments were provided by reports of his work at York, where he was well regarded, as a visitor from the Old Testament might be: impressive, indeed venerable, but a sort of extra. But for him it was different, a new hope. He was not naively hopeful about the new Universities as such – could not be, given what he had said about Robbins – and there were things he was sardonic about. The social sciences, for instance, especially as represented on academic committees, and paying political regard to the imagined demands of the national interest. '"We *are* the nation", I said.' He was scornful of the professional unionised student of the time, and was not inclined to see herd-behaviour, drinking, noise, promiscuity, ·untidiness or any other manifestation of basic self as anything but that. He had a practical turn which enabled him to cope with most situations: 'So I opened the door and said what the BLOODY . . .?' Before the rare expletive I imagined student rioters falling back, abashed. He was also aware that as a notorious figure he was automatically the focus of idle curiosity. He needed small classes, but many people turned up, for the spectacle. 'I *bored* them. Next week there were only twelve.' 'How did you do that?' 'Oh, I gave them a long analysis of Mallarmé. The best poem.' 'Oh? Which is that?' 'You know: the Toast to Gautier.'

But I come back to his loneliness. I think it weighed on him. He had not sought it, but he had created it, and in its inevitability he had to accept it; but I believe it was a grief to him. It sprang from his integrity, which was also his spikiness. I remember once Lord Annan wrote in a letter to a journal (I think it was the *T.L.S.*) 'But is Dr Leavis *kollegial*?' Lord Annan was the head of a great academic institution, and had to pay proper attention to that social virtue, and it was a question to be asked. And I remember that in the hall in which I ate my dinner, shocked and dismayed after Tillyard's admonishings, I could have looked up and read over the high table *Ecce·quam bonum et quam iucundum fratres habitare in unum.*

I also remember Leavis's look when I put my question to him, and his answer, correcting my simplicity or rebuking my cynicism. The collegial ideal did exist for him: it was painfully real because it was never realised. He conceived an ideal community, a Cambridge of the nineteenth-century mind, the Cambridge that Sidgwick and Leslie Stephen represented in their time – and that he represented in his time. It was a type-case of his whole intellectual system (or faith). Because he effectively represented it, it was to that degree 'true', and it was kept true every time someone else responded to his 'This is so, is it not?' by saying 'Yes, but.' But to a cynical, or even a positivist mentality it was no more than a personal fantasy. And in his own time the ethos of Cambridge had ceased, for others, to be represented by Sidgwick and Stephen, residual Puritans who had kept a faith in faith. It was represented by what was consciously a group spirit, in the circle which took Moore's *Principia Ethica* and strangely converted it into the authority for an ethos which placed 'personal relationships' above the service of any other ideal. At its lowest the Bloomsbury ethos fostered the coterie, or even the political cell: it prolonged into adult life the herd-loyalties – including hero-worship – of the school, but displaced them from the sanctioned corporate enterprise on to the private loyalties of the group that selected itself as an élite. But it was a specialisation of the herd-mentality, complimenting itself for being above the rest of the herd, and this accounts for Leavis's detestation.[3] But he did have his answer to those who, like myself, with good but mistaken intentions pressed on him that the world is as it is and he was simply seeing the consequences.

He had thought his way through that. He was the only man I have known in that lonely posture of whom it could not easily or truthfully be said that he was an egoist, or a flawed personality; and this was partly a matter of intellection. In the last books, from the one on Dickens to that on Eliot, and the last of all, on Lawrence, he was constantly exploring the moral problem involved in being a self, and a self at odds with others and tempted to assert its absolute selfhood in opposition. Like everyone else, he needed a way out of that threatened impasse: remission from the prison of the ego postulated by Eliot, from which Eliot himself could only find a release through the grace of God. Leavis wanted another kind of grace, and found it formulated in Blake's and Lawrence's notion of the completed identity which had grown to be perfectly itself. The formulation seems to me a doubtful one; I don't trust Lawrence ultimately on that issue; indeed I find I would rather trust Leavis himself. What he retained, beyond the notion of the growing identity, was the old-fashioned notion of the pursuit of truth, preserved at a time when the possibility of ultimate truth has been abandoned for the substitute, 'pluralism'. Leavis did not, when he asked 'This is so, is it not?' expect to get the bland modern reply 'So for you, perhaps. Not for me, I'm afraid.' He was engaged in the common pursuit of true judgement, and he insisted that it was possible and necessary: a duty.

It was that, I believe, which makes him, or should make him, a secular saint of the modern University. He did also think he had Blake's and Lawrence's sanction finally to be what he was and to speak from the middle of that. To the ordinary person that is an impossible risk, and most of us take good care not to let our mere selves have free rein. Leavis could, when necessary, just let fly; but I have the clear impression that he really hated rows, tried to avoid them, and went into them only because he felt he *must*. It was the ulterior thing that guided him, and he managed (I believe) not to let his passions or his personality seriously misappropriate or deform his ideal. No observer could say that they did not affect it at all, but it would be unreasonable to expect that: he was human. There is no pure distillate, 'integrity', that can be run off and displayed in a bottle like an essence, uncontaminated by anything else in the personality. It is inextricably mixed with other things. His anger and his obsessiveness, the obverse of his earnestness and courage, were part of his integrity. So: the aim he had set himself, and his long pursuit of it; his evident lack of worldly success and the little store he set by that; his willingness to accept personal privation; to acquire a galling notoriety instead of proper respect and gratitude; to be a scandal and a stumbling-block to fellow academics when he ought to have been an inspiration – all that had purified his will when it might merely have soured his temper; so that when he spoke out, he spoke with unique weight.

So much is true; but it sadly confirms that my most appropriate memory of him is of a slight figure walking quickly through the Cambridge streets, looking neither to right nor to left, and speaking to nobody. I also remember him skating on the frozen Cam in the winter of 1963. Other people were tottering about, falling down, picking themselves and each other up, laughing and shouting. A few expert couples swept along with arms linked, exchanging self-possessed words with each other. He was on the old-fashioned long skates of the Fenman, leaning forward like a racer, yet withdrawn from it all. As he went through the crowd he created both a space and a silence about him. He was quite a small man, and lightly built. He ate very little and seemed to live mostly on sunlight. But he had long legs, which carried him with a kind of eagerness: he had a quick, long, light stride. He looked ahead, at his own height or a little above, and one learnt not to be offended at being cut. Partly he was always thinking, and in a world of his own; partly he must have learnt that if he stopped to be addressed by every bore along his way he would never get anywhere. So he went quickly by: in his late seventies I saw him, hatless and tieless as always, drop aside into the road from the pavement, run briskly past a group of loiterers, and then resume his even, lengthy stride. One image obstinately remains in my memory, which must have glorified it, as memory will: I was startled, but on second thought not at all surprised, to find that just such a memory has remained with Raymond Williams. Once Leavis strode past me, eyes blazing, just outside the Pitt Building as I was going in, and I let him go ungreeted, as usual. As I went up the steps I saw large raindrops making dark circles on the stone. I turned to watch him. He had gone on down Trumpington Street, and as the rain began to fall he moved into an easy loping run, springing up into the air, bound after bound like a deer, till he passed out of sight.

Notes

1 'De mortuis nil nisi verum' he once said to me, pausing in the doorway, and giving his little pre-joke sniff.

2 He had this gift of italicising. 'My wife's a *scholar*, you know', he once said. Impossible to convey all that he packed into the word, but respect, amazement, amusement and reprehension would be among the ingredients.

3 It is relevant that the *Scrutiny* group was often pictured as a coterie or sect. But the extraordinary severity with which the Leavises treated their friends and pupils may have stemmed from a determination not to relax into easy mutual accommodation. If the group ever existed, it certainly didn't survive.

11

Round and about the
Pelican Guide to English Literature

BORIS FORD

I do not remember that the reviewers of the *Pelican Guide to English Literature*, when it was originally published in 1955–8, linked it with *Scrutiny* or the Leavises. The *Guide* seemed to make its way without that assistance – or impediment. But more recent comments have tended to go along with Francis Mulhern's view, in his book *The Moment of Scrutiny*, that the *Guide* was the product of a 'second *Scrutiny* generation, led by Cox and Ford'. Thus David Nokes, reviewing the revised *New Guide* in the *T.E.S.*, wrote that the original *Guide* 'represented a high water mark for Leavisite literary criticism'. And Marilyn Butler, in her review in the *London Review of Books*, wrote that the *Guide* did 'more than anyone except Leavis himself to disseminate Leavisite views', though adding that this was at best a 'practical' achievement at a 'humble and humdrum' level, especially as the 'Leavisite tradition' seemed to her in 1982 both 'dated' and 'wilfully limited'.

And so it may be interesting to consider how far the *Guide* was explicitly designed as some sort of offshoot of *Scrutiny*; and to ask what the Leavises thought of it.

If the formidable weight of most histories of literature might lead one to suppose that they were conceived and excogitated in a weighty fashion, this was certainly not the case with the *Pelican Guide to English Literature*. I was, at that time, Chief Editor at the Bureau of Current Affairs and the Director was William Emrys Williams. Bill Williams had long been one of Allen Lane's closest colleagues and he went off to Harmondsworth once a week to an editorial meeting. One day, in 1950, he came into my room overlooking Green Park and said that at yesterday's editorial meeting

103

Lane had proposed that they should publish a history of literature and that he thought the simplest notion would be to republish the *Concise Cambridge History* edited by George Sampson. Bill Williams, who had been a W.E.A. tutor in literature before the war and was by way of being Lane's literary guru, opposed the idea of redoing the *Concise Cambridge* ('dead the day it was published', was his description), with the result that he was sent off to think of a better idea within a fortnight. We talked it over and the upshot was that I agreed to produce a few rough notes which Williams would try out on the Editorial Board. And he added, in his relaxed manner, that we might as well think in terms of a number of volumes, 'for we don't need to stint ourselves'.

On sitting down to concoct my few rough notes, I reflected that I was commendably ignorant about histories of literature. At school I had studied English literature in the sixth form with Denys Thompson and the first books he had perplexingly asked me to read were George Sturt's *The Wheelwright's Shop*, the Lynds' book on the U.S.A., and Stuart Chase's *Mexico*. Eventually, after this circuitous route, we arrived at some literature, which we read and discussed in great detail, our eyes firmly on the text. Very occasionally I was told to read a chapter or two of Légouis and Cazamian's history; they had the advantage, I gathered, of not having studied literature in the English academic fashion. Indeed, in their introduction they speak of themselves as 'outsiders' who have 'an independence of mind due to their foreign training' and who 'have approached [English literature] consciously and of deliberate choice, as men rather than as children'.

When I went on to study with F. R. Leavis at Downing College, we were only referred to this or that history of literature for cautionary purposes. My memory of Leavis's tutorials is that they were liable to hop about from writer to writer and period to period, demanding wide reading and considerable agility in his students. These tutorials were an incalculable mixture of perceptions and hints, of demonstrations and probing questions, of ironies and unfinished expostulations (with a sudden intake of breath, mouth open, and then a wry smile); and this made them compelling and inspiring. But I am sure Leavis would have agreed that his supervisions alone would not have produced the astonishing results that Downing achieved at that time: 4 Firsts out of 8 men in Part I in 1938, and 4 out of 7 in Part II the next year. We also depended on the very methodical teaching we received from Gordon Cox and Geoffrey Walton, and the formidable tutorials for the Moralists and the French and Italian texts with James Smith. This quartet was incomparably richer than any history of literature. And anyway, Leavis was a quite distinctive historian of literature with an uncanny sense of the human and moral texture of society, and of the nature of literary influence and indebtedness. To have *heard* his chapter on the Line of Wit was a bracing experience indeed.

I went down in 1939 and eventually found my way into army education. But I managed to keep in touch with the Leavises; they were, albeit under invariable pressure, the most voluminous letter-writers to the end of their lives. In 1941, on a visit to Cambridge, Leavis invited me to review the one-volume *Concise Cambridge History* for *Scrutiny*. Doing my homework for Bill Williams ten years later, I re-read my rather jejune piece and found that I had concentrated on the fatuity of Sampson's attempt to rehabilitate the beliefs and partialities of a former age as embodied, embalmed, in the 14-volume *Cambridge History* of 1907–16: a work notable for containing virtually no quotations and in which one can see, volume after volume, English literature as the new Academic Institution. In my review I was somewhat ribald about this, and in particular about Sampson's attempt, in his new chapter on contemporary literature, to project these standards forward as a basis for evaluating subsequent literature ('Henry James was the Gentleman of Shalott', 'Lawrence . . . a lower-class parody of Byronism', and so on). And then, to my surprise, I was reminded that I had ended my review by putting forward proposals for the kinds of 'histories and manuals which one would be glad to have on the shelf, . . . those which undertake a critical survey of the subject . . . for the general reader, who needs some help in seeing the larger pattern, . . . and those which present factual information'.

During these few days I visited the library to take a swift look at the histories I had ignored as a student and at the newer histories published since: *Chambers' Cyclopedia* (1844), an attractively improving and moral anthology, with biographical/historical accompanying texts; Saintsbury's *Short History* of 1898, offering itself as 'a storehouse of facts' and resembling a well-tended graveyard of noble monuments; then, after the *Cambridge History*, there was a long lay-off in the industry, until Dobrée's *Introductions to English Literature* (1939), five volumes of bibliographies and backgrounds of a stolid character which felt, and indeed by then was, out of date, for the bibliographies were not frequently enough revised; and finally, starting in 1945, the *Oxford History of English Literature* in the hallowed Oxbridge number of 14 volumes, not many of which had appeared (in the wrong order) by 1950: scholarly, knowing, urbane.

Those were the volumes which the library yielded up. They were variously factual, reverential, uncritical, scholarly, academic, and virtually unreadable if one were thinking of younger readers in sixth forms and universities, or general readers like teachers, civil servants, social workers, and house-bound wives, those voracious takers-out of books from public libraries. Moreover, these compilations seemed to bear little relation to the way literature was now being studied in schools and universities. They felt unused and unusable.

What, then, was likely to be appropriate to the 'general educated reader' who buys Penguin Classics in vast quantities, the reader presumably of George Eliot and T. S. Eliot, of Lawrence, Jane Austen, Shakespeare, Auden, Keats . . .? They would expect to be addressed in a congenial and lively fashion. In particular, I thought, they would want, and be glad of, help in finding their bearings: where, they might ask, is the *life* of literature to be found today? what is this Gawayne poem which is virtually unobtainable (in 1950)? what is the 'Line of Wit'? how does one tackle Milton, and how might one enjoy him? what do the Augustans have to offer to non-classicists? how about Dickens – sentimental? vulgar? creative genius? is Auden worth quite so much fuss? what does *Scrutiny* represent? It seemed to me that we must address ourselves to the questions and interests of today's and tomorrow's readers, and do so by discussing individual works of literature in detail, with copious quotation, so as to point to significance and distinctive quality, to nuance of tone. Pelican readers, I imagined, would want to be helped to respond to what is living and contemporary in literature, whenever it was written.

Within a few days I had typed out an outline plan for Bill Williams. I quickly arrived at a total of 7 volumes, starting with Chaucer (I had studied no pre-Chaucerian literature at Cambridge and so was too ignorant to include it) and coming up to more or less the present day. The distinctive feature of the proposed *Guide*, I felt, would be the structure and balance of each volume, with its two major surveys of the cultural and social background and of the literature of the period, followed by a number of detailed studies of individual writers or of individual works, and finally a fairly copious appendix of biographies and bibliographies.

I handed over this outline to Williams, and he seemed pleased with it. Indeed, he said he would put it forward, with my permission, as his own, and when I gently demurred, he explained that Allen Lane worked on the astute principle of accepting ideas from anyone but commissioning the book from someone else. And so it proved. Bill Williams's proposals for a 7-volume *Guide to English Literature* were accepted by the Editorial Board.

'And now,' said Lane, 'whom shall we get to act as general editor? How about Bonamy Dobrée?'

Fortunately Williams was able to fend off that unexpected idea; and then he had the sudden notion that his Chief Editor at the Bureau of Current Affairs was a literature specialist, on whom, moreover, Williams could keep his Penguin eye. Swiftly agreed. I met Lane and Glover, his editor at Penguin Books, and was told to get on with it and have the first volumes ready in two years. I had no contract, though I think I received a letter indicating the miserable terms that we would receive – for contributors writing chapters of some thousands of words, it amounted to a few pounds per edition of about 30,000 copies. 'Don't worry', Lane replied to my protest. 'If they are any good, they'll get Chairs out of it.' As for me, I was to receive £100 or £150 per volume, depending on its size.

The key to the *Guide's* coherence of tone and critical approach was obviously going to depend on the selection of contributors. It was imperative that they should already share critical assumptions and have similar ideas about how to tackle a given author and his writings – I could hardly set up seminars to achieve this kind of agreement. In addition it would obviously help if I knew and had worked with many of them, for I perceived that steering 7 teams of anything up to 20 contributors in each team would prove a daunting task. All of this meant, in the nature of things, that very many of these contributors were likely to have studied at Cambridge, and I hoped that some of them would have written for *Scrutiny*.

My memory of the exact sequence of developments is hazy. But I am sure I decided not to talk to Leavis about the project until I was certain that the plan of the *Guide* would appeal to the contributors I had in mind. So I consulted three people: Lionel Knights, for many years an editor of *Scrutiny* but also a distinguished academic with strong W.E.A. and extra-mural commitments; Leo Salingar, whom I had known well at Cambridge and since, and for whose work on Marlowe, Shakespeare and Tourneur I had the greatest admiration; and Kling, G. D. Klingopulos, who had been an exact contemporary of mine at Downing and for whom the Leavises, especially Queenie Leavis, felt much respect and affection. All three proved enthusiastic, though I remember Lionel Knights was unnerved by the scale of the undertaking and didn't envy me the task of bringing it to fruition.

So, strengthened by these responses, I went to talk to Leavis. At this period, meeting Leavis had become for both of us an absurdly clandestine affair. For many years I had been on amiable terms with both the Leavises. As an undergraduate I had been a regular taker of tea and of Queenie's excellent cake at Chesterton Hall Crescent. During the war I had visited them, even stayed with them, from time to time. But shortly after the war I received an impressive, if perplexing, postcard from Queenie which read: 'Mrs Leavis informs Mr Ford that he is no longer an acceptable visitor to her house. Any communications from him will not be answered. Q. D. Leavis.' I had not the least idea what this was about and wrote to Dr and Mrs Leavis to say so. I received no answer. Some time later I was in Cambridge and decided to visit Leavis in Downing. He was somewhat embarrassed, but as always courteous. We discussed this and that, and eventually he said that his wife was upset by what she described as my complicity in Raymond O'Malley's 'mishandling' of Ralph's education at Dartington – this had been a most distressing and deplorable business which cost Raymond their long and close friendship and in which I had been peripherally involved. And so, he concluded, it would be simpler if I were to communicate with him and meet him at Downing; and perhaps I would not mention this to anyone lest word of it got back to Queenie. 'As you know, she's fighting for her life', he added, 'and this makes her impatient at times.'

This secrecy about our correspondence and meetings was maintained for a number of years. And then I moved to Cambridge to take up the post of Education Secretary at the Press. We lived in a succession of rented houses, and then heard that the Leavises had decided to move from Newton Road, where they now lived. So I wrote, rather hesitantly, to Mrs Leavis, asking if we might look over their house with a view to buying it. To our relief she replied in a friendly fashion, inviting us to come round. So we took tea and excellent fruit cake; and Queenie showed us the house, talked about its snags and attractions, while Leavis sat back, amused and fairly silent. As it happens we didn't buy the house because they couldn't find another to suit them. After waiting some months, we eventually bought a house two or three doors away in Newton Road and became neighbours of a sort. But Leavis still found it simplest to meet in Downing.

The meeting about the *Guide*, however, took place in the earlier, clandestine epoch. He said very little and that very cautiously. I couldn't tell if he was not wanting to offend me or if he simply had no views on the matter. I asked if he would contribute a chapter or if I might perhaps reprint one of his essays in the *Guide*, and on this he had a decided view. Eventually he remarked that he doubted if the project were feasible: there were not enough people of the necessary calibre, he felt; and the best of them wouldn't want, or be able, to do that kind of writing. He cited the great difficulty he and his wife had had in recent years, trying to find people to write for *Scrutiny*. However, he wished me luck; but essentially the *Guide* was not his kind of undertaking.

I think I felt somewhat depressed by Leavis's doubts, though I had probably expected them. However, I went ahead, sending out dozens of letters with a degree of optimism that I now find extraordinary. I first enrolled the authors of the main literary survey in each volume: John Speirs, Leo Salingar, Gordon Cox, Arthur Humphreys, Denys Harding, Kling, and John Holloway. They became the lynch-pins of each volume, and with their help I planned the individual chapters and selected likely contributors. I find, on making the count for the first time 25 years later, that there were 136 separate chapters in the 7 volumes (including the 2 surveys and appendix in each volume); and these were written by 77 individuals, of whom 27 (about 1 in 3) had contributed to *Scrutiny*, however modestly. Very few people to whom I wrote refused to take part. This formidable team included 'insiders' from the *Scrutiny* 'movement' like Lionel Knights, Denys Harding, Wilfrid Mellers, John Speirs, Derek Traversi, as well as 'outsiders' like T. S. Eliot, Lionel Trilling, Quentin Anderson, Edgell Rickword, Geoffrey Grigson, Nikolaus Pevsner. If I ask myself why they took part and Leavis didn't, I think it is to uncover a disturbing trait in the man. He was, without doubt, a genius, whereas none of the many other critics were that, however distinguished or excellent their work might be, and perhaps geniuses are liable to feel awkward in company not of their own choosing; or maybe Leavis and his wife were temperamentally unable to commit themselves to so uncertain a project, which they had had no part in devising. But when all is said, it seems to me that Leavis's refusal to take part was an unworthy act of pride. Or it revealed a strange temerity or caution, as if he hesitated to move outside his role of 'guardian' of a minority literary culture to a wider and more general readership, perhaps from fear that this would involve over-simplifying and falsifying what he had to say; for *Scrutiny*, after all, sold about 1200 copies and the *Guide* was going to hope to sell hundreds of thousands of copies. Perhaps he feared that this entry into a world of mass sales might inescapably contaminate us all with a spirit of vulgar superficiality?

In fact, the problem of writing for the *Guide* was not how to simplify in the sense of 'writing down', but how to write with lucidity, how to avoid assuming too much familiarity with texts and with existing criticism, how to manage without recourse to a wealth of *recherché* allusions and subtleties of association. I believed (really as an act of faith) that a great many people who had been nurtured, in varying degrees, on *Scrutiny* and associated writings might welcome the opportunity to apply its rigorous, selective, minority-orientated approach to the collaborative task of writing, for a much wider readership, a comprehensive account of English literature that would still be selective and critical. I think I might even go further and suggest that one of the tests of a responsible 'minority' concern for literature is its readiness to communicate with the non-specialist, with the educated but critically less sophisticated reader who reads for enjoyment and for meaning. The sales of Penguin books, indeed of Leavis's own books in papercover, confirm that there are potentially very many more such readers than were dreamed of in Chesterton Hall Crescent.

An experience from my undergraduate days gave me an inkling of a hope that Leavis might agree to take part in this kind of undertaking. The undergraduates had become, in 1938–9, quite militant about some features of Parts I and II of the Tripos, and we presented a set of moderately radical proposals to the Faculty Board: to separate the Chaucer–Shakespeare paper into two, to allow more scope for contemporary literature, etc. And in our dissatisfaction with Faculty lectures, we organised for one year a rival programme of lectures, which were given by junior lecturers, college tutors, and Ph.D. students, like Lionel Elvin, Hugh Sykes Davies, Arthur Humphreys, Gilbert Phelps, and Leavis. It was a mixed bunch, one might say, as the *Guide* was to be. One of Leavis's seminars, held in Downing, was on Rosenberg's *Dead Man's Dump*. He read the poem, in that intense, precise, infinitely subtle manner of reading of his, and then he talked about the poem with a commitment and simplicity of understanding that was profoundly revealing. Finally he read the whole poem again. The very many undergraduates who were there were unusually hushed and I felt sure they were as moved as I was by the experience. Leavis's contributions gave powerful support to the student cause; and our action proved surprisingly successful. In a similar mood, he might perhaps have been willing to support the undertaking represented by the *Guide*.

In his review, David Nokes wrote of the *Guide* that 'with its appearance, a critical crusade, begun and developed in the pages of *Scrutiny*, was confirmed as the new critical orthodoxy.' I doubt if I, if any of us, would have put it quite like that, and Leavis would have been duly affronted. What we would admit, I think, is surprise and pleasure that a large work of serious critical intentions should have proved valuable for so long; and that Penguin Books should have decided, at a time of very different fashions and orthodoxies, to commission a revision of the *Guide* (including the addition of three new volumes) so long as it retained its distinctive critical character.

A few months before this revision was broached Leavis died. Queenie Leavis replied to my letter, with thanks. 'My husband was nearly 83, he had done his work, and in his last painful months longed to die, so one should not repine.'

12

Seeing a man running

RAYMOND WILLIAMS

One February afternoon in the hard winter of 1963 I was walking south on King's Parade, wrapped and hooded in an army sheepskin against a driving crosswind full of grain snow. The street was empty until, a hundred yards ahead of me, a man came running around the corner from Pembroke Street. As he came nearer I could see that he was only lightly protected against the weather, his shirt collar wide open, his jacket flapping as he ran.

There was never any difficulty in a physical recognition of Leavis. I could already see the deeply tanned skin and the strong set face. But it was only a few weeks since I had been told, pointedly, by two separate elderly dons, that in Cambridge you didn't speak to an acquaintance you happened to meet in the street. I had felt rebuked. In my own country, along the Welsh border, we do not think of passing anyone, friend or stranger, without a salute or a greeting. If we are not busy we usually stop for a talk. I had been back in Cambridge, as a senior member, for less than two years. The social coldness, I supposed, went with the intellectual atmosphere and the east wind. So what should happen with this respected acquaintance, who had now stopped running and was walking towards me?

As he came close he looked intently into my face. I nodded and raised my arm. The intent look hardened. He passed without a word. My instructors had evidently been right. Then there were sudden running steps behind me and as I swung round a hand was laid on my arm.

'I'm sorry, Williams. I didn't mean to cut you.'

I had read that expression often, but I had never before heard it used.

'That's all right. It's a terrible day.'

'It isn't that', he said, his look hardening again. 'But I have to get to the bank before it closes.'

'Of course.'

He took his hand from my arm and ran on. I crossed the road, though I had no need to.

Twenty years later, after many hours spent with Leavis, in meetings, in passing conversations, in longer talks, both before and after that day in the snow, I remember this incident more sharply than any other. It is very small in itself, but I think of it as symptomatic of such relationship as we had. Many people working on Leavis, as it is called, and an increasing number working on the relationship between his work and my own, come to ask the answerable questions, about what is in the books, and then find it difficult to believe that there are further questions I cannot answer at all: what our relationship was like, as colleagues seeing each other quite often; what we said to each other about the themes we shared and the issues which so evidently divided us. Faced by polite but insistent disbelief, when I have said, truthfully, that we never really discussed them, I have sometimes tried recounting this small incident, but to find it meaning nothing to them.

'Surely? Surely?'

'But no.'

When I came to a lectureship in Cambridge in 1961, Leavis was not far off retirement. His attitudes to the English Faculty, and those of most of the Faculty to him, were set rock hard. Yet that image alone will not do. There were regular eruptions: a reported remark about a colleague that he had made at a lecture; a combative letter to the Chairman; a fierce argument at a meeting. I have never known a social situation in which a group seemed so obsessed by one man. Everybody, it seemed, had a Leavis story, and made it his first business to pass it on. His contemporaries, especially, dispensed such stories, at least to me, in the tone of that advice of the elderly dons about talking in the street. Meanwhile I, in effect, knew nothing. Whenever I met him he was unfailingly polite. In most cases, in the Faculty arguments, he seemed to me to be right. At the same time, you cannot come in on the last couple of chapters of a history like that and delude yourself that you understand any of it as

well as those who had been living it through, with all their circum-
stantial though also (I found as I went on listening) largely uncertain
and contested accounts. It was not my shared history, though I
had an oblique and unavoidable relation to it, through the work.

Of course among the stories I was sedulously told were some
which included what he or one of his circle – the more usual word
was 'gang' – had said about me. Since at that time, just after *The
Long Revolution*, I was getting stick from almost everybody, I was
merely curious. Could it really be the case, as I was confidently
told, that someone very close in that circle had said that I was a
prime example of the boy educated at state expense who had turned
to bite the hand that had fed him? This was so incongruous with
what I had understood of the work that I was unwilling to believe
it, though I would have enjoyed some relevant analysis of that
'state expense'. Yet many people did again and again misunder-
stand, at times almost wilfully, their actual relations with Leavis
and some of his most basic attitudes. I was much later told that he
had demurred at this description of me. Yet the politics were a
problem, as I discovered much later again, when a left-wing
lecturer, in trouble at his university, asked me to collect some
eminent supporting signatures, and insisted that I approach the
Leavises. I spoke to Mrs Leavis on the 'phone. She refused angrily
and in political terms.

As I look back now I see a gradual unfolding, in my own mind,
of what the full Leavis position had come to be. The young researchers now upbraid me for being so slow in seeing it. They may
be right. But what I get, to the end, in the work but even more in
my direct contacts with the man, is a sense of something wholly
unresolved, into which that fierce energy was still being poured.
At the surface level there was a very strange mixture of the deliberate and the reckless, but below that again there was a condition
I have only ever seen in one or two other men: a true sense of
mystery, and of very painful exposure to mystery, which was even
harder to understand because this was the man of so many confident
and well-known beliefs and opinions. Perhaps I merely mistook
this. But it was the sense I always got from those infrequent but
unforgettable hard and lost stares into some distance.

No memoir can touch those levels; certainly no memoir of mine, who as I got to know him knew that I was not getting to know him. It was easier at a relatively public level. At one of the first Faculty meetings I attended almost the entire business was a very long argument between Leavis and the Chairman of the day about the propriety of asking a question about one of the previous summer's examination papers. He was repeatedly told that the question was not admissible, and repeatedly, with extraordinary forensic skill, he kept asking it. I look back on that now from a Faculty still riven by disputes but in which there is a special annual meeting to discuss the examiners' reports and, where necessary, the papers. It was how it so often went. I could align with Leavis because of what I took to be the position from which he was arguing. Then at another meeting it would be wholly different. There is a mood which sometimes grips university teachers of English, when they take on a fierce collective existence as examiners: a hard pleasure strengthened by an unchallengeable sense of duty as they mark, mark, mark people; execute extraordinary intellectual exercises of grading. The common pursuit, the collaborative spirit, I would think, looking across at Leavis and expecting some shared sense of the problem: the marking had to be done, while the system was there, but was this mood necessary to it? It was a shock when I sometimes saw him going along, though clumsily, with the cold distance of the exercise. Standards, standards. It was a shock comparable with that moment, which impressed some others, when during a discussion of a man proposed for an invitation to lecture he suddenly said, extending his hands: 'He is not one of us.'

The official business in which I had most to do with him was when a new paper on the novel had been proposed for Part II of the Tripos, and I, as secretary, had to convene a committee on it. I spent, in all, hours on the 'phone and in the street persuading Leavis to join it. He was quite sure he would not be wanted; I insisted that he especially was. He joined, eventually, and was very sensible and helpful. It is true that there was one major argument, but it was conducted in my view – others disagree – in a wholly appropriate university spirit. The crux was whether the paper should be the English novel, or the novel in general. He wanted the English novel only. A majority were against him. The example of the Tragedy paper was raised: to understand English tragedy it was useful or even necessary to set it beside the Greek and the French. Leavis would not budge. A general paper on the novel would amount to radical misdirection.

'But Dr Leavis', someone said, 'to understand the twentieth-century novel we have, for example, to read Proust and Kafka.'

'I have read them.'

'Then should not the students have the chance to read them!'

'It would be a misdirection. There is nothing relevant there.'

'But surely that would be for them to decide.'

'It would be a misdirection.'

'Because of reading in translation?'

'That too.'

'Then what about American novelists? Faulkner, for example.'

At this point I have to hold on to my seat. I have the clearest memory of what was said next, and of the mood in which it was said: one of fierce pleasure in the argument but also of surprising conviction.

'Faulkner!', Leavis said. 'When the Americans moved in on Europe, after the War, they had to have a great novelist. That's who they chose, Faulkner.'

Nobody knew, at the time, what to say after that. The general argument continued. Leavis could see that he was losing. Finally, with that open pleasure which usually accompanied what he supposed a decisive point, he turned to me in the chair.

'I put it directly to you, Mr Secretary. The coherent course would be the English Novel from Dickens to Lawrence.'

He knew quite well that this was the title of my main current lecture course. He knew also, I think, that the course was an attempt at a sustained argument against *The Great Tradition*.

'All right', I said, 'I think it is a coherent course. But a majority of the committee want some foreign novelists included, and I think their arguments are strong. Part II, after all, has that important extending dimension.'

'No, I am putting it to you, directly.'

'I could vote for either. They would be very different. But at the moment I'm an officer of the Faculty, trying to get the committee's decision.'

'To you', he repeated.

The meeting resumed. Eventually a compromise was arrived at: broadly what Leavis wanted as a core, but the other works admitted. He wrote after the meeting and said that I had 'done wonders with that committee'. But when, through a later group, a specimen paper was produced, and it became clear that the compromise wasn't going to work easily, or perhaps at all – as has indeed proved the case – he denounced the whole idea, attacked it in print, said less about the early history of the proposal than I thought he might have done, built the case, as so often, into a general indictment of this misdirecting and excluding Faculty. He had lost, as so often, in a cause that meant everything to him. It was then difficult for him to admit how much, in practice, he had taken part and tried to take part. Long after he had publicly admitted general defeat, in his proposals for an English course, he went on trying to influence more local directions, and by the sixties, by some of the younger lecturers, was being positively invited to contribute. But it was too late, in all important ways. He wanted such collaborative work; it had been his ideal. But though he was often helpful at meetings, he both hated and projected the repeated experience of being in a minority.

'If you had voted for Dickens to Lawrence', he said later, 'it would have turned the committee.'

'I said I would vote for it.'

'You said for either.'

'Because that is my position. What I mainly wanted was a paper on the novel. Either would make a great difference to the Tripos.'

'You could have turned it.'

'No. The majority was clearly the other way.'

'You were not prepared to stand out and be isolated.'

'I have done that often. But on this it didn't apply. I wanted that paper, in either version.'

'I am taking the sense of your work.'

'Yes, and it is nearly all in a minority position. But isn't that the problem, working in any institution? So long as I can teach as I want, I have to accept a framework built by a majority I don't agree with.'

'No, you don't have to accept it.'

'Accepting it as you have. To continue the work. To put these other ideas in.'

He shook his head. He would not accept what he took as a mere excuse, nor apply the general point to himself. There was this kind of barrier, again and again, whenever the central issues were approached. He had worked a lifetime in a Faculty he opposed and despaired of. In a different mood and from different positions I was starting something of the same. I don't blame him for finding the problem insoluble. I have found it increasingly insoluble in these latest years. But we couldn't share that sense, at any time. Everything came out from him directly and *ad hominem*, while I was trying to talk about systems and structures, and of the problems of choice while we were inevitably inside them. He at least couldn't question that 'inevitably', having made the same kind of choice, but neither could he admit it. The whole cast of his mind was that of the heroic isolated individual who was nevertheless appealing, in terms, for Cambridge, for the common pursuit, for more open discussion, for taking part; always appealing and acting in both ways, in a very complex whole situation. It is that figure, and that problem, that I see as real, by contrast with the distantly idealised version of the lonely and punished hero, and more especially with the popular version of the intensely disagreeable, unco-operative and troublemaking man.

I have one other substantial memory. During a later episode of contested Faculty business he invited me to tea at his house. Though that was the supposed occasion, none of my attempts to discuss the business was responded to. Instead he told me the whole story which I know he told to so many: of the War, of the Faculty in the twenties, of Wittgenstein, of Richards, of the reception of his wife's first book, of the years of *Scrutiny*, of his increasing exclusion, of the illnesses and the problems of money, of other (named) people losing or renouncing their way. Most of those who have heard it will know how compellingly it was told. It was a sustained structure of feeling through the only apparently random episodes. It was essentially composed, in a literary sense. I responded to the events, though remembering the other versions I had heard of some of them. But I also responded, for myself and as he and others had taught, to their telling.

'You should write this', I said.

'That has been said before.'

(Always that edgy kind of reply. I once wished him happy birthday, and he said: 'I see you've been reading *The Times*', and I said: 'No, I don't read *The Times*; I just knew it was your birthday.)'

'It has the involving strength of one particular kind of novel', I said.

He looked away.

'With this difficulty', I added. 'That one is wholly convinced by this powerful single-perspective account, until one remembers the possibility of appearing oneself as a character in one of the later chapters.'

He looked across at me, angrily. It seemed an entirely impertinent, even insolent remark. Was not the real feeling all back there, in the account he had given me? What kind of pretension was it to suppose oneself as mattering in it? I was speculating all this, from the look, but I hadn't mainly said what I had as a personal point; it was meant to be a point about the method, about the composition, about what that kind of self-centredness is when it reaches a certain intense generality, enfolding and apparently addressed to a special and consenting kind of reader, and then the inevitable surprise of finding actual people and events – oneself or others – absorbed and presented in this same powerful procedure.

'I must tell you . . .', he resumed, and the complex story began again, in a new episode.

There is not much else to tell. Thinking about method disturbs this whole process. Whose story is it anyway, as we are all seen and by that famous method 'placed'? Yet among mainly sad or baffled memories there is one that still makes me laugh out loud. We often sat side by side at Faculty Board meetings. He was mainly, in my opinion, polite and attentive, though the rows that also occurred are more strongly remembered. Often, through the duller business, we would both look out through the huge window. We once whispered to each other, simultaneously, that the wind had changed. In one very dull patch I looked down and saw him intently examining the backs of my hands, which are covered with hair. He had spread his own hands out in front of him; the backs were quite smooth. At the other end of the table they were trying, as I remember, to nominate an examiner for the Winchester Reading Prize. He went on staring at our hands and when he saw that I had noticed, he smiled.

'Nothing scriptural, for God's sake', I said under my breath. I don't think he heard, but he nodded, and there was a 'Good' from the other end of the table. The examiner for the Winchester Reading Prize had been appointed.

In the year that Leavis died I gave an unofficial memorial lecture for him. Nothing official had been arranged in the Faculty, but I wanted the occasion to be marked. I set down simply 'F. R. Leavis' on the Faculty List. I see from the notes that I spent most time discussing his kind of Practical Criticism and the phase it had offered to represent in Cambridge. I tried to describe the largely unrepeatable combination of close verbal analysis and intense moral argument. There is a sharp, underlined note rejecting what seemed to me the retrospective accommodation: 'a marvellous critic, pity about the man and all those "extra-literary obsessions"'. For the man was all intense concern and conviction, at levels inaccessible to separated argument, though vigorous argument and demonstration often proceeded from them. I took my own theoretical distance from this, as a method, and argued that in any case imitation of the method, without that original constitutive centre, must be weak. I emphasised his quite exceptional wholeness of response, but took that commonplace phrase to its relevant source: a lived, serious and intransigent project, which could not and would not be theorised in any of the positions and terms it claimed. Thus the man was not separable from the critic: for him a virtue, but for the rest of us a problem. *Ad textum, ad hominem*: the personal method that had been offered as a whole educational project had to be taken back or forward, to quite other kinds of history, argument and analysis (especially of language). It is not what might be said at an official memorial lecture, but it was the recognition I wanted to make of a unique and irreplaceable man, taking those two adjectives more seriously and more literally than in their use in tributes.

The last time I actually saw him he was running along the Madingley Road with a fistful of letters to post. I had often seen him doing this, in his last years, and thought about the wide correspondence into which he put so much vigorous writing, idiosyncratic and impersonal in that wrought, intense, precarious fusion one keeps recognising, at every level, but not in ordinary terms understanding. I was in a car and there was traffic about, but I slowed down and waved. His face was set hard with the effort of the run. He did not look across, as he continued running.

13

Taking tea with Mrs Leavis

NORA CROOK

When I came up to Cambridge in 1959, the first three things I
heard about Mrs Leavis were that she had been a beautiful young
woman, that she had recently had a near-fatal bout of cancer, and
that she was vitriolic. As it is a good rule, in general, not to hate
anyone on someone else's recommendation, even a friend's, I was
prepared to believe two of these points and to reserve judgement
on the third. The following spring (I think) I heard her lecture to
Downing College's Doughty Society. I remember little of the
lecture (except that *Middlemarch* figured largely) for I had read
few of the books to which she referred and was not ready for it,
but I do remember her presence – slim, brisk, with an upright
carriage and a mobile face, which now and then gave one glimpses
of the young girl she had been. She was then about fifty-three. I
remember, too, the following interruption from the floor:
'I disagree with your calling *Isabella* a non-political poem.'
'Oh, indeed? Why?'
'The two brothers are capitalists.'
Mrs Leavis paused; an unfathomable look crossed her face, and
she resumed the lecture without a word. I was glad that she refused
to be drawn; the interruption was a piece of coat-trailing; anyone
in the room, including the interrupter, could have made the obvious
retort: a few stanzas of nineteenth-century radicalism don't make
a political poem. Yet I also felt glad the young man challenged her;
the stanzas are among the most memorable in *Isabella*, and the view
that Keats was apolitical was then so widely accepted that it was
salutary to have it denied, however naively. I have often wondered
if this incident lodged in Mrs Leavis's memory, as it has in mine.
Certainly twenty years later she spoke to me warmly of Keats'
political maturity, though not specifically of *Isabella*. If the young

man started off a train of thought in her mind, this would have been characteristic. Contrary ideas were seldom merely rejected – they either remained to irritate or were assimilated.

The foregoing anecdote may give the impression of someone less willing to engage in debate and, if necessary, modify her views than was in fact the case. Far more typical was this extract from a letter of 1975 when my husband was writing up his Ph.D. thesis on 'S. Johnson's Idea of the Imagination': 'I must admit I couldn't believe in the subject, apart from the fact that Dr J has been inflated, and over-researched on, by pedants and criticasters, in my opinion. Still, I am open to conversion, of course.' When she heard what my husband's research had taken in – it included Johnson's understanding of mathematics – she found it believable. (Mathematics interested her: 'What a good subject for a girl!' was her comment to my sixteen-year-old daughter, who was showing talent in that field. 'I wanted to be a mathematician when I was your age.') We also had an argument, lasting for years, about comprehensive schools. She held that, while they might increase opportunities for a greater number of children, the academic ones were bound to suffer. In the end she acknowledged that my children, at any rate, had had good schooling at the local comprehensive.

It was to be another eighteen months after that lecture before I met her. She was supervising third-year Newnham students in Practical Criticism. The nominally one-hour supervisions lasted two – Mrs Leavis believed in giving value for money – and often finished with a large tea. She hated a dead silence. She had plenty to say, and if no one spoke up, would go on talking. But when anyone interrupted she did not mind; indeed, one got the impression that this was expected. Nor was she offended at being corrected – no real teacher is, provided it is done without malice. I remember her making a silly slip; she said, *à propos* of Wordsworth's *Elegiac Stanzas* that 'Him whom I deplore' referred to the artist. 'But Mrs Leavis', I interposed, with the assurance of one who had 'done' the poem for Higher Schools Certificate, 'Surely that refers to his brother John, drowned at sea.' She looked: 'Yes, yes, of course you're right – it couldn't possibly be Beaumont', and seemed almost pleased. The occasions for her correcting me were more numerous.

I once asserted that the Appalachian folk song *Nottamun Town* revealed its American provenance by its 'syncopated rhythm'. 'No, it doesn't. Where did you get that idea from? I'll sing it.' Which she did, in an untrained but clear, true voice.

The introduction of *Nottamun Town* into our supervisions reflected Mrs Leavis's lifelong interest in the relation between folk literature and the literature of art, 'a subject that seems completely neglected in university English courses though very interesting and of course in respect of medieval literature Elizabethan and Victorian quite essential to our appreciation of both traditions', as she wrote to me in March 1975. What else did she try to teach us? It is hard to describe without sounding bitty. 'Above all, the impression left on me by her supervisions', says a friend, Sophie Gairdner, 'was of her being totally in possession of the text under discussion, and coming to it afresh. She was a reader and re-reader all her life.' She also remembers the educative effect of listening to the Leavises arguing out their differences over Dickens, Mrs Leavis putting her head through the kitchen hatch. She used two 'Matthew' poems – 'The two April Mornings' and 'The Fountain' – to illustrate the difference between a distinguished poem which nevertheless fails to communicate entirely (the former), and a complete success (the latter). She tried to steer us away from categorising poems as merely bad or good. In Yeats' 'Two Songs From a Play' for instance, the lines 'Odour of blood when Christ was slain / Made all Platonic tolerance vain / And vain all Doric discipline' were, she said, glamorous-sounding but unpleasant nonsense. But the lines 'Whatever flames upon the night / Man's own resinous heart has fed' seemed to bring the poem to a satisfying conclusion, and deserved a better context. We were unsophisticated when it came to gauging the attitude of a writer towards his subject and audience. One of the good out-of-the-way things she introduced me to was Prior's 'Jinny the Just', that small masterpiece of mingled irony and sentiment. 'Her will with her Duty so equally stood / That seldom oppos'd she was commonly good, / And did pritty well, doing just what she wou'd.' We maintained that Prior was satirising the egotism of Jinny. 'Oh, do you really think so?' she asked disappointedly. 'If you are right then it's commonplace and rather nasty. I had hoped Prior meant us to see her as truly good-natured.' Hating to be right, under such circumstances, one went back to the poem, and thought again.

One day in 1964, by which time I had two small babies, an invitation arrived for all the family to come to tea with the Leavises, now moved to 12 Bulstrode Gardens. The babies crawled about, picking up cotton-reels provided by Mrs Leavis, and handing them to Dr Leavis, who thanked them courteously. Other invitations followed. Mrs Leavis loved getting up treats for little children – organising Easter Egg hunts, creating dolls' houses, decorating ex-sugar-cube boxes to fill with spicy home-made biscuits. As they grew older, she would send these foster-grandchildren of hers – of whom there were many others – books which her young family had enjoyed or which she had ust discovered. I would often get a letter asking if my children would like a copy of this or that Puffin. Her choice could be unusual: she once gave some Maoist stories containing such dialogue as 'Is it not wonderful that our fathers do not feel the heat or cold while they are working for the Cultural Revolution?' She felt that these would stimulate curiosity; furthermore, they satisfied her demand that picture books should be inexpensive and beautifully illustrated. (She often lamented that the *Père Castor* and *Orlando* books which had cost shillings in the 1930s cost pounds in the 1970s.)

In early 1970, Mrs Leavis had a near-fatal attack of pneumonia, which left her with a weakened heart. She was told to rest. A quieter kind of intercourse between us ensued. I would visit her at tea-time, often by myself, and we imperceptibly became friends. (I never called her Queenie, though I asked her once why she was so named; it is an anglicisation of the Hebrew *Malka* meaning a queen.) Sometimes there would be other visitors – her daughter Kate and son Robin, or friends like Christopher Parry, former editor of *The Use of English*, Dom Hilary Steuert, who had introduced Dr Leavis to Gray's *Impromptu* ('Owls would have hooted in St Peter's choir / And foxes stunk and littered in St Pauls'), Brian Worthington, Head of English at Clifton College, Miriam Margolyes, the actress. There were many others – I mention only some of those I met. Sometimes she visited me.

12 Bulstrode Gardens is a solid post-war house, without intrinsic charm. Mrs Leavis had, however, imprinted it with her own taste, which, without being eccentric, owed nothing to fashion. An antique bureau, cream-painted walls, patchwork of her own making, plain bookcases of white-painted or blond wood, a rush-bottomed chair, gaily-coloured posters, blue-patterned Victorian crockery, 1930s slipware by Michael Cardew, loose covers in a Morris design, yellow and rust predominating, a few plain rugs, clean-lined modern dining-chairs, a vermilion-stained cupboard – all these disparate elements combined to produce a hospitable atmosphere – simple, natural and cheerful. She loved colour, hence her preference for Finnish design (she greatly admired Finnish culture in general) over the more clinical Swedish. Dr Leavis would sometimes emerge from his study, draw the tea for us, and join us for half an hour. At the end of the visit, Mrs Leavis would give us delicious produce from the garden and larder.

I mention these domestic details because it is essential to any reading of her character to recognise that she was a housewife and mother as well as an intellectual. Indeed I see her life as a heroic attempt to combine roles which, the world's experience tells us, are contradictory. She wished to fulfil herself by being a support to her husband and through partaking in the ordinary mysteries of child-bearing and family life. At the same time she wanted a partnership of equal but different intellects. And finally she wanted achievements for herself. I think the foregoing suggests why, though often approached, she would not ally herself with any feminist writing, though she had a certain respect for such groups as the publishers of the American journal *Signs*. Most women find it a strain to combine even two of the above roles I have outlined. Mrs Leavis tried for all three, and pulled off the experiment amazingly successfully, considering the bad luck she had with illness and death. Her example was energising, as was her precept. She made me feel that I could do anything, even though, in the event, I didn't. 'Why don't you offer to edit *Tom Cringle's Log* for Penguin Books?' was one suggestion 'With your Jamaican background it would be just the thing.' If I have lazed away my youth it isn't Mrs Leavis's fault.

Her health improved, her career budded, and her letters to me became full of books planned, lecture-engagements in Belfast, Edinburgh, Newcastle, Clifton. But she travelled vicariously as well; she was always avid for details of one's holidays; these would spark off a train of vivid recollections. 'Did you see whole haystacks being quanted along on wherries by aged men with side whiskers?' she wrote, on receiving a postcard from the Norfolk Broads. 'We went sailing there for our honeymoon in 1929. My husband asked one such [aged man] if he would like a cup of tea; he replied very slowly and politely "No thankee sir, I'm just going whoom to my beloved, and I'll have a cup of tea with her." . . . My husband's grandfather, Elihu Leavis, lived in a cottage in the village of Denver, near Denver Sluice, roasting his meat on a spit at the open fire, and you could see the stars up the open chimney, and of course he had a well in the garden.'

Here are a few fragments of conversation, chosen for no better reason than that they may surprise.

'I enjoyed Buster Keaton. So much better than Charlie Chaplin, who always invited pity. I remember a film where Buster Keaton fell into a swimming pool fully dressed. My husband said, "It's wrong to laugh at him – there's nothing ridiculous. Every movement he makes is so beautiful." I disliked the Marx brothers – so gross, all that rudeness to women.'

'Trollope understood misery. The best parts in *Can You Forgive her?* are the scenes of family unhappiness in Vavasor Hall.'

'Gluck's *Orpheus* is one of my favourite operas. When I was near death in hospital I had an obsession that if only I could sing the whole of *Che Farò* I would come back to life again, and it was the turning point for me. There was an unconscious logic about this because of course *Orpheus* is about a husband calling his wife back from the dead, which was what my husband was doing.'

Mrs Leavis: 'When I was in hospital, I was next to a Carmelite nun. *I* had to tell her all about the sex in the newspapers.'
My husband (gently teasing): 'But what on earth made you do that? You make it sound like a moral imperative!'
Mrs Leavis (laughing): 'No, no, she saw these newspapers in other people's beds and didn't know what they were about, so asked me. She was so innocent!'

In 1977 Dr Leavis's health gave way. It was an intensely painful time, especially as he knew he would never finish his current book. Mrs Leavis nursed him throughout, day and night. The award of the C.H. brought some diversion – it was a recognition which meant a great deal to the family. After his death in April 1978, she was truly bereft. 'What should I do?' she asked, 'I want to write a memoir of my husband; there are things that only he and I knew, and I can't bear to think of anyone else not getting it right.¹ But then there's my own work – there's so much to do, and I'm seventy-one.' I said she should do her own work. She received this opinion dubiously.

Dr Leavis's death had another effect on her. There was now no one alive who knew the full extent of her share in their common endeavour. Inadvertently I may have played a part in bringing home the full force of this to her. In either late 1979 or early 1980, I made some remark about Dr Leavis's being influenced by Schweitzer. 'Where did you get the idea that my husband had a special interest in Schweitzer?' she asked on my next visit. I mentioned a parenthesis in the Appendix to *D. H. Lawrence, Novelist*: 'There are two reviews of *The Cocktail Party* I should like to see – one by Lawrence, and one by Albert Schweitzer.'

'That was me!' she exclaimed, 'I was in the kitchen when my husband was working on that essay, and I suddenly called this out to him. I chose the two names as being as far apart from each other as it is possible to be. "Oh, can I use that?" he said. I said "Of course" – we shared everything, we always were feeding each other ideas.'

On that occasion she told me of her part in *The Great Tradition*. 'When my husband showed me the draft for my comments, I said: "It needs a first chapter to set the whole thing off." He agreed but he hadn't the time to write it, so I said I would. He then re-wrote it – putting things the way he would write, you know, so that the styles matched. And the footnotes were mine too. Didn't you know?'

'No', I replied. 'How could I know? How could anyone know?'

At this point I must record that neither then or at any time in twenty years did I hear Mrs Leavis say anything that could possibly be construed to mean that she and her husband were rivals, or that she blamed him for lack of recognition or that she was anything but proud of their partnership and believed it to be a true one. I mention this only because two mutually destructive attempts to denigrate the Leavises' partnership have recently been published. One suggests that their public comradeship was really a 'furtive instance' of plagiarism on Dr Leavis's part, motivated by 'sexual or pect jealousy' (John Sutherland, *T.L.S.*, 9 April 1982). The other, contrariwise, surmises that she browbeat him into incorporating her writing into his work in order to push him forward – a laughable suggestion if one recalls Dr Leavis's established reputation at the time of *The Great Tradition*.

This is not the place to discuss the recent allegation that she was a hindrance rather than a help to her husband, but I take the opportunity to express my conviction that without her, his work would have been narrower in its scope. 'There is a wrong sort of catholicity of taste', Dr Leavis used to say. The corollary of this is that there is a right sort of catholicity, and her influence was consistently towards this latter sort. (She was a rapid and voracious reader, which enabled her to be always putting him onto good half-forgotten books and minor classics, like *Pudd'nhead Wilson*, *Belchamber* and *The House with the Green Shutters*, to name three that I am certain of. Among her recommendations to me over the years were Leigh-Fermor's *The Violins of St Jacques*, Kingsley's *Hypatia*, Randall Jarrell's *Pictures from an Institution*, Karen Blixen's *Out of Africa*, Renoir's *Renoir my Father*, S. N. Behrman's *Duveen*. Of course she did not regard these as all being of the same status.)

The last years brought disappointments and compensations. A projected book on Victorian novels of religion failed to materialise. But she was more in demand than ever as a lecturer. There was the devotion of her children. And her first grandchild was born.

She was working on Solzhenitsyn and Mandelstam in the New Year of 1981, struggling against arthritis and ill-health. She had had several black-outs. Old friends, like Adrian Bell the novelist, had died. When I asked her if she would lecture to the Literary Society of the Cambridgeshire College of Arts and Technology, she said: 'You had better get me quick – I might not be around for much longer.' I had never heard her speak like that before. The talk took place in February. It was to be her last public engagement.

A few weeks later I had a telephone conversation. She was going into hospital. There was, she said, the hope of an operation which would put her heart to rights; she would be back to normal and able to finish her work. 'You will visit me in hospital, won't you?'

But the next I heard was a 'phone-call from Kate to say that she had died. The funeral was a very private affair, only family and a few friends. Just as for Dr Leavis, there was no service, which is what she wished. We sat in the crematorium chapel, and I thought of this woman who had so long counteracted the devil, which is death, by brisking about the life. It is a talent for the sake of which the possessor deserves to be forgiven much. Most of us are *memento moris* to one another. But Mrs Leavis deserved only gratitude from me –

> Tread soft on her grave and do right to her honor
> Let neither rude hand or ill tongue light upon her
> Do all the small favors that now can be done her.

– for she had given me nothing but affection, encouragement and bracing friendship.

Note

1 'Where do people get their notions from?' she once asked exasperatedly 'Here's someone writing that my husband was gassed in the First World War, when he wasn't at all. Why can't people check with the family?'

14

Some recollections of the Leavises

MICHAEL TANNER

I had not even heard of Leavis when I arrived in Cambridge in 1955 to read Moral Sciences, as Philosophy was then called. Friends who were reading English told me that he was narrow, dogmatic and quarrelsome, and I was too busy during my first year in Cambridge getting my brain to work after two years of National Service to attend lectures in faculties other than my own. But in the course of my first long vacation, when I was trying to think intelligently about literature for the first time, I took *The Great Tradition* down from the shelves of the local public library, and the result was something like a religious conversion. I had never come across such a congenial tone, in the first place. I couldn't wait to go to his first lecture in the Michaelmas Term of 1956, and it lived up to my expectations. He distributed sheets on which were printed pieces of both poetry and prose (fiction and criticism), and proceeded with his judgement and analysis, with many an *obiter dictum* and half-audible remark about other English dons, of a kind that has often been recalled and usually misquoted. I became and remained in the crudest sense a Leavisite during my three years as an undergraduate – and have often been taken to be one ever since.

When I became a graduate student, working in the then almost wholly neglected field of aesthetics, I went along to his room in Downing and asked whether I might sit in on his seminars. Characteristically he replied, thinking that I was an English under-graduate; 'Yes, but don't tell your Director of Studies – he might not approve.' The seminars, which I attended daily, including Saturday mornings, were haphazard affairs. Though they were ostensibly geared to a particular topic, they ranged widely, and Leavis mainly discussed whatever was uppermost in his mind. A transcript of them would not make impressive reading. But the intensity with which he spoke, the courtesy and tact with which he coped with the most inane remarks from the audience, and the extraordinary seriousness with which he dealt with the matter in hand, were exemplary. Often he was distracted by current controversies; and I found it impossible to take helpful notes. But the overall effect was much more striking and lasting than that may suggest. However random the progression through an hour, or through an accumulation of hours, one gained an incomparable grounding in what he considered to be the central issues in criticism, and in the reasons for his regarding them as being so momentous. It was really much more like being present at the table-talk of a great man than attending a class.

In one sense, then, Leavis was scarcely, at least by this stage, a teacher at all, if that suggests a Socratic ideal of eliciting from his audience reactions which were then discussed. And even then I had the feeling that an attempt at argument with him would be unlikely to be profitable. Courteous as he was, he rapidly resumed the line of thought which a questioner had interrupted. And of course there was, as the world well knows, a great deal of mocking and bitter reminiscence, a reliving of the battles which he had been engaged in during the previous thirty years, and a contempt for almost all professional students of literature which led one to wonder how he could continue to envisage hopefully a nucleus of intelligent, disinterested critics whose effect would be widespread. That apart, two features of the classes which other memoirists elsewhere haven't mentioned stick in my mind. One was his frequently reiterated stress on the need for wide reading: 'Cultivate promiscuity', as he used rather quaintly to put it. The other is that, although there was always at least one priest present, he didn't ever attempt to disguise his dislike of Christianity. Years later, when I sent him a copy of *The Listener*, in which a talk of mine on Johnson was reprinted, he wrote to me: 'Poor Johnson! Not even he was immune. – However hard they [he was referring to the editors of a periodical in which he was then regularly appearing, which combined Leavisism with a strange brand of Wittgenstein-derived Christianity] try, they won't succeed in assimilating me to Christianity or The Anscombe' [the Catholic Professor of Philosophy at Cambridge who had contributed to the journal].

Although I was so regular an attender of his classes, I had no personal contact with Leavis until the spring of 1961, and then it was purely by letter. Lawrence's *Phoenix* (now *Phoenix I*) had just been reissued, and Leavis reviewed it in the *Spectator*. In the course of his review, he stated that Lawrence's supremacy as a critic was demonstrated by his essay on *Death in Venice*. That struck me, and still does, as absurd, and I wrote a rather angry letter to the *Spectator* saying so, and why. They didn't print it, so I sent a copy of it to Leavis. He had no idea who I was – I made no mention in my covering note of my attendance at his classes. But by return I got a long and extremely friendly letter, in which he said that he actually very much admired *Death in Venice*, 'which I re-read frequently in my autographed copy'; that he had read Mann in German up to and including *The Magic Mountain*, to which he had reacted 'How German! I'm not Germanically given.' He added that a careful critique of Mann was something that he would very much like to undertake, but that there were too many other demands on his time. I was impressed by the rapidity, candour and modesty of his reply, and correspondingly disappointed when early in the next term's lecture course on The Novel he mentioned *Phoenix*, and praised it on precisely the same grounds that he had done in the *Spectator*.

My next contact with him was more than three years later, though in the meantime I continued to attend his seminars and, having become Director of Studies in English at my college, which resisted the idea of a *bona fide* fellow in the subject, sent along the few students I had to the classes too. Then in 1964 Leavis resigned his honorary fellowship at Downing, because that college eventually appointed as his successor someone of whom he strongly disapproved. Since the Leavises had moved to a part of Cambridge remote, by local standards, from Downing, I wrote to him offering him one of my rooms in college to hold his seminars in. He gratefully accepted the offer. Each morning he would arrive at nine o'clock and continue uninterruptedly until one, after which he normally stayed for a chat. That arrangement didn't last long; I became involved in a controversy about my college's refusal to appoint a 'real' fellow in English; the national press, at a low ebb for news, conflated that with Leavis's resignation, and he felt it would be against my interests to be known to be closely associated with him. For the remainder of the sixties I saw him rarely, but I established contact with Mrs Leavis, and persuaded her to teach for the Novel paper and nineteenth- and twentieth-century literature in general. The men whom she supervised, usually singly, would return at about six o'clock, having arrived for the supervision at two, and sorely in need of alcoholic tranquillisation. Their supervisions consisted of torrents of information, urgings to read many novels, including very large numbers of foreign works, many of them pretty obscure – she always lent them her copies of them, and quite often gave them one of her reserve copies, which she tirelessly acquired from stalls in the market – and astonishingly wide-ranging surveys of the development of the novel in all the European countries and the United States. She annotated the students' essays very fully, but didn't discuss them much in the supervisions. Usually, the men said, at about four o'clock Leavis would enter with a cup of tea for his wife. I was surprised at the uncharacteristic lack of hospitality, until I discovered that it was a prearranged signal, invariably ignored by Mrs Leavis, for her to stop: she suffered from severe heart trouble, and had been forbidden to over-exert herself.

In the late sixties the Leavises began to invite me to lunch quite often. It was always an enormous meal. Mrs Leavis deplored the fact that each time there is a World War the housewives of England take the opportunity to reduce the number and choice of courses they serve. She and their daughter Kate produced an astonishing number of alternatives, all of a superlative quality. During the meal, when Leavis himself never had anything more than a bowl of soup – he told me once that it was convenient for people to think it was because he had been gassed in the First World War, but actually it was because of the state of tension in which he lived – Mrs Leavis did most of the talking, keeping up a remarkable flow of anecdote, and laughing a great deal, her mirth often being occasioned by remembrances of prudery and priggishness. I recall her account of how an extremely distinguished literary critic was discovered by his bedmaker to be keeping condoms in his bedside table (this was in the early thirties), and how they were taken to the Master of his College, 'one of those innocent classics who composed Latin verses about schoolboys bathing nude', and that he had to have explained to him what the condoms were for. Leavis's mind often seemed to be elsewhere - he had no doubt heard the stories often before. Finally, when Mrs Leavis was unable to persuade me and any other guest to eat any more, she and Kate cleared away the dishes and retired to the kitchen, while Leavis took over the conversation. While he always talked in a confidential, rapid style, he was less interested in reactions than in the expression of his views. I always had the feeling that he was very lonely, longing to talk, and to air many of the unprintable witticisms that played so large a part in his conversation and his letters. Once when I, discouraged in my attempt to write a large book, felt I would be cheered up enormously if he agreed to let me dedicate it to him, he first replied no, because it would offend several people, one persistent author in particular, who were currently making the same request. After a few days a further letter came, in which he said that he'd changed his mind, and added about the prolific author: 'I can afford to hurt X's feelings - he has so many of them.' Though his wit was typically sharp and even cruel, he also had a Johnsonian view of the absurdity of most enterprises, including his own, about which he was often dismissive.

As, during the later years of his life, we became much closer, his monologues became longer, more self-searching, and more painful, though he always maintained that he would be a fighter to the end, and that the depressing state of the world in general, and of English studies in particular, didn't lead him to despair. Once he said: 'Knights thinks I'm miserable. I'm not miserable!' with very great intensity. During the middle nineteen-seventies, as he approached and passed the age of eighty, he still carried out an exhausting and unpaid weekly visit to York University, which gave him great happiness, though I always felt that he needed to over-estimate the effect that he had there. It was an absolutely crucial element in his being that he should teach - the way his last books, including most

of *The Living Principle*, got written was by producing them first
as lectures for York.

Something that many of his pupils have written about, but which
seems impossible to convey adequately, was the overall imperson-
ality of his conversation – his over-riding concern with literature
and civilisation – combined with the truly incredible warmth that
streamed from him, a warmth that was unquestionably directed
towards the person he was talking to, though it didn't manifest
itself in any specific interest in one's personal life. In many ways a
very old-fashioned person, he seemed to find it impossible to
express overtly the affection he felt. It was part of his fastidiousness
that he didn't go in for advertising his feelings, but they were imma-
nent in everything he said, so that there was an exhilarating glow
which invariably left me, after even a short conversation with him,
feeling refreshed and revitalised. Another aspect of that fastidiousness was that he really did find bad or indifferent writing too
painful to read, so that he never attempted to emulate Mrs Leavis's
astonishing sorties into the mediocre or worse. I remember one
occasion on which she was telling me how many of Trollope's
novels I ought to read, even though a great deal of most of them
was poor, because there was a valuable chapter or two embedded
somewhere in the middle of them. As she talked, she passed me a
daunting series of them, urging me to take them away to read.
Leavis, who was sitting on the other side of me, gave me a con-
spiratorial glance, and as Mrs Leavis handed them to me he covertly
extended a hand which received the book she had just passed to me.
While she went on, until she died, ransacking the world's literature,
his reading became, I think, more and more confined to the books
that he regarded as ultimately valuable, and he often castigated
himself for having failed to notice what was there on his innumer-
able previous readings. 'People talk about the Leavises', he once
said to me, 'but actually my wife and I are completely different
critics.' Mrs Leavis was always making discoveries, and her conversations about literature invariably included references to books
that I hadn't heard of, but which were interesting, she said, for the
light they cast on some neglected aspect of Victorian religious con-
flicts, or their conceivable influence on Melville. Leavis rarely

advocated anything new, though his late attachment to Montale's poetry was intense. His reading outside of literature was, by this stage, haphazard. This was something I had occasion to take him to task for in his last literary controversy, when I animadverted on his claims for an insignificant work of philosophy which he had chanced upon in Heffers', and for an amusing but lightweight attack on the social sciences. He was unrepentant, but he wrote to me, prior to publishing his reply to my article: 'Perhaps I judge too much by my own limitations. These are certainly *very* restrictive: I'm not being "modest" when I say I'm very slow. There is such a lot of literature, and so little help in dealing with it. And who can draw a line round the Study of English Literature (*Life and Thought*!)?' – the last few words refer to a series of papers once so named in the English Tripos. He continued: 'What I'm avowing is that I'm not "philosophical" in the innocent literary sense (now archaic) of the word. I'm "engaged" and embattled – and terrified.'

In 1977, not long before his eighty-first birthday, it was clear that though he was not in the least senile, he was in a more exhausted condition than I'd known him in before. It's worth quoting in full the last letter I received from him. I wrote to him asking why he had omitted from the chapter on 'Elites, Oligarchies and an Educated Public', as it appears in *Nor Shall My Sword*, an account which he had given, when he first published the essay, of an encounter with an American graduate student in Oxford who had made Leavis feel very strongly how helpless one sometimes is in trying to cross a culture-gap, in this case in connection with the men who had 'gone over the top' in the First World War. I wrote that I thought it was one of the finest passages he had ever produced, moving, personal, and yet not at all drawing attention to himself. He replied by return, as always:

'I'm very glad you feel as I do about that excised passage. I was troubled about it. I was at school till the term before war was declared. I had refused to join the O.T.C. and defied the Headmaster, old Rouse – but I was the school athlete. I wasn't sophisticated or articulate. My father's articulateness accounted for that – and the effect of his personality. He dominated every company he was in, though he wasn't overbearing. Simply a centre of human power. He said to me in the Kitchener days 'You'll do as you decide, but I advise you not to join the army.' That's how I felt. I couldn't be a pacifist (that word came in then); I knew that the Germans mustn't be allowed to win. But . . . I worried about the 'ought'; the problem was insoluble. I joined the Friends' Ambulance Unit. Stinking blankets and lice, and always a job to do that was too much for me. But after the bloody Somme there could be no question for *anyone* who knew what modern war was like of joining the army.

I didn't want to come home, and couldn't communicate with my father – whom I loved.

As for the excised passage, I was afraid it might lead some readers to suppose I was talking about myself. So in the end I cut it out.

I'd listened (e.g. in the Somme salient) to the barrages, tormented by concern for the men on *both* sides.

Thankyou for the offprint. I can't tackle it at once. For one thing, I've no margin of energy. I'm in my 80's! And I'm very tired; so much so, that I can't make up my mind whether what I've written will bear publishing. Perhaps I'm past it, and this state is permanent.

This is the explanation.'

The next time I saw him was to have lunch with him on his eighty-second birthday. He was obviously appallingly tired and said nothing during the meal. Afterwards he spoke desultorily, and then, uniquely in my experience, dropped off for a nap. When the other guest and I got up to leave, Leavis insisted on accompanying us to the end of Bulstrode Gardens, and apologised for having got us there 'under false pretences'. The next day I went on holiday, and when I 'phoned up on my return Mrs Leavis told me that he had had a series of cerebro-vascular accidents. For a period of about a month, during which I saw him only once, he was sporadically extremely active; in between he was sunk in unapproachable and terrifying gloom. I can't imagine seeing anyone look so desperate. All he said was 'I'm not feeling chirpy.' Not long after he became completely quiet and docile, and spent nearly all the time in bed dozing. I would go round and see him occasionally; he seemed to like to have someone to sit with him, and Mrs Leavis did nearly all the time. His death was a relief. But I shall never cease to miss him.

15

F. R. Leavis and the schools

FRANK WHITEHEAD

It is widely held that F. R. Leavis had an important and far-reaching influence on the teaching of English in schools. Actually, given the avowedly educational intent of the herculean effort which had *Scrutiny* at its centre (to put it baldly, a desperate attempt to recreate the educated reading-public which mass civilisation had destroyed), I find it a little surprising that Leavis himself devoted so little of his immense energy to the problems of school education. That he attributed a key significance to work at this level can be seen from the two paragraphs near the end of *How to Teach Reading* (1933) which begin: 'With the universities ignoring their function it would, of course, be idle to hope much of education in general. But what has been said has obvious applications at the school level, and much might be done if it were permitted, if there were teachers educated to do it, and if the examination system were not allowed to get in the way' (p. 48). Yet in the early volumes of *Scrutiny* all the significant contributions on schools were left to other hands. One thinks for instance of L. C. Knights' 'Will Training Colleges Bear Scrutiny?' (December 1932), a seminal article about the training of teachers; his 'Scrutiny of Examinations' (September 1933), an analysis of the effects of mass examining in the School Cerificate which, alas, remains as topical and relevant as ever even to this day; and Denys Thompson's 'What Shall We Teach?' (March 1934), which likewise broke fresh ground in its specific references to school conditions accompanied by highly practical suggestions. Leavis in the meantime had made two forays into this area (and they were to be his last).

In 1933, in joint authorship with Denys Thompson, he had published *Culture and Environment*, a book designed explicitly though not exclusively for school use and for several decades studied principally in the sixth forms of grammar schools. Then in August 1933 a 4-page leaflet was produced headed *The Scrutiny Movement in Education*. This contained a report of a meeting held at Cambridge 'at the end of the last May term'. The summary of the opening address[1] stated that it had always been intended 'that a positive movement should develop . . . to propagate and enforce a clearly realised conception of education and its function', a function exemplified by reference to 'the implications and reception of *Culture and Environment*'; it was emphasised that 'the inevitability (and desirability) of drastic social change makes an active concern for cultural continuity the more essential'; and the aim proposed was defined more specifically as 'to form among those teaching or intending to teach in school, college, university and adult education . . . a body of people actively conscious of the common function and bent on a concerted effort to further it'. At the end of the discussion it was 'agreed that any elaborate machinery of organisation was to be avoided' and that 'such organisation as was worth having would develop spontaneously – in local "cells", so to speak – with a minimum of incitement'. Further announcements were promised in *Scrutiny* in due course, but none ever appeared. The tone of the leaflet suggests that this venture, had it borne fruit, would have resulted in a rather narrowly-based association of the already-converted, taking as its appointed aim the dissemination of propaganda for the diagnosis of society's ills set out in *Culture and Environment*. As such I am sure it would never have achieved as much as the less dogmatic movement slowly and laboriously built up in later years under the guidance of Denys Thompson.

In defence of Leavis's caution in regard to schools, it should be said that he himself had little if any experience of school problems; and that his own schooling had taken place, just before the First World War, at an exceptionally favoured and highly selective boys' grammar school. Moreover his own expressed conviction that: 'In any period it is upon a very small minority that the discerning appreciation of art and literature depends' (*Mass Civilisation and Minority Culture* (1930), p. 1) disposed him to focus attention particularly on sixth forms in grammar or public schools, seeing them as a potential reservoir for the recruitment of alert undergraduates capable of forming the nucleus of the desiderated 'educated reading-public'. All the same, throughout his university career a high proportion of Leavis's pupils made a career in teaching (usually grammar-school teaching), though so far as I have been able to gather this was not the result of any explicit advice or suggestion on his part. There were of course the indications in his earlier writings (one has been quoted above) that he saw school teaching as offering a worthwhile field of endeavour; but it seems probable that the main incentive was of a more negative kind – the *Scrutiny* ambience made it plain that, as compared with the possible alternatives for English graduates (advertising, journalism, the B.B.C.) teaching did at least give some guarantee against the likelihood of corruption and contagion.

In 1935 I went up to Cambridge to read English as a noncollegiate student at Fitzwilliam House. From 1936 to 1938 I was able to attend Leavis's university lectures, and these (along with Mansfield Forbes' final term of lectures before his premature death, and I. A. Richards' spell-binding performances) were the high point of my Cambridge education. At that date, at any rate, Leavis was an excellent lecturer, and the lecture room (rather smaller than that allocated to Richards) was always well filled. If there were any of the disparaging asides about his university colleagues which I am told he later interspersed into such occasions I have not remembered them. Three points seem worth stressing. First, since the negative or adverse aspects of Leavis's critical judgements have so often been trumpeted, I must insist that the major effect of listening to him was to introduce me to the enjoyment and appreciation of many works and authors I should never otherwise have turned to; thus, his dealings with Shelley may have seemed harsh in certain respects, but what they did for me was to direct me to the merits of *The Masque of Anarchy*, *Peter Bell the Third* and *The Triumph of Life*. Second, he was an excellent reader of poetry, who seemed to be intent on allowing the poet's words and rhythms to speak *through* him, as it were; I remember particularly his superb reading of passages from Pope. Third, although some of the material of his lectures had already appeared as articles in *Scrutiny*, he always seemed to be thinking out his argument afresh as he went along, and the first-hand quality of his commentary on the texts he referred to convinced one that he had re-read them and reconsidered his response specifically for this lecture.[2] This recollection seems to be in place here since the seriousness and disinterestedness so evident in teaching of this quality may well have played a part in influencing some of his students towards a teaching career.

I was never a pupil of Leavis's, but my school English-teacher had procured for me an invitation to the famous Friday afternoon teas at Chesterton Hall Crescent, and I am afraid that, like some others, I availed myself of this hospitality with a shamelessness which in retrospect makes me wince. In spite of the hard core of acolytes nervous of putting a foot wrong, these gatherings were often pleasantly relaxed social occasions, graced by occasional visitors whose homage Leavis clearly relished, and capable of embracing conversationally quite a wide range of topics. Thus I remember Leavis confessing to spending a considerable amount of time listening to the wind-up gramophone that was in evidence and, on being challenged, naming the composer he listened to most (it was Haydn). Inevitably, literary topics figured largest, however, and Leavis was the most frequent speaker. I have a vivid recollection of one Friday when Leavis delivered a damning comment on Auden's poetry and driven by some brash impulse I asked him whether perhaps Auden did not deserve credit for having attempted what Edmund Wilson in *Axel's Castle* had urged as the contemporary poetic necessity, namely some fusion between the personal and the social. My intervention was clearly not well received by the assembled gathering, and Leavis's' demurral, though polite, was unyielding. Later, however, he took me on one side and spent at least a quarter of an hour explaining to me, with a patient kindliness to which I had absolutely no claim, just what was suspect about Auden's socio-political preoccupations. I felt then (and still feel) that this passionately disinterested concern that the truth should prevail is one essential prerequisite of the great teacher. Why then does some misgiving linger when I remember that afternoon's exchange? I can explain it only by referring to a seminar conducted by Leavis a few terms later as part of an experimental programme organised by the English Club in an attempt to persuade the Faculty that it would be beneficial if lectures and supervisions could be supplemented by rather larger seminar groups with more opportunity for the cut and thrust of differing opinions. There were about fifteen of us foregathered in an appropriate-sized room, and we all had a copy of a text proposed by Leavis himself, I. M. Parsons's anthology of twentieth-century poets entitled *The Progress of Poetry*. The first poet in Parsons's volume is Hardy, and Leavis opened the proceedings by asking why we thought Hardy was there. There was a long silence. Eventually in desperation I suggested that perhaps he had been put there to demonstrate the starting-point. This was the wrong answer, though it seems to me in retrospect that its very wrongness could have been made the opening for a profitable discussion. Instead Leavis simply asserted (a viewpoint which I think he probably modified later) that the reason for Hardy's presence was that he had lately been very much over-valued as a poet. Throughout the rest of the session, although Leavis asked questions from time to time, no other member of the group ventured to open his mouth, so that what we were treated to was a monologue, fascinating, almost infinitely perceptive – but a monologue all the same.

After graduating in 1938 I did my teacher-training in 1938-9 at the University of London Institute of Education, and about half-way through the year in the course of a brief visit to Cambridge I found myself again at Chesterton Hall Crescent at one of the Friday afternoon teas. I remember Leavis questioning me about my London tutor Dr P. Gurrey (whose 1935 book *The Appreciation of Poetry* had included commendatory references to *How to Teach Reading*), and my uncomfortable impression that Leavis's real interest was in learning whether Gurrey either was or might become a 'disciple'. I wasn't able to answer at all satisfactorily, principally because I had begun to feel that from Gurrey and his colleague Maura Brooke Gwynne I was in process of learning something important the nature of which I wasn't yet clear about. Trying to pinpoint it to myself now I have an image of an early lesson I tried to teach to a fourth-year form at the South London boys' grammar school where I did my teaching-practice. From E. G. Biaggini's book *The*

Reading and Writing of English I had taken two paired passages of prose, one bad, the other reasonably good, and I was trying to build up on the blackboard, using pupils' answers to my questions, a parallel list of judgements (essentially intellectual in nature, I'm afraid) on the quality of the writing. It was the first lesson of mine which Gurrey had come to watch, and it wasn't going very well. At the end of it I expected him to give me some inkling as what I was doing wrong, or how I might try to improve my performance. Instead he shook his head regretfully, and said: 'No, you haven't got it.' And that was all he would say. Eventually, partly from his lectures and seminars, but even more from watching him and Miss Gwynne teaching classes of varying ages and abilities, I concluded that 'it' was something to do with the unsuspected ability of pupils to read, respond, write and act out of their own powers and volition if given opportunity, encouragement and the right stimulus. Laboriously, in my own later teaching–career and in my writings I set my energies to trying to combine this fostering of the young person's innate creativity with a concern for those standards of discrimination which *Scrutiny* had upheld so valiantly in face of the vulgarity of the modern publishing and entertainment industry. But greatly though I always admired Leavis, I am rather doubtful as to how far he would ever have understood Gurrey's 'it'.

The mechanisms of the subsequent slow extension of Leavis's influence upon school English-teaching (Denys Thompson's founding of *English in Schools* in 1939, his editorship of its successor *The Use of English* from 1949 to 1969, the formation of local *Use of English* discussion groups in the late 1950s leading to the formation of the National Association for the Teaching of English in 1963) cannot appropriately be dwelt on here. What matters is the history of the ideas themselves, the critical thinking about society and about literature as it was transmitted, modified, and (inevitably) diluted in the course of its passage through other minds; and since the body of thought as a whole has an essential unity I cannot avoid a certain arbitrariness in attempting to tease out merely a few of the strands.

Regrettably the central strand I must start with has failed in the long run to establish itself in any form which Leavis would have acknowledged. The analysis of modern society in *Culture and*

Environment, though derided or ignored by the reviewers, was taken up with enthusiasm in the thirties by a significant minority of English teachers, and further extremely telling ammunition for their teaching was provided in 1939 by Denys Thompson's book about newspapers (*Between the Lines*) and in 1943 by his even more carefully documented book about advertising (*The Voice of Civilisation*). In the 1950s, with the increasing concentration of press ownership, the advent of new gramophone-record technology, and the gratuitous introduction of advertising on television, the entertainments industry began to plumb depths inconceivable in the 1930s, and concern about its influence on the young became more widespread among the teaching profession, so much so that in 1960 the National Union of Teachers called together an important conference on 'Popular Culture and Personal Responsibility'. This was followed up in 1962 by Raymond Williams's useful (if occasionally muddled) Penguin Special *Communications*, which included among its 'proposals' some specific and helpful teaching-suggestions. But in the later sixties and early seventies the English-teacher's sense of the necessity for *resistance*, generated so inexorably by *Culture and Environment*, was gradually and insidiously eroded in ways the history of which still waits to be written. Something must certainly be attributed to the writings of Richard Hoggart, to the publications of the Birmingham University Centre for Contemporary Cultural Studies, and to that blandly diversionary book *The Country and the City* published by Raymond Williams in 1972;[3] in their various ways all these tended to blur, with dubious sociology and inappropriately crude class-concepts, the powerful impact of Leavis's original cultural analysis, to whose amazing prescience life in the 1980s bears almost uncanny witness. It is perhaps enough to say that in relation to 'popular culture' all too many English teachers have today been corrupted by fashionable media voices, so that although (for example) in many classrooms newspapers and advertisements are given some attention, the lesson is all too likely to end up with an exhortation to write an account of a school football match in the style of *The Daily Mirror* or *The Sun* or to devise and execute an advertising campaign that will sell your own newly-named brand of confectionary bar.

F. R. Leavis and the schools

More long-lasting in its influence on schools has been the detailed literary criticism, rooted in close attention to the words of the text, which was at the heart of Leavis's teaching and writing for the central thirty-five years of his life and which continued to loom large even in the more philosophical and prophetic books of his final decade. Yet even here some caution is needed if misunderstanding is to be avoided. 'Practical Criticism' in the form in which it has reached the schools is commonly thought of as the 'unseen test' in which the sixth-former is thrown upon his own resources to evaluate and comment on a poem or extract whose provenance has been kept from him. I believe myself that such exercises (and the examination paper in 'Interpretation and Comment' which they normally prepare for) do have a valuable role to play in training the reading-capacity of sixth-formers; but in the form in which we know them they owe more to I. A. Richards and his use of the notorious 'protocols' than to Leavis. Undoubtedly Leavis took valuable hints from Richards (perhaps rather more than he was later disposed to acknowledge); and in the 1940s he was content to use the term 'Practical Criticism' as exemplified in his comment in *Education and the University*: 'By training of reading capacity I mean the training of perception, judgement and analytic skill commonly referred to as "practical criticism" . . .' (p. 69). In his undergraduate teaching, however, Leavis seems to have gradually become increasingly dissatisfied with a tendency to isolate 'exercises in judgement and analysis' (necessarily limited to short poems or passages) from the wider context of critical study of an author, a movement or a period; and it may (I suspect) have been this kind of dissatisfaction that led him to abandon the projected book of examples of 'judgement and analysis', segments of which appeared at intervals in *Scrutiny* between 1945 and 1953 and which were eventually collected together in the Part II of *The Living Principle* (where they seem not wholly in their right setting). In any event the term which Leavis came explicitly to prefer was 'criticism in practice'; and it was fitting therefore that the reading-sheets issued by *The Use of English* for use with sixth-formers from 1949 onwards should have borne this title.

More than from any other printed source, though, it must have

147

been from *Revaluation* and from *The Great Tradition* that English teachers, and ultimately their pupils, learned how to develop and apply their own reading-capacity to poems, prose and novels – and not only, of course, to the works Leavis himself discussed. At the same time this body of criticism (as well as the later books on Lawrence and Dickens) can be seen to have had a radical and welcome innovative effect on the choice of set texts for 'A' Level English – a movement, one might almost say, from *Eothen* to Eliot's *Four Quartets*. Moreover Leavis certainly took an interest in the movement towards greater enlightenment in this area. In 1955 I published a selection of Crabbe's Verse-Tales designed for sixth forms, and since it was entirely due to Leavis's lectures and his comments in *Revaluation* that I owed my own introduction to the later Crabbe, I took the liberty of sending him a copy. In due course there came back a punctilious acknowledgement with the comment: 'I think the book was very much worth doing, and it seems to me that a good English master may be counted on to do some recruiting for Crabbe – about whom there is more to say than I said in *Revaluation*.'[4] Further evidence of Leavis's concern for the promotion of good sixth-form teaching comes to hand in a letter from one of his former pupils who reports between about 1964 and 1973 having 'on several occasions visited him with his prior agreement accompanied by groups of sixth form students', at first from a highly selective grammar school, later from a comprehensive school. This provides a suitable context in which to mention Leavis's opposition to comprehensive schools, including his own testimony that Mr Thorpe's declaration in favour of them was one of the reasons for his resolving, in the 1960s, 'not to expose myself to being counted in future as a loyal backer of the Liberal party' (*The Human World*, 15–16 (1974), 98). I think there can be little doubt that Leavis's stand on this issue was adopted with the motive of defending the grammar schools – perhaps above all, indeed, of defending the standards of their sixth forms. In its historical setting this was not an ignoble position, though one may believe it (as I do myself) to have been a mistaken one.

There is a related area, however, where I find it impossible to exculpate Leavis – namely his failure to put on record any concern for the education of the less able and less privileged pupils in our school system. I don't believe there was anything callous or unfeeling about his omission; one might indeed simply say that his mind was always too busy with matters which seemed to him to take a higher priority. Experience had never brought home to him the devastating incapacity suffered by someone who, in our print-dominated society, has not succeeded in learning to read and write. (And from the cultural point of view it must admittedly seem to many of us that the ability to read Mickey Spillane or a Mills and Boon novel is a distinctly dubious advantage.) But what seems particularly regrettable is that there were, in fact, always present at the heart of Leavis's thinking two insights which, had they been brought to bear upon the education of 'the ordinary child', might have had revolutionary implications. In the first place (and this comes into the open more obviously in his later commentaries on Blake) there is Leavis's recognition of an essential continuity between the artist's creativity and that manifested in daily living by the ordinary person. I quote from *Nor Shall My Sword*: 'Genius for him [i.e. Blake] is a peculiar intensity and strength of representativeness: the artist's developed, conscious and skilled creativity is continuous with the creativity inseparable, he insists, from perception itself, and from all human experience and knowledge' (p. 13). Secondly, there is the emphasis which Leavis placed, throughout his writing career, upon 'language' as in itself a 'culture', an organic human achievement which 'has its life in use – use that, of its nature, is a creative human response to changing conditions, so that in a living language we have a manifestation of continuous collaborative creativity.' The persistent failure of the state educational system to recognise and build upon such potentialities in the common people, its compulsion instead to become 'an influence foisted upon them from outside, a constraining agency' is something which was diagnosed repeatedly by George Sturt both in his published writings and in his Journals; and it seems a pity that this was given so little emphasis in Leavis's social analysis. There are of course no easy solutions to be offered; more promising than any other that I know of, however, is the mode of approach developed by David Holbrook (one of Leavis's former pupils) in his book for teachers *English for the Rejected* (1964) and in his four work-books for secondary pupils *I've Got to Use Words* (1966). The distinctive feature of Holbrook's work here is the provision of positive and practical suggestions for fostering the ordinary child's creative linguistic powers, while at the same time ensuring a proper concern for quality of experience by feeding into the classroom situation plentiful listening-to and reading-of a medley of traditional rhymes, ballads, modern jingles, poems and stories which speak to the living interests and preoccupations of the pupils. Without this concern for quality of experience, 'creative writing' can too easily, alas, become little more than a bored and sterile doodling with the emotional superficialities purveyed so insistently by comics, advertisements and television programmes.

One further reference to Leavis is called for. Early in 1966 I wrote to him in my capacity as Chairman of the National Association for the Teaching of English inviting him to come as a member of the British contingent to the month-long Anglo-American Seminar on the Teaching of English which was to be held at Dartmouth College, New Hampshire, in August/September. His refusal was both prompt and courteous: he was already committed to an arduous lecture-tour of American universities that autumn. Another disappointment was that, although at our initial planning meeting we had had the benefit of L. C. Knights's presence and advice, he too was unable to be with us at Dartmouth owing to prior teaching-engagements at another American university. Nevertheless in the final N.A.T.E. party the *Scrutiny* connection was well represented – two former editors, Denys Thompson and D. W. Harding, were there, while former pupils of Leavis included Douglas Barnes, Boris Ford, David Holbrook and Esmor Jones. Despite this wealth of talent on the British side, the seminar proved a disappointing occasion at which there was very little genuine meeting of minds with the American representatives. (These included a few academics, no school-teachers, and a high proportion of educationists and administrators – I well remember how baffled some of them were by the high valuation the British team set upon the of writings of D. H. Lawrence!) It is my own considered judgement that John Dixon's influential report on the seminar[5] had a harmful effect upon English teaching in England, largely because it distracted from that seriousness of attention to the experience of literature in schools which the deteriorating cultural situation in Great Britain since 1966 has made ever more essential.[6]

For I am convinced that it is more difficult to teach English well in the 1980s than it has ever been before, not merely because of disgraceful government policies which starve schools of the books they need, but also because the debasing influence of comics, the gutter-press, advertising, American films, commercial television and the pop-music industry is more vicious today than it has ever been. Against these adverse conditions thousands of teachers of English day after day put up a fine struggle to keep alive the values which our literary heritage both transmits and continually redefines. There are three facets of Leavis's legacy to us which can help in this struggle. First, there is the superb body of literary criticism itself, unequalled in its sensitiveness, in the justice of its judgements, and in its ability to send us back to the literature itself to read again with fresh insight and to evaluate again for ourselves on the basis of our own response. Admittedly it is a defect that none of this criticism relates to work written since *Four Quartets*; but the second important facet of the legacy is that it provides a method and a model which we can apply for ourselves, according to our own capacities, to other works. And indeed as teachers we *need* to do this continually and to do it as well as we can – to post-1945 poetry, fiction and drama, to children's literature, to the literature of emergent African and Caribbean countries, and also to any serious film and television drama that we can manage to identify. Moreover (the final facet) the model has the inestimable advantage that it is not merely a technical form of criticism; it is concerned with a sensitivity of response and a responsibility of judgement that sets it at a far remove from the American 'New Criticism' with which some commentators at one time confused it. The point can best be made by quoting Leavis's own words: 'I don't believe in any "literary values", and you won't find me talking about them; the judgements the literary critic is concerned with are judgements about life' (*Nor Shall My Sword*, p. 97). Practising teachers won't have any difficulty with the concept; I wish I could say the same about all the educational pundits.

Notes

1 I am indebted to L. C. Knights for the information that the unnamed speaker was Leavis himself.

2 In contrast I attended by mistake the opening lecture of a course by E. M. W. Tillyard two years running; the second delivery of it was a carbon copy of the first, even to a repetition of the same feeble and tasteless pleasantry about Hazlitt's *Liber Amoris*. Tillyard was the most powerful member of the English Faculty then and for long after; for pompous self-satisfied banality he was also, in my experience, unrivalled.

3 For the beginnings of a critique of the influence of Hoggart and Williams see my two articles 'Culture, Class and Society', *The Use of English*, 22, 2 (1970), 122–7, and 'A Quite Alarming Blankness', *The Use of English*, 25, 3 (1974), 252–7. Despite the first-hand testimony so carefully and cautiously assembled by George Sturt in *Change in the Village* (and corroborated quite independently from a different English county by Flora Thompson in *Lark Rise*), the concept of the 'organic community' has been particularly seriously misrepresented, to such an extent that when in 1980 Denys Thompson published a comprehensive anthology assembling for the first time a survey of the whole historical evidence (*Change and Tradition in Rural England*) this passed virtually unnoticed. See also John Fraser, 'Reflections on the Organic Community' in *The Human World*, 15–16 (1974), 57–74.

4 The letter continued in a certain characteristic vein: 'I took him away with me to Aldeburgh this summer, and read through most of him again, looking out (when I looked up) over the estuary. My oldest son who is a musician was much annoyed at seeing B. Britten Esq sitting "composing" at his window on the front whenever we passed. I myself don't forgive the gentleman for his disgusting treatment of Peter Grimes. He knows what sort of libretto he wants no doubt: but he might have left Crabbe out of it.'

5 *Growth Through English* (1967).

6 For a perceptive treatment of the issues at stake see David Allen *English Teaching Since 1965: How Much Growth?* (1980).

16

F. R. Leavis and the sources of hope

DAVID HOLBROOK

After a number of attempts to examine the experience of F. R. Leavis and his influence, I found the air too full of ghosts and demons to deal with the subject in any way of reminiscence or anecdote. Into this perplexity thrust a recording of his quite magical reading of T. S. Eliot's *Marina*, a poem to which he evidently responded, because of the hope expressed in it. Yet in his own writing, he became more and more equivocal about hope. Yet, if there is no hope, what was the point of setting out in the first place? Is there any hope of English studies moving hopefully beyond Leavis?

We owe Leavis a great debt for his insistence that judgement in art relates to problems of choice and value in life, and for making English studies a serious and important discipline. Anyone teaching English returns again and again in gratitude to his literary criticism. And yet there seems to be something wrong: something which must be examined intellectually, and so I intend to stick to the argument here, in relation to that problem of hope, the parted lips, the new ships.

The conflict in Leavis's mind, over whether or not there was any hope, is clear from a reply printed in *The Human World* to some observations on the matter by Ian Robinson (no. 15–16). Robinson had more or less accused Leavis of falling into despair, and this prompts Leavis into a tormented reply: 'I should say that I am more pessimistic than he appears to be if my reaction to the menace that faces mankind (but which is faced so little) didn't belong to a level that makes it unnatural to talk of either pessimism or optimism.' His 'menace' does not mean, of course, the threat of nuclear war, but the triumph of what he called 'technologico-Benthamite society' and 'egalitarianism'.

In the course of this reply Leavis quotes Lawrence (three times) saying 'the whole great form of our life will have to go' and also quotes him saying 'There is nothing to be done' – though Leavis says that it is 'impossible for us to wait inertly for the overt disaster – which is now imminent'. The menace, however, is 'apparently irresistible', and the word 'menace' is also repeated *passim*. It is very difficult to follow what Leavis does mean, except that he found some small hope in his seminars at York University: otherwise he spoke wildly of the future: 'But I don't want to save our civilisation – on the contrary, I want to save humanity and life from it and its accelerating developments as it completes its conquest of our lives.'

Leavis, at one point, speaks of a 'community' which shares his views: yet he never seems to have been happy with any close colleague and he was uneasy with anyone who ever disagreed with him. In *The Human World* he answered Robinson in a diagnostic way, *ad hominem*, virtually accusing him of some mental disorder: Robinson has offered him 'the same grotesque gratuitousness, the same violence of infelicity' elsewhere: 'It is some automatism that intervenes in *his* thought and works havoc, and he should look to it: the aetiology should be discoverable.' It is really no answer in a philosophical debate to declare your opponent is sick.

The reply, '"Believing in" the University', makes very depressing reading. I cannot feel about my students in the world, or about the university, or about my own children, and their future, in that doom-laden way. Leavis talks of 'new shoots' but there seems very little hope or promise in his later views. The reason for this tendency to be Jeremiah-like and to prophesy doom arose, as I shall try to argue, from a lack of confidence in his own insights into philosophy.

'This is clearly a critical time.' Thus Leavis in his preface to *Education and the University*. That book was full of hope. 'Such prepotency as this country may hope for in the English-speaking world of the future must lie in the cultural realm', he said in the same preface, demanding that a university English department be a 'focus of the finer life of cultural tradition.' The university that made such an effort to be this would have a chance of becoming 'if not the Athens of the English-speaking world, the unmistakeable main focus of the Athenian function it had done so much to confirm to this country' (p. 11).

Towards this goal, Leavis defined 'critical analysis and the training of sensibility' later in the book. This was in an attempt to correct the 'futilities, misdirections and wastes commonly incident to academic literary study'. The misdirections and wastes, it would seem, are still with us: a supervisor writes on a student's essay, 'You had better think how to condense the essay for the purposes of the examination. I suggest that you adopt the structure of this essay and produce numbered points under each heading: once you have done this you should be able to memorise the argument.' Today, students seem less well-educated in the Humanities in general when they come up, less well-read certainly, while there seems too little time during their three-year course to read even the major texts – let alone the peripheral material that is today prescribed for them. By judicious selection and by manipulating the system (as by substituting one long essay on – say – Yeats for everything from 1830 to the present day) they can obtain an honours degree without having really been educated as good readers, adequate to belong to the ever-imagined 'reading public': the narrowness of reading in literature at 'A' level is now protracted into the degree level, even as, by the new professionalism, exam-question papers, lecture lists and dissertation titles appear increasingly pretentious, as if the third-year undergraduate could cover with facility every work, theme and theory in the business at the drop of a hat. We know from our own students, however assiduous and brilliant, that this is just not so. As Leavis said, the student has to make his choices, hedging his bets as best he can.

Ours is also at large clearly an even more critical time: both culture and environment have become increasingly hostile to human values and integrity. What 'active principle' means in *Mansfield Park*, or why Emma Woodhouse suffers so much at the realisation that she might have done harm to others, are questions which have to be approached with diligence as if they were foreign to our ethics. It is as if the Crawfords, or the company from Mrs Brookenham's drawing-room (in *The Awkward Age*) had taken everything over – so that it becomes difficult for the student accustomed to the modern novel to grasp that superficial and unprincipled people may be felt to be 'evil' (to use Jane Austen's term) because they make it more difficult for others to find and realise their own integrity. They may cause 'wasted lives', and this is why we, in attention to creativity, in a humanities subject, have to understand how they are placed, in great art.

In the idea of a university, and in the concept of a 'discipline of sensibility and intelligence' as Leavis sought to define it, there is something that we must hold on to, which relates to moral issues in our civilisation. We owe Leavis a great debt for having made this so plain it must remain uncontrovertible, even if today 'English' seems to have lost its way and sense of purpose, despite his life's work.

But what we must have is a perspective which can take us beyond Leavis's position, and sustain us so that we can escape his despair. And here we have, I believe, to say that in a strange way, Leavis's very integrity, his purity, was his downfall. He had a notion of his task and stuck to it, even when it proved to be not the best way to the truth, and something more was needed.

The struggle to preserve the humanities is a battle of ideas. It is a question of pursuing truth: *quaerere verum*. To seek the truth, both of the objective world 'out there', and of the subjective or 'inner' world, was the original *telos* of ancient Greek classical thought. We belong to the subsequent civilisation and we are in its *telos*. It remains to be seen whether this impulse to pursue the truth was the supreme dynamic of the human mind. But as the phenomenological philosopher Edmund Husserl declared in his *Crisis of the European Sciences*, we have to take on this *telos*, and, in deferring to it, become 'functionaries of mankind'.

One of our major tasks is to restore to the quest the search for insight into the subjective realm, that half of reality which has been seriously neglected since the triumph of the scientific revolution in the seventeenth century, and the predominance of the 'objective' ideal, which can only find as real the outer (and dead) things. Only then can we overcome the alienation which men feel, as they now seem to be in a universe (that delineated by Newtonian physics and Cartesian science) in which man's culture and achievements have no place, and in which no meaning is possible, because everything is only matter in motion operating by chance and necessity, in which 'everything exists and nothing has value'.

Leavis intuitively glimpsed that he was on the fringes of a philosophical revolution. He was interested in Collingwood, who tried to restore teleological perspectives to the concept of life. He read Marjorie Grene and Michael Polanyi and saw that there was a possible post-analytical position from which reductionism and mechanism might be challenged, and a whole field of 'continental' philosophical biology – as in F. J. J. Buytendijk – which indicated a new place for man in nature. He realised the importance of being anti-Cartesian, and anti-Benthamite, because it was necessary to uphold 'being' (as celebrated by Blake, Dickens and Lawrence) against quantitative, functional concepts of man. Roger Poole was right to argue that Leavis, in emphasising the importance of the experiencing 'I', the individual consciousness, and the significance of the unique living choice of each man and woman, was an existentialist critic, while his attention to 'felt life' in literature as the focus of our discipline, as a humanities subject, has also a phenomenological emphasis; since it deals with phenomena of consciousness such as symbolism. Leavis in his talk of 'significance' meant 'meaning': and, as Husserl indicates, our essential problem is to find something in which to believe.[1]

Leavis, however, was so afraid of 'philosophy', and so hostile to philosophy, that he failed to examine his own position. Philosophy to him was a limited discipline of attention to single, mathematical meanings: p stroke q. The philosopher was incapable of a 'whole' response to poetic language, and would misrepresent such meanings by asking for them to be made explicit – when they were always ineffable. So, when Roger Poole acclaimed Leavis as an existentialist, Leavis not only rejected this, but proclaimed that Poole must be 'an enemy', doing terrible harm at his University, because he was a philosopher.[2]

The reason for this hostility to philosophy was the desire to keep the 'English' discipline unsullied by analytical, 'intellectual' approaches. Leavis's aim was 'to deal in doctrine, theory and general terms as little as possible' (*Education and the University*). He gives a brief outline of his assumptions (pp. 18ff). He assumes that we can, in 'attempting at an ancient university an experiment in liberal education, count on a sufficient measure of agreement, overt and implicit, about essential values, to make it unnecessary to discuss ultimate sanctions, or provide a philosophy, before starting to work ... and I believe further that what is unnecessary is best avoided'. As Geoffrey Strickland shows in *Structuralism or Criticism*, a widespread growth of intellectual approaches has tended, in many places, to make more good reading and criticism seem old-fashioned, though, at the same time, the best thing some of the theories have done is to raise important questions of how our reading works upon us. We can no longer assume, however, as Leavis supposed he could, that there are fundamental assumptions we can just take for granted.

Moreover, this is even more true in criticism, and it is there that, now, looking at Leavis's late criticism, we may begin to have serious doubts. If we examine the long analysis of *Four Quartets* in *The Living Principle* what we find is that even though he renounced philosophy in such a determined way - Leavis relies heavily on philosophy, to provide his 'essential values'. He employs - as in fact anyone must in a humanities discipline - what must be called a philosophical anthropology.

This philosophical anthropology is compounded of fragments from Blake (e.g. the distinction between 'self-hood' and 'identity'), from D. W. Harding (e.g. Eliot's 'desperate personal need', and the principle that to be afraid of death is to be afraid of life), from odd scraps of Polanyi, F. J. J. Buytendijk, and German terms, picked up from Lord knows where, such as *Ahnung* and *Nisus*: and then fragments from D. H. Lawrence.

Moreover, in rejecting F. H. Bradley and T. S. Eliot's use of Bradley, Leavis assumes an attitude to reality and the self, a concept of how we find reality. Taking in Collingwood, he declares that life is 'process'. In his psychology, using a strange invocation of Coriolanus, he declares that being enclosed in the self-hood can be insanity: and throughout he uses a 'diagnosis' of T. S. Eliot as a 'case', to reveal his self-defeat, and ultimately his 'sin against life'. In fact, as I try to show elsewhere, Leavis's fundamental concept of 'identity' (which has to do with believing of one's works 'they are not mine' because one does not 'belong to oneself') was developed by Leavis from a book by one Davies on Blake which was, at the moment, discussing Blake's beliefs about the resurrection of the body. A similar vagueness of origin and meaning hovers around *Ahnung* and *Nisus*: the *Ahnung* is at one moment a pulse in the universe, a dynamic obliging a responsibility to life, and at others a moral drive or conscience within people: at one point it is even the visionary experience among the roses at Burnt Norton.

The exegesis on *Four Quartets*, in *The Living Principle*, whatever one thinks of it as a demonstration of criticism, rests upon absolute principles which belong to philosophy (if we take this to be a philosophy of being). If life is process lived in time, then if one's poetry is to be creative about life the aim must be to stay in time. If to fear death is to fear life, then any expression of a fear of death reveals a lack of courage in the face of life. To yearn for a spiritual reality out of the body, outside 'life' and time, is to yearn for a 'nullity'. (St John of the Cross? The *Bhagavad Gita*? 'I saw eternity the other night ...'?) All these are premises or principles upon which Leavis's adverse judgement of Eliot's poetry rests: yet, obviously, they cannot be argued within 'literary criticism' itself.

The literary criticism is another matter. I do not feel in that long analysis that Leavis shows that Eliot reveals, as he says, contempt for the rustic folk at East Coker, or displays self-disgust here and tormented self-derision there. I do not accept that the spiritual experience leads to a nullity, or that the view of human effort is nihilistic, or that the opening lines of *Little Gidding* are 'dead'.

But more seriously, the overall ultimate critical judgement, that Eliot's greatest work leads to a self-frustrating, shameful cowardice in the face of life, and nullity, is impelled to its ('inescapable') conclusion on philosophical and psychological principles which simply do not hold water: and which are offered in no 'open' Socratic manner, for scrutiny and argument. The local critical analysis may be offered in a spirit of 'This is so, is it not?' But the philosophical principles – that since life is time a poet must not yearn for a realm out of time – are offered as unquestionable axioms.

Despite twenty years' reading of case-histories and theories of subjective psychology, I cannot find evidence to support Leavis's most fundamental distinction between 'identity' and 'self-hood'. My reading of philosophical anthropology does not support his view of what it is that underlies our capacity to find reality (though the concept of 'the living principle' is a useful one). Leavis's psychological concepts are home-made, amateur, and dogmatic: apart from Harding (with home he also fundamentally disagrees) he refers to no sources in subjective psychology.

The same is true of his philosophy: and though I am no philosopher, I can see that he misemploys Collingwood, Buytendijk and Polanyi: they are often not saying what he takes them to say, and they do not support his case as he supposes them to do. If *The Living Principle* is a demonstration of English as a discipline of thought, then it will simply not convince those who need convincing.

This is not to deny the important insistence: 'The aim is to keep as close as possible to the concrete, and to deal with general considerations in terms related as immediately as possible to practice . . . given [he goes on] the measure of actual and tacit agreement about ends that cannot be counted on for working purposes.' We must agree that 'Here, in this work, we have the function that is preeminently the university; if the work is not done then it will not be done anywhere' (p. 24). But the unsatisfactoriness of the *Four Quartets* essay itself is enough to show that it would be worse to go on working without examining more deeply *what it is one is doing* and what are the 'general considerations' upon which it is all based.

For the 'battle' can only be won, in Husserl's perspective, as a battle of ideas. Leavis's error was to try to put the world right by university departments: by training a band of teachers: by the demonstration of literary criticism in practice. This was a fine idea, and he conducted the programme with integrity.

But unfortunately that very integrity, his adherence to the idea of 'concreteness', led to his self-defeat. Of course, we need always to bear in mind that the poem or work of literature doesn't exist until it is 'there' in the 'criss cross of utterance between us'. But once it is, there is, to use his own term, its 'upshot', to discuss: and the principles upon which we possessed and evaluated it. This inevitably leads us into the extension of the debate into the wider realm of philosophical anthropology. There was a time when Leavis seems to have seen that this must be so.

Earlier, Leavis had, in his sketch for an English school, in *Education and the University*, made it plain that 'English' needs as a subject to see itself in a wider context, as a humanities subject. No one would suppose, he said, that a 'literary education' would be satisfactory by itself. 'One of the virtues of literary studies is that they lead constantly outside themselves, and, on the other hand, while it is necessary that they should be controlled by a concern for the essential discipline, such a concern, if it is adequate, counts on associated work in other fields' (p. 35). This, indeed, is the basis of a proper 'liberal' education: something better than classical Greats is, however, necessary in this broader approach, so Leavis in his sketch postulates an intelligence framed in English which will be able to deal with issues in any humanities subject better than those trained in those subjects:

Some critics will still insist that the proposed scheme cannot produce the properly trained man, the man properly trained in anything; that it might be said to aim explicitly at the production of the amateur. The reply must be: call him what you like; we want to produce a mind that knows what precision and specialist knowledge are, is aware of the words not in its own possession that are necessary, has a maturity of outlook such as the study of history ought to produce but even the general historian by profession doesn't always exhibit, and has been trained in a kind of thinking, a scrupulously sensitive yet enterprising use of intelligence, that is of its nature not specialised but cannot be expected without special training – a mind, energetic and resourceful, that will apply itself to the problems of civilisation, and eagerly continue to improve its equipment and explore fresh approaches. (p. 59)

There is a great deal of idealism in this: did Leavis ever find such a mind (and approve of it when he did?)? But it indicates how a student might, through his English studies, develop, say, an interest in Jane Austen's preoccupation with the dangers of people being so lacking in 'active principle' that they can hurt others and disturb the harmony of a close society; or contemplating how (in Isobel Archer) the idealistic impulse to be independent and make a work of art of one's life can come to grief when it meets cultured egoism masquerading as noble cultivation; or study Shakespeare's deep sense of the question of whether so unrealiable a creature as man, living in his sensual and mortal body, tormented by perplexities of appearance and reality, can achieve good government. If a 'literary' student tackles these problems fully, he must surely find himself involved in other disciplines to which such questions inevitably lead: questions of what human 'model' or make-up we accept: questions of integrity and how we know when we are being true to ourselves: questions of where the sources of our values may be found – and such questions require philosophy and psychology: albeit of kinds which can engage with meaning and values.

Leavis sought to promote 'the prospecting and ranging mind', by stimulating '"extra-literary" readings'. It was a valid aim, but it is a pity he did not take his own advice, for when he is using certain principles to reject Eliot, he should have considered what 'precision' was and what 'specialist knowledge' was. To hold positions, as he does, about 'life', 'time', and 'reality' requires at least the willingness to subject these to examination as precise as may be, and to the specialist concerns of those who explore them. This (Leavis recognised) was especially true for the youths he was training: 'So much in his intellectual after-life may depend upon the start a man gets and the habits he forms at the university.' In his sketch for an English school, Leavis proposed 'a specially accessible library, containing a number of copies of certain books': 'e.g. the best of Christopher Dawson, *Middletown*, Ian D. Suttie's *The Origins of Love and Hate*, and such works of sociology, anthropology, history, political thought and so on . . .' (p. 61). The drawing up and revision of this list, he declares, 'would be a valuable experience for the seniors concerned'. Indeed it would – and in this comment a great deal lies, by implication, not least from a critic whose posthumous work was to be entitled *The Critic as Anti-philosopher*.

For me the most significant item in the proposed list is Suttie's critique of Freud. Obviously, then, Leavis saw that one essential area of concern was the question of the model of man which we adopt. It is clear by implication that Leavis recognised that the movement out into philosophical anthropology was inevitable and necessary.

What was Leavis's view later, as expressed in the article 'Mutually Necessary' in *New Universities Quarterly* (1976)? He says there that he has always been sceptical about seminars on Wittgenstein's linguistic philosophy for 'English' students. One would agree with him that for the 'both intelligent and serious' literary student 'one difficulty is that there is too much literature demanding attention'. The literary student 'must aim at being intelligent about the large changes in the philosophical climate as they have affected cultivated sensibility in the last four centuries'. He wanted to avoid the waste of time represented by members of seminars turning to Russell's *History of Western Philosophy*. But then he seems to think the problem is insoluble: one can't rely on the philosopher proper to recommend books suitable for English students. But then (as he found) both Ian Robinson and Michael Tanner dismissed contemptuously the one book he found which he thought did point to a revolutionary movement in philosophy which seemed to him to offer a new perspective to the humanities student.

However, he says that Ian Robinson has assumed wrongly that he must have known about the part Marjorie Grene's *The Knower and The Known* had played in a 'would-be revolutionary movement': but he hadn't known. Tanner on his part finds Leavis's judgement of Marjorie Grene and Polanyi inadequate. He declares that Leavis's quotations from Marjorie Grene show her 'disastrously confused' while what Leavis finds in Polanyi he dismisses as 'truisms'. Leavis saw that Cartesianism is a 'disastrous doctrine over a very wide area of fundamental issues', and he was grateful to Polanyi for having overcome dualism. Leavis says that

Polanyi is an epistemologist [who] insists that what for philosophers is 'mind' is 'there' only in individual minds, and that an individual mind is always a person's, and a person has a body and a history. His mind is the mind of his body, and his body is the body of his mind. The dualism that has defeated so many epistemologies is eliminated here. (*The Living Principle*, p. 39)

I believe that Leavis was right, and that Michael Tanner and Ian Robinson were wrong. The matter cannot be argued within the compass of a contribution of this length, but it seems clear to me, after a good deal of ranging in the field, that what Leavis perceived in Marjorie Grene's work was a glimpse of a whole world of ('reflective') philosophy, to which English philosophy is either indifferent or hostile – simply because it operates in a different perspective. Whatever Marjorie Grene's limitations, her work cannot be dismissed as contemptuously as Tanner and Robinson tend to reject it. Take for example her book *The Understanding of Nature*: this was produced from a series of seminars with philosophers of science at Boston and appears as a volume in Boston studies in the Philosophy of Science: clearly her contributions were thoroughly tested in this context. In a chapter on 'Aristotle and Modern Biology' she writes about those elements in scientific work which correspond to our critical response in the teaching of literature: the 'rootedness' of aesthetic recognition in taxonomy, in 'the perception of real this–suches' (she is relating the emphasis of the biologist C. F. A. Pantin, that biologists recognise species by 'aesthetic recognition' to Aristotle's view of the relation between knowledge and perception, seeing a *this–here* as a *such–and–such*):

... the grounding of scientific knowledge, and especially of scientific discovery, in perception (rather in sensation or the bare observation of bare particulars) is beginning at last to be acknowledged by philosophers of science. In a general way, perception as the paradigma of discovery was the *Leitmotif* of Hanson's writing [N. R. Hanson, *Patterns of Discovery* (1965)]. The 'primacy of perception' as our chief path of access to reality was the central theme of Merleau-Ponty's work [M. Merleau-Ponty, *The Phenomenology of Perception* (1962)]. A similar theme dominates Straus's phenomenology [E. W. Straus, *The Primary World of Senses* (1963) and *Phenomenological Psychology* (1966)]. And in Polanyi's *Personal Knowledge, Tacit Dimension* and other essays ... one has, as distinct from those more general intuitions, a carefully articulated epistemology which explicitly makes of perception, understood in a Gestalt-cum-transactional fashion (not unlike Aristotelian aesthesis), the primordial and paradigm case of knowing, and explicitly makes the achievement of perception the primordial and paradigm case of discovery. (p. 100)

In Polanyi's terms, in all knowledge, as in perception, we rely on subsidiary clues within our bodies to attend to something in the real world outside. However 'abstract' that something be, both the bodily base and the from–to structure characteristic of sense perception persist.

Discussing the philosophy of Helmuth Plessner in the next chapter, Marjorie Grene discusses the difference in our perception of animate and inanimate things. We need a concept here which is not only *spatial*: it has to do with the whole way in which an organism 'takes its place' in an environment. Plessner uses the term 'positionality', and this has to do with the way a living thing 'takes its place' in the world and in a sense 'knows' itself (as a cell 'knows', immunology tells us, which is its own stuff and which is alien). We know living things in a different way from how we we know the non-living: they 'confront' us: and in this we find the clue to our way out of the Cartesian dichotomy.

Within our Cartesian heritage, there is no alternative for any form of life, except to be either a mere body spread out in space, completely 'external', *or* a bit of subjectivity, completely and secretly 'within', or an unintelligible combination of the two. It is this conceptual framework which has prevented us from developing an adequate philosophical biology, an adequate sense of man's place in the world: and surely our understanding of ourselves and our place in nature constitutes a central problem of metaphysics in our time, as Marjorie Grene argues. And, as I would put it, it is the area in which we must try (as under the injunctions of Edmund Husserl) to find something to believe – for the trouble with the Cartesian–Newtonian universe is that, reduced to 'matter in motion', operating by mathematical laws but also by chance and necessity, it has become a cosmos in which there seems to be no place for man and his achievements – the achievements of consciousness and culture. As Husserl declares in his *Crisis of Modern Science*, we cannot live in such a world.

Once we glimpse concepts from 'continental' philosophy like 'positionality' and centricity, we begin to see that a new way of knowing is necessary, a way of understanding 'life' better. Discussing Plessner Marjorie Grene says: 'For a body with this kind of boundary structure is not simply divisible into inner and outer;

it is, through its relation to its boundary, *both* directed *out* beyond the body that it is *and* back *into it* again' (p. 325). I have gone far enough into Marjorie Grene's excursion into 'reflective' or 'continental' philosophy for my purposes. I believe we may bring together here a number of areas of thought which indicate a radical movement, such as is explored by Roger Poole in his *Towards Deep Subjectivity*.

Erwin Straus's rejection of Pavlovian behaviourism is important and belongs to the phenomenological movement in which we also find Maurice Merleau-Ponty, thought by many to be a more serious philosopher than Sartre. In science and psychology we have parallel developments in books like *Against Reductionism* edited by Arthur Koestler and Robert Smythies and the work of Liam Hudson as in *The Cult of The Fact*. Marjorie Grene picks up R. O. Collingwood's concern to reintroduce teleological considerations in science, while her *Approaches to a Philosophical Biology* surveys the work of Adolf Portmann, Plessner again, F. J. J. Buytendijk, Straus and Kurt Goldstein. One of her best essays, of great relevance to English studies, is on 'Hobbes and the Modern Mind' in *Philosophy in and Out of Europe* which also contains notes on Heidegger, Jaspers, Sartre and Merleau-Ponty. There is a great deal more to say here about psychotherapy, which has followed the existentialist and phenomenological path, of which an excellent historical–critical account is given by Rollo May in *Existence – a New Dimension in Psychiatry* edited by Rollo May and others. In this he tries to outline the relation of the existentialist movement (now strong in its influence on psychotherapy) to Freud, Kierkegaard and Nietzsche.

What Michael Tanner dismissed as 'truisms' do, in all this body of thought, provide a clue to the escape from intellectual traditions which have inhibited our thought about man's nature throughout the period of the scientific revolution and the consequent 'dissociation of sensibility'. Taken as a whole, the movement which offers such an escape from positivism cannot be simply rejected out of hand (see, for example, the two massive volumes on the phenomenological movement by Herbert Spiegelberg, and his *Phenomenology in Psychology and Psychiatry*, which deals with a long series of continental thinkers, too many to list).

F. R. Leavis and the sources of hope

As Roger Poole says, the new reflective philosophy and the sub-jective disciplines that emerge from it do not yet have an adequate terminology or satisfactory disciplines: but – like Leavis's kind of literary criticism – they are beginning to approach to human truth as the established analytical, positivist approaches do not, having become sterile. They grope towards the philosophy of being which established philosophy denies us.

We owe an enormous debt to Leavis in that, from his own work in English, in developing it as a humanities subject, he caught a glimpse of this revolution. Some years ago, I was able to conduct a series of seminars with students, research graduates and staff in the psychology department at Cambridge, very informal, in which we discussed poems and passages from fiction, alongside passages from psychoanalytical writings on symbolism, on 'reflective' philosophy (e.g. from Martin Buber on the I–Thou) and on the nature of knowing. To our surprise, the series 'worked' and gave several young people (as they tell me now) a very welcome glimpse of modes of thought beyond reductionism, and of other possible 'models' of man beyond that assumed by strictly empirical-psychology. This series of discussions is being tried now at the School of Education at the University of Bath. (Leavis, of course, did not believe in' mixed courses' and would not have approved.)

All this points in a different direction altogether from that area of philosophy with which Leavis found himself so much in conten-tion: the area in which people like Wellek asked him to define his 'norms' or in which Tanner presses upon him the word 'probative'. '"Verifiable"... must have, if used of literary critical judgement, an utterly different meaning ('value') from that which it has in natural science – and at the mathematico-logical end of discourse from which the thinking of the philosophers seems in general to begin, and continues to treat as the inevitable basic mode.' You can't prove a value-judgement in literary criticism, it is true, though you can move beyond the mere assertion of personal conviction, as by what John Wisdom called 'the collocation of naturalistic descriptions'. ('Seems good to A, to B, to C, and on further consideration . . .'; see *Philosophy and Psychoanalysis.*)

167

Leavis however, saw the only way forward in terms of training individuals in the capacity to make *judgements*. 'The continuance of the literary tradition in a vigorous state depends on a tiny minority of persons of keen and articulate critical sensibility, and its being influential depends on a much larger reading public that respects and responds intelligently to the judgement of the elite minority.'

But there is another task, and that is of promoting understanding – the understanding of meaning. And this is not a task which involves the training of an élite: it is a struggle in the realm of ideas, 'out there' in the public world. While the world resents an élite, it would welcome the pushing forward of the boundaries of ideas. In the essay 'Mutually Necessary' Leavis's argument with Tanner sinks into yet another debate on T. S. Eliot's *Four Quartets*. And here we must record the unfortunate example Leavis's last struggle with Eliot provided. In *Education and the University* Leavis made a response to *Four Quartets* a keystone; as an example of the sensibility and intelligence at work on literature. In *The Living Principle* he devotes many pages to an analysis of Eliot's poems which alternate between showing what a fine poet he is, and declaring a decided 'No' to what he takes to be the meaning of the poem.

In this, there are a number of passages of literary criticism which seem to me just wrong – for instance, that where he tries to show that the opening of *Little Gidding* is 'dead'. But there are also many passages where Leavis, who has proclaimed himself anti-philosopher, makes those absolute philosophical and psychological statements to which I have referred. The literary criticism of Eliot is offered in a spirit of 'this is so is it not?' But the principles about time and life are not: they are offered as absolutes. And this lies behind Leavis's final despair.

The principles – even the most critical and puzzling ones, as about 'identity' and 'self-hood' – are not subjected to critical analysis, or allowed to be the subject of Socratic dialogue. In his eagerness to produce a (hostile) judgement against Eliot, thus Leavis falls short of *understanding*: in places, even in literary criticism, he fails to understand the poem, as when dealing with the peasants in East Coker, the fishermen in *The Dry Salvages* and the passengers in the underground railway train elsewhere in *Four Quartets*. That we allow, as literary judgements are always contingent. But a failure to examine one's own models and principles in philosophical anthropology can lead to a disastrous lapse in self-knowledge. His account ends in a strange confusion; in the essay 'Mutually Necessary' he really seems to end up believing that much of Eliot's guilt-feelings were about him, Leavis; that he is the ghost met in the air-raid in *Little Gidding*, and that Eliot's deep shame also relates to him, Leavis.

Following this astonishing passage in *New Universities Quarterly* Leavis says 'I stand, then, by my account of *Four Quartets*', and, moreover, 'I stand also by my contention that "English" should be a liaison-centre, and that in the "co-presence" needed to make it that, no discipline of thought is more important than the philosophical to that quite different one, the essence of which I have tried to define.'

But the 'defining' cannot be done with philosophical cogency, as (Leavis says) he has been trying to persuade a 'philosophical elite'. That may be so, but all the same, if thought and 'the philosophical' are important, the terms invoked in dealing with man's nature and his relationship with reality must be under open review: and this cannot be done if a critic remains doggedly 'anti-philosopher' merely.

Alas, my students find the analysis of *Four Quartets* in *The Living Principle* no demonstration at all of English as discipline of thought: they find it a demonstration of confusion and wilful unwillingness to understand Eliot, in order to support a hostile rejection which was intended to deny Eliot his place in twentieth-century letters.

Leavis reverts to Polanyi's essay on 'The Logic of Tacit Inference'. He was right that there lies a clue in Polanyi to a relevant epistemological problem. But Leavis ends with a quotation from Malcolm's *Memoir* of Wittgenstein, which includes the following phrase: 'what is the use of studying philosophy ... if it does not improve your thinking about the important questions of everyday life ...'.

The purpose of both philosophy (or what I would call philosophical anthropology) and English *is* to improve our thinking about questions of everyday life – not least by helping us to improve our capacities to understand meaning. It is not a matter of training an élite but of offering ideas, and demonstrations of ideas in their application. In this it is necessary to offer the ideas, too, in the spirit of 'this is so, is it not?' as well as the 'judgements'. Judgements are, actually, less important than the demonstrations of understanding, though in the end they, too, rely upon the question of our models of man, our sense of man's place in nature, and our metaphysical beliefs too. Both judgement and understanding relate to the pursuit of truth. Something seems to have gone seriously wrong with Leavis's sense of what he was doing, because both his judgement and understanding seem seriously impaired in his essay on *Four Quartets* so that, in both, truth is the main casualty. He fell into this confusion, I believe, because the break-through in philosophy which he glimpsed, and urgently needed, was denied him, by traditions, and the resistence of those colleagues who failed to share his glimpse of its possibilities. But now, to restore our hope, even in the face of his ultimate pessimism, we need to attend to the revolution in philosophical anthropology to which he pointed and of which as a philosopher of being, he gave so marvellous an example.

Notes

1 See 'The Affirmation of Life: the later criticism of F. R. Leavis' in *Universities Quarterly* (Winter 1974).
2 See F. R. Leavis, *Thought, Words and Creativity: Art and Thought in Lawrence* (1976), p. 92. If Leavis was trying to demonstrate how literature and literary criticism could be real 'thought', it is disturbing to see how unfair he could be, and how far he could fall short of genuine engagement in a discourse – in this case the important debate on what is meant by 'life'.

17

Leavis: an appreciation

JOHN HARVEY

Opinions about F. R. Leavis have been so fiercely divided that most discussions of him could hardly be called debate. The year of his death is a sad but appropriate time to attempt an appreciation of the personality, and the work, which made so great a difference to English criticism.

He is known as a harsh critic; but the harshness and pessimism in his work are scarcely surprising when one considers the start he had to his adult life. He came up to Emmanuel College, Cambridge, with a scholarship from the Perse School in 1914, and had barely matriculated when war was declared. He was a conscientious objector, and joined the Friends' Ambulance Unit as a stretcher-bearer. His work was at least as dangerous as that of the combatants, and it wouldn't be easy to imagine the impact of it on a nineteen-year-old: he had to be always where the fighting was worst and the injuries most appalling. I believe that on one occasion, after being shunted all night from one goods yard to another through a city being bombed, shut in cattle-trucks crowded with the wounded and dying, he was for a month unable to speak at all. He returned from the war severely shell-shocked and scarcely able to talk, and for the rest of his life suffered from insomnia.

It hardly then needs special explanation that, resuming his studies, he got only a II.2 when he took Part I of the History Tripos in 1919. He changed to the newly-formed English course, which had just escaped from its first position as an option within the Modern and Medieval Languages Tripos and was presided over by the kindly belle-lettrism of 'Q' (Sir Arthur Quiller-Couch). Leavis took the English Tripos in 1921. On the morning of his first examination, on 23 May, his father was crossing the road after wishing him well, when he was killed in a traffic accident, with

Leavis standing by; Leavis sat his papers, and got a First. In a letter to F. L. Attenborough, the fellow in English at Emmanuel, 'Q' reported of Leavis's Tripos:

Leavis did quite well in the Tripos, especially in the earlier papers which were consistently good. There was quality in them too: and if they were, here and there, a trifle thin, one felt that the man had spent time in trying to express himself well. On the last (the Criticism) paper he collapsed. But knowing the circumstances, and finding on enquiry that in the Mays his Criticism paper had led the whole field, I hadn't the faintest compunction in signing him up for a First – even apart from the pluck of the whole performance, which was astonishing. (I lost my father in my last year at Oxford, and know what it means.)

'Q's letter was presumably a reference for the research studentship which Leavis was presently awarded; it continues, shedding an interesting light on the impression the young Leavis made:

I suppose Leavis was too shy to worry me personally for advice: and you know that under pretty constant bombardment by those who are not shy I haven't the time to look up those who are. But I should be happy to make amends if given the chance of supervising his work for a research degree. He has suggested a very good subject, and I know enough of him to be pretty sure he would make a good fist of it.

We have had by Heaven's grace some very good men among our few early researchers in English (Dobrée, Colleer Abbott, Miles, Herman). I believe that when their stuff sees print we shall be able to claim a modest success: and it would be pleasant to admit Leavis to the team.

There is some poignancy, now, in the impression the letter gives of the intimacy and confidence of the new subject.

Leavis's Ph.D. thesis, on 'The Relation of Journalism to Literature', is perhaps most interesting for its appreciation of early pamphleteering literature – by Milton among others – the genre in which, later, Leavis himself developed a genius.

He took his Ph.D. in 1924, and in 1925 began teaching as a Faculty probationary lecturer. His first lectures were on eighteenth-century literature, but in his second year and after he taught chiefly on modern poetry and modern novels: he was, conspicuously, the only member of the Faculty to offer teaching on twentieth-century writing.

By the time his lectureship expired – he gave the last course in 1932 – he had criticised with sufficient effectiveness for various colleagues to wish him out of Cambridge, and there was a generous rallying-round to try and secure chairs for him in South Africa and Australia. Believing that if his ambitions for English teaching were to have any real effect, it must be at Cambridge, he hung on, existing on the small fees from supervising. Not surprisingly his supervisions were in demand, and in the year in which his Faculty post ended he was invited to direct studies in English at Downing. At Emmanuel, his relations with H. S. Bennett, who had been appointed Director of Studies in the year that Leavis began his probationary lectureship, had become bitter. Leavis was never elected to a fellowship, and it is clear that beyond the research studentship ($£150 for two years) he was not supported by the college. He used to say that he first heard his teaching was no longer wanted at Emmanuel when he came into college at the end of the vacation and found his study had been reassigned and his books heaped in the corridor.

In 1935 he was elected to a college lectureship at Downing, and in 1936 to a fellowship, and to a lectureship in the English Faculty. He had missed several previous appointments and been pressed to go; but on this occasion 'Q', who normally ducked Faculty business, was sufficiently concerned to travel up from a house-party to attend the final meeting of the Appointments Committee. Even the lectureship that 'Q' secured for Leavis was, though tenured, only a 'part-work' appointment, carrying half the normal salary. Leavis did not begin to receive the full stipend of a lecturer until 1946, when he was fifty-one.

Leavis had married in 1929 and begun serious publication in 1930. In 1932 the periodical *Scrutiny* was started by L. C. Knights and Donald Culver, largely with the aim of getting Leavis into print: he contributed the leading critical articles in the first two numbers, and in the third became an editor. Much of his *Scrutiny* writing was done with an eye also on book publication, and from 1930 on there followed the steady progress of critical books, almost all of which have been continuously in print since they first appeared.

His principal books were *New Bearings in English Poetry* (1932), *Revaluation*, a critical history of English poetry (1936), *Education and the University* (1943), *The Great Tradition*, an account of the nineteenth-century novel (1948), and *The Common Pursuit* (1952), a collection of critical essays. Two particular ways in which his criticism was decisive were in his early championing of T. S. Eliot and D. H. Lawrence, and in his arguing of the proper organisation and function, and the importance, of English literature as a university subject. But also influential were his appraisals of Milton, Keats, Shelley, Dickens, George Eliot, Hopkins, James, Conrad . . . Those who think him negative or narrow should consider the number and diversity of the authors to the appreciation of whom he has made an important difference. *The Common Pursuit* is perhaps the best book to go to, to see quickly the range and the principal themes of his thought, and the originality, pith and force of personality of his prose. His best writing combines a collected thoughtfulness of great precision and weight with both vehemence and an intense dry vivacity, making him the strongest individual voice, in English discursive prose, in the last four decades.

As an undergraduate I was able to go regularly to his seminars at Downing in the early sixties, when he would have been close to seventy. What I remember of his person is of course the famous open-necked shirt and sandals, worn through all weathers; the extreme fitness and litheness, and the skin as tanned as a gardener's; after the baldness, the train of grey hair worn long at the back. And principally, what is not described in descriptions of him, the extremely handsome and strong head. His gaze was disconcertingly level, penetrating and dry, and a mere reconnoitring glance, as he came into a room, could be frighteningly sharp. In his talk, what at the time made the strongest impression was the amused and more or less scathing personalities: 'The Vice-Chancellor asked me what I thought of Professor Y . . . but he came back to it a third time, so I said, "Well, if you really want to know, I think he's vulgar – brassy -- and a bounder!"' 'If a talented monkey could write novels, these are what you would get: it's the same mimicry – and the same lasciviousness!' I cannot register in type the effect of his

accent, an odd deliberate cultivated Cambridgeshire, lingering on
final vowels ('brass-y') with peculiar damningness.

The great strength of the seminars was his commentary on the
old dating-sheets he had to hand. He would go through the
miscellaneous excerpts and stanzas characterising and identifying
from phrase to phrase in a way that not only enhanced and 'placed'
the passage itself, but also made immediate and formidable the
whole past ethos out of which the passage came. The zest and
illuminatingness of this extempore criticism, simply of whatever
cropped up on the sheet, is not I think to be guessed from his
published work, where he writes normally with the driving urgency
of a particular 'thing that needs saying'.

Less valuable, and occupying the larger part of the seminar
hours, were the general reflections that became, through a term,
repetitive. In my time his main theme was T. S. Eliot ('Tom.
Petering out like that! How many poems has he written since the
Four Quartets?!'), and in particular Eliot's 'corruption, decay and
inward mess'. Circlingly, against I suppose strong resistances, he
was developing the negative diagnosis of Eliot's 'case' which is
expressed, in a veiled way, in his late criticism. Periodically he
would reproach himself for talking all the time; but his retorts to
questions were prompt and final, and we were too daunted and
entranced to co-operate in debate.

Three years before he retired he was conceded a readership, and
this was the most recognition he ever had in Cambridge. After his
retirement he was a visiting professor at several universities, including, happily, Bristol and York, where the shaping of the English
courses had been greatly influenced by his thought. He continued
to publish criticism of considerable force until the year before he
died.

Leavis's early criticism was chiefly of poetry. He wrote on many
poets, and I could not represent adequately, in summary, his judgements on writers as diverse as Jonson, Milton, Pope, Wordsworth.
But in any case both the perceptiveness and the provocativeness of
his local comment are well known now, and what rather needs to
be urged is the coherence and impressiveness of the general

thought evolving through the consecutive essays – in a fundamental investigation constantly renewed and extended.

The greatest problem of criticism has always been in coming to a good understanding of the relationship between literary qualities and the values of life in general; the major errors have come either from treating literature too simply in terms of general ethics, or from trying to explain literary values in dissociation from other values. What Leavis developed was a language for evaluating emotion – in terms essentially of one's attitude to one's own emotions: was one nourishing them for their own sake or for the pleasure of the ego, or were they truly defined by their object? Underpinning the particular discussions, he had a general account of the interdependence between fine distinctions of emotion and fine distinctions of language in any culture. He was then able to demonstrate that the nuances of suggestion that made particular words right or wrong in poetry did so because they conveyed acceptable or unacceptable attitudes to emotion in the process of expressing it. Involved in this criticism was a picture of the individual nature, which could either be shapeless and chaotic, at the mercy of every whim of the ego, or could have the delicate whole organisation that would make fine and right feeling possible: the coherence and delicacy of this organisation being married, again, to the coherence and delicacy with which language was used – ideally in poetry.

Of course such an account does not cover all the ground; Leavis had a subtle supporting analysis of metaphor, and of the kinds of whole movement a poem can have. He distinguished between language that asserts or gestures towards its meaning, and language which, through a complex analogical play, comes closer to embodying its meaning; and between writing in which new experience is dulled by being fitted into familiar forms of expression, and the more startling and sometimes 'difficult' kind of writing in which language is from the outset determined by new experience, and also is the completion and focus of that experience. Also, though Leavis would not be drawn into explicit political comment, his analysis had a political dimension in the connection he always saw between the idiosyncrasy of the best poetry of a period and the best encouragements, and the blindnesses, of the particular milieu in which it was written.

My summary is dense but crude, but it does, I hope, suggest the subtlety of Leavis's attempt to see the connections between the way we value poetry and the way we value anything. The reader will find that Leavis's formulation actually is more sensitive and more complete than any given previously – whether by Sidney, Johnson, Coleridge or Arnold, and it is possible to argue that in this central question of critical thought, Leavis 'got it right'.

In the forties and fifties he became increasingly interested in the novel, and the impact of his criticism shows in the number of classics that owe a large part of their present currency to him – *Hard Times, Nostromo, Portrait of a Lady, The Rainbow*. However he did not often give to novelistic prose the searching particularity of analysis he had regularly given to poetry, and his general description of fiction does not have the powerful keenness and coherence of his earlier criticism. His account of fiction presses the argument that a great novel is to be appreciated as a kind of poem, or 'extended metaphor': he refers only negatively to the conception of the novel as a world of 'real' people governed by the probabilities of 'real' life. In his detailed criticism, on the other hand, it is clear that his genius is for conveying the accuracy of the novelist's insight into the way in which, from day to day, people make their own fates – it is a genius adapted best to the realistic psychological novel, and his long chapter on George Eliot in *The Great Tradition* is a masterpiece of criticism.

The claim Leavis made for the novels he especially admired was that they gave the most profound criticism available of the phase of civilisation that had produced them. This conception of what masterpieces do – the creative criticism of civilisation – saves literature from being either imprisoned in its own time, or lost in 'eternal verity', and it is realised with great impressiveness in his commentaries on *Little Dorrit* and *Women in Love*. But, as Leavis's primary criterion, it has the air of meeting all needs – while it does not, for instance, meet all the issues raised by great tragic art. (At no time in his career did Leavis discuss at length *Hamlet, King Lear* or *Macbeth*.)

The criticism of civilisation – of our civilisation – was at all events Leavis's own preoccupation. Article after article in the early numbers of *Scrutiny* recorded how technological and urban over-development, and the predominance of a new rootless 'mass' culture, had almost destroyed the old world of humane values, which had its roots in the 'organic' agricultural community. In a world of broken-up and deadening work, aimless leisure, and mass cultural disinheritance, education became supremely important, and in education the study of literature had special value because literature was the finest life of the civilisation which had gone – yet stayed alive and influential while the literature was read. From this position Leavis developed his whole educational programme, concentrating on the university syllabus in English literature: for which he had clearer and more productive intentions than anyone else. The broader social analysis was often attacked, especially by Marxist critics, as romanticising the past in the interests of a super-ficial understanding of industrial society. Leavis, in reply, argued that the Marxist view was superficial, since the communal posses-sion of industry, though desirable, could not in itself compensate for the whole lost world of 'organic' values. His criticism of the various political philosophies, as not having a sufficiently fine appreciation of the human values they were supposed to serve, may have been just; but the connection between the 'organic community' and the sophisticated literature he most admired was often extremely indirect. He wrote as though he wished he could have lived in such a community; and yet it is hard to imagine that he would have been satisfied there.

In his later writings Leavis rested value chiefly on a union of qualities – spontaneity, wonder, creativity, disinterestedness – which he found presented with most power in the directly combative art of Blake, Dickens and Lawrence. These late books (*Nor Shall My Sword*, *The Living Principle*, *Thought, Words and Creativity*) have been much criticised, and it is true that in them Leavis uses his key authors as occasions to develop his own criticism of 'technologico-Benthamite' civilisation. But though the books are for that reason unsatisfying as literary criticism, it is surely fair to consider also the larger argument they urge; and what then strikes the reader is the new degree of hopefulness in Leavis's thought. His main investment is no longer in a rural community that cannot be restored, or in an anti-industrialism ensuring nothing but defeat: he concentrates rather on attempting to define the qualities of spirit it is most vital to preserve, however conditions may alter. In his recent Dickens criticism the engineer–inventor Daniel Doyce (in *Little Dorrit*) has a positive halo one couldn't have imagined in Leavis's earlier work. This strain of qualified optimism gives, if anything, greater weight to his intense, disinterested, not apocalyptic and not defeatist anxiety for civilisation.

I have tried to give some outline of Leavis's thought, but I have not sufficiently conveyed the peculiar character, the 'feel' of his writing – the unremitting urgency of insistence, the perpetual mental strife, in one arena after another, *for* this, *against* that. The at once questing and warring force in all his prose makes one ask: what *is* the large impulsion that drives his criticism on? Probably there is no one short answer but, as at least bearing on the question, I mention two antithetical themes which run through his criticism like arteries.

When he is writing about individuals, the term he returns to, time and again, is 'ego'. The novelist on whom he writes best of all is, I think, George Eliot, and George Eliot has a marked severe inquisitive watchfulness as to the poses and indulgences of the selfish ego – its insidious invasion of real emotions, its unobserved action in the best natures, its contamination of conscience. This especially is what she is passionately interested in, and best on, and what in her Leavis is best on. And clearly he is so because that energy of introspective moral vigilance was something that he had himself independently. It is very marked for instance in his essay on *Othello*, where Othello's egotism is pinned down and indicted with an emphasis and searchingness that go beyond the Eliot essay that must have inspired him ('Shakespeare and the Stoicism of Seneca'). But however strong Leavis's case may be, it is hard to believe that any other critic would have located the tragic centre of the play in Othello's *egotism* to the extent that he does: he makes the play's presentation of jealousy seem narrower than it need; and also, by making it what we expect from Othello, he takes away the shock of the egotism in Othello's reaction to having killed his wife.

When he criticises George Eliot, it is precisely for giving in to her ego – in the self-dramatisation that mars her noble heroes and heroines. In his criticism of Milton, he is fundamentally criticising the grand style because he sees it as the style of a grand egotism (he insists that Milton's egotism is grand). In very many of Leavis's famous demotions and demolitions, the root fault found is failure to restrain an exceptionally powerful inborn egotism: such a failure is behind the self-enjoying 'afflatus' of Shelley's verse, behind the maddened contempt in Swift's satire. And as I indicated earlier, Leavis's whole theory of the close relation between quality of language and quality of feeling is based on an untiring alertness to the subtle ways in which the ego interferes with feelings and words.

The 'ego' is his serpent. And the corollary of this, in his writing on Blake and in his more recent criticism in general, is the special value – really a kind of holiness – given to the innocent, wondering condition of being 'ego-free'.

The other, complementary theme is indicated in the special charge the word 'civilisation' has for Leavis. The negative side to that concern shows in his despair about the twentieth century; the positive shows in the way that, with poet after poet, when he defines the quality that moves him most, it proves to be the fineness of a whole culture – 'Marvell's seriousness is the finer wisdom of a ripe civilisation.' It might suggest an uncharacteristic impracticality to say that in all his criticism Leavis is fundamentally in quest of an ideal society: but there is a quest, and I think a real impatience or even hunger in his keenness to seize hold of and convey the distinct qualities of different phases of culture. Henry James mattered for Leavis chiefly because of his 'constant profound pondering of the nature of civilised society and of the possibility of imagining a finer civilisation than any he knew', and that concern was Leavis's also. In the poetry of Ben Jonson he admired most the strain in which 'the English poet . . . enters into an ideal community, conceived of as something with which contemporary life and manners may and should have close relations.' And he said of Alexander Pope's vision of the conditions and values of Augustan society, 'his contemplation is religious in its seriousness'. What is both idiosyncratic and profound in Leavis's own best writing is the presence of a religious impulse which in another age might have been directed to God, but is here directed to civilisation: this being for him not just a secular matter, as his full discussion of Pope shows. (The more overt and general religious motive in the later books I find also more vague and more uneasy, the reiterative, coiling, self-quoting prose giving, through all the insistence, an odd effect of frustration.)

It is not surprising that such an abiding preoccupation with the damage done by the single ego should be complemented by a passion of concern for the large but delicate, collaborative, personal-and-impersonal creation that a civilisation is; the juxtaposition does not, of course, 'sum up' Leavis. As to 'ego', clearly he was a man who had himself a formidable energy of will and ego, and was troubled by these things and always at war with them (as he was always at war): all his writing has that tension, and shows I think also that his victory over ego was at best an equivocal one.

Both his life of perpetual antagonism, and his invoked sanctuary of 'civilisation', perhaps go back to his experience of real war. In the trenches and the hospital trains, through the interminable horrors, civilised life – having as true and profound a basis as possible – must have been something that he yearned for with a force and depth one could not exaggerate; and presumably this concern is tied especially to literature because what he did to escape, when he could, was to read. Reading had *been* civilisation for him.

This thought, so large in its scope and so generous in its appreci-ation of literature, was, as is generally known, produced in an immediate drama of critical and personal hostilities that often suggested a smaller intensity. The Leavises wrote always as though from a small armed citadel, without allies, under a permanent vicious blockade. To some extent, of course, this really was their situation – I imagine that in the early years it had very much been so – but there is no doubt that they also found it congenial, and that in later years at least they let matters arrange themselves so as to make their isolation more complete. At the end of their career, while their work had demonstrably had wide influence and recognition, they felt they had been betrayed by almost everyone who had worked closely with them. This was tragic, but a component of the tragedy was the ease with which they severed long-established ties – with people who, they must have known, admired them very greatly.

If the isolation was in part congenial, it was also productive; in the Retrospect to *Scrutiny* Leavis acknowledged that it had been easier, as a resented outsider, to *be* a critic; and it may also be that the sympathetic and generous side of his nature, disappointed and blocked in actual relations, was able to expand only with literature – and did expand there wonderfully, giving his criticism, which draws so much of its energy from exasperation, its paradoxical largeness. But hard-pressed urgency in fighting for a particular case often meant, also, that he did not try to tell the whole truth about an author, and often did not give the classically complete and well-judged criticism that he – and hardly anyone else – could have given. He did write such a criticism of George Eliot, but of Lawrence he did not. What especially thrived, in his willed and beleaguered isolation, was a generalised pessimism which closed his curiosity, and narrowed the truth of his more ambitious literary and social thought.

But to present matters only in such a sombre light would be unjust: it would endorse the widely current picture of him as a man morose with injury, when the main impression he made was of someone extremely hard-bitten, but also extremely alive and lively. So far as I have seen, his teaching sessions have been described as solemn occasions, which they were not. He would open his mail in the lecture hall, and comment. A quality that made a strong impression, and hasn't been recorded, was his mischievousness. Of the famous first lines of 'The World', by the Welsh poet Vaughan, that used to be so plangently quoted,

> I saw Eternity the other night
> Like a great ring of pure and endless light,

he would say: 'Well – the man who said that could say anything.'

Of Shakespeare's plays he would recommend especially *Measure for Measure*: 'What play can you say is greater?' – a puckish grin – '*King Lear?*' As he mounted his bike and accelerated, he remarked once: 'My wife thinks that Mrs Gaskell is a great novelist. But she isn't a great novelist – she's a *bore*!'

He closed his last official lecture in Cambridge with an attack on the view that the good and bad qualities of literature were some sort of moral absolute – a naivety sometimes attributed to him. To clinch the point, he quoted Santayana's observation on ethical absolutism, to the effect that saying something is good in itself or bad in itself is like saying that whisky isn't intoxicating to you or intoxicating to me but stands there dead drunk in the bottle. Then he made some difficulty in switching off the light at the lectern, muttered *sotto voce* '"Put out the light"', and left.

Note: Leavis at school

Since the available accounts of Leavis's education refer only to his attendance at the Perse School, it should be recorded that he had previously gone, for a period of a little over a year, to the Cambridge and County School. He started there in 1910, and was especially prominent in the debating society, in his second term opening a debate on the abolition of the death sentence (the school magazine notes 'the motion was proposed by F. R. Leavis in a very able manner. The speaker laid great stress on the finality of the death sentence and on its fallibility'). Under arrangements which were I understand fairly regular then, his excellent performance in the local examinations led to his transfer to the Perse.

The Cambridge and County School Magazine for the Michaelmas Term 1911 contains what is I believe his very first publication, a memoir called 'Little-boy-man' which had won the school's essay prize. It commemorates an elderly acquaintance or relative who had been a bookbinder, and who had a quietly philosophical sense of humour. In view of the popular representation of Leavis as a man by nature ungenerous and waspish, it is pleasant to note that the memoir is affectionate, moved and self-effacing. It runs:

Little-boy-man

He is gone, thank God! he is gone to that everlasting and unbroken rest for which he longed. At the bottom of one of those dismal specimens of stationery, which respectable folk think it only proper to circulate at the death of a near relative, ran the obvious and unnecessary legend, 'His end was peace.' Had it been, 'His end was welcome,' there would have been some point, for his last days were afflicted by one of the most painful diseases which nature can inflict upon man. It is scarcely eight short months ago that he was spending, in peace and happiness, the evening of a quiet life; it is scarcely eight short months since the terrible blow fell, and turned content to hopeless misery, and yet how much suffering was crammed into eight short months.

Yes, he is gone! And yet I see him now, seated, pipe in mouth, in the armchair at the corner of his hearth, peering at the evening newspaper through (or was it under? I never could tell) his glasses. 'And why that ridiculous title?' I hear the reader, justly incensed at these wanderings, ask.

A very small visitor once exclaimed, in a moment of inspiration, and with all the frankness of youth, 'Uncle, you're a little-boy-man!' It was indeed a happy remark, for the 'little-boy-man' could scarcely have exceeded five feet in height, and his ruddy face was as cheerful and as free from care as a child's. He stumped through life with a philosophic calm, disturbed by nothing, and wishing for nothing but to stump out of it in the same contented way.

He had been a bookbinder at one time in his life, and, having thus learnt to appreciate a good book, he was very well-read. Often he would come out with extremely quaint remarks. Being asked, by one intimate friend, how he did, he replied that he was all right in other respects, but was 'suffering from a paucity of bullion.' On another occasion, while conversing with a friend who took charge of his financial affairs, the latter remarked to him that some capital which he had invested would be returned in so many years. 'Ah!' he replied, 'It will be in time to build me a handsome mausoleum.' What made these remarks the quainter was the cheerful, philosophic way in which they were uttered, every syllable being pronounced distinctly, as if it were weighed carefully in the mind before being spoken, and the apparent absence of humorous intention.

Often have I seen him riding in from, or starting out for, the country on his tricycle, puffing at his beloved pipe, and pedalling in the deliberate manner with which he did everything. These expeditions were undertaken chiefly that he might follow his hobby of butterfly-hunting, in which he was very skilful. As a result of his labours, he had at home a magnificent collection, and knew most that was worth knowing about insects. In my younger days, when I felt less compunction in the taking of a bird's egg, or the catching of a butterfly, it was to him that I carried my treasures to be examined. Often have I taken to his house an especially gorgeous butterfly, confined in a glass jam-jar, in which some leaves had been thoughtfully placed, much, I now fear, to the discomfort of the unfortunate inmate. 'That, my boy,' he would say, and I still fancy I hear the deliberate verdict, 'Is one of the Nymphalidae, a Vanessa io, or, in vulgar parlance, a Peacock butterfly, a very common species.' When his net was not to be seen fastened to his tricycle, a fishing-rod would be in its place (for his temperament made him an excellent angler) or, in autumn, a stick for black-berrying.

Such he was, a dear old ruddy, round-faced man, and one of those few of whom nothing evil can be remembered.

And he is gone; though I can hardly believe it!

F. R. L.

18

No compromise

D. W. HARDING

Leavis as I remember him in 1925 was a sensitive and friendly man, easily approachable by an awkward undergraduate, vigorous but gentle, with a courtesy that went beyond manner because it was based on considerateness. The friendliness of the fortnightly supervisory sessions was not a matter of mutual interest between him and his pupils but outward-looking, a shared interest in a common task of which the importance could never be in doubt. My fellow student and I came away from supervision exhilarated, and equally sobered, by a glimpse of the high standards that were valid in reading literature and that he, with us, was aiming at. They were not the standards of specialist scholarship or range of knowledge, in which a tutor easily surpasses his pupils, but of perceiving and entering into the strength and delicacy, the subtleties and the simplicity of great writers in their handling of experience. Appreciation of the excellent in literature was the main thing, though there was the necessary converse of dismissing the pretentious, the falsely simple or sentimental, the bogusly intellectual. As I remember, what he thought bad was less closely examined than the good and the objections to it less cogently demonstrated, with the result that the weaker or more hurried students (and we were all hurrying through a vast syllabus) could easily pick up inadequately argued dismissals. To this day I have never read Browning with any attempt at discrimination since my stereotyped sixth-form admiration met the contrary force of Leavis's brief endorsement of Santayana's devastating essay. I was only the meeting-point of two external forces, as I was similarly about Shelley, until a chance circumstance obliged me to read him for myself.

I have heard it said that in later years, with larger groups in seminars, Leavis resorted to monologue and became repetitive and rigid – understandably in view of the burdens he was carrying. In the supervisions I knew, with just two students and their essays, he was flexible, notably willing to meet unforeseen questions and discuss, there and then, points on which he had no prepared position. About imagery in *Macbeth* I asked naively whether after all Johnson was so wrong in objecting to the meanness of 'peep through the blanket of the dark' – what was the value of such a metaphor just there? Leavis broke off from his prepared line of commentary and immediately began to think it out – the suggestion of the darkness as thick and smothering, 'thick night', the later 'light thickens', 'peeps' with horrified fear – I forget the details, but the moral was that simple questions were worth raising and would be met without any defence by status. The instructive contrast came when a lecturer at another college, having generously agreed to look over an essay by any of us who attended his course, came on my doubt whether his theory of tragedy explained our tolerating such painful episodes as the death of Desdemona. 'But you must not consider the *other* characters – you must think only of the Tragic *Hero*!' He had exceptionally thin wrists and he slapped his desk where I sat beside him, with such petulant emphasis that I thought the hand might snap off. Like any prudent boy I saw that I was up against authoritative doctrine and said no more.

In alternate weeks my partner and I took our essays to H. S. Bennett, the Director of English Studies at Emmanuel. At that time Leavis was not only a willing colleague of Bennett but on terms of close friendship with him and his wife; the breach with the Bennetts, occurring after Leavis's marriage, must have been crucial for his later unhappy relations with the English Faculty, not from any hostility on Bennett's part (he was lastingly regretful about the break) but from loss of the respect, or at the very least toleration, that any colleague of Bennett's would have been given. Though Bennett's own field was Chaucerian studies and Middle English his range of interest was broad and he was tolerant – friendly towards totally different enthusiasms (those of M. D. Forbes for instance) and unperturbed, if quietly amused, by iconoclasms that issued, as Leavis's did, from genuine and intelligent conviction. He was at the same time so well liked and respected by the more conventional and orthodox members of the Faculty that had Leavis maintained their early association it is hardly conceivable that he could have been so relentlessly discouraged and so nearly ostracised. I made no secret of remaining deeply grateful to Bennett and affectionately attached to him, and Leavis never seemed to hold that against me.

Although the relation between Leavis and the English Faculty was extraordinary, he would in any university have been an uncomfortable colleague for many people in English studies at that period. He was out of sympathy with the older dons, not then extinct, for whom literature was one of the elegances, a liturgical contribution to the sonorities of the combination room. Nor had he any affinity with the ordinary decent people for whom the study of literature is an academic occupation in the same way as geography or biochemistry is for others. For Leavis literature was a necessity or a moral urgency, as prayer may be for religious people; not only was his academic subject part of his identity – the geographer's too may be that – but the details of his activity within it, the perceptions, discriminations, appraisals, were meshed closely with his identity as a moral person, 'moral' in the sense of the whole range of his values. Least of all could he tolerate a would-be sophisticated lightness of touch about literary values; the donnish cult of P. G. Wodehouse, for instance, was for him not just a silliness but a real offence against the standards that its devotees professed in other literary contexts. Though the 'morality' with which he was concerned could never be detached from its literary embodiment, never paraphrased or codified, it meant that divergent judgements could never be dealt with lightly as differences of mere opinion or taste. Literary appraisals that he thought wrong, failures to make discriminations that he thought vital, obtuseness to essential qualities – on such points his disagreement was, in effect, a personal reproach.

This 'serious' view of literature was implicit also in the work of Forbes and Richards in the 1920s when they were major influences on Leavis, but Richards turned to the pursuit of a distinguished career and Forbes dropped out into quasi-creative alternatives or distractions. Leavis alone of the three (and they essentially were what made 'the Cambridge English School' different from other university departments of English) filled all through his life the role he indicated when, deploring my admiration of Scott-Fitzgerald, he spoke of his 'literary-critico-moralist reaction' to my estimate (2 February 1952). For him that role came first. Any status, prestige, official reward or appreciation had to be conferred on *that* role as he performed it or not at all. Most people accept the condition that occupational status will depend on their slightly modifying their approach or convictions to fit more comfortably into the majority pattern; intimidation by the picket line is only the jagged tip of a massive and blander infrastructure of pressures and inducements by which all the occupations keep their members more or less in line. Leavis bitterly and openly resented the Faculty's failure to give him senior status; he wanted it, but he wanted it for the role he had defined, without having the corners rubbed off for social comfort.

He refused to modify his personal response to a literary work – his insights and appraisals – by any deference to the standard evaluations, however smoothly worn, of academic literary criticism or to over-estimations of contemporary work, however fashionable. (Naturally neither I nor anyone else would agree with all his judgements, but our disagreement, to be valid, would have equally to do without the support of embalmed opinion or of current flock behaviour.) In either case he often had to go against a large, loosely associated body of the right people, whether literary journalists and their cultivated friends or academics engaged in English studies.

Pleasant and likeable as these people so often are, their networks have some drawbacks. With nothing like the formal control of writers' associations in totalitarian states they still work, gently and unthinkingly, towards establishing and maintaining a broad consensus, often with the greatest amiability. Evelyn Waugh's biographer records that *Brideshead Revisited* was first published in a small edition limited to presentation copies, an 'extravagance' to which Waugh's agent agreed 'because he knew that he and the publisher were on to a winner'. The reception of the work 'was so enthusiastic that one can almost use the word ecstatic with precision. It came mostly from friends, it is true, but these friends contained a considerable proportion of people with claims to high and inalienable critical standards, Henry Yorke, Graham Greene, Desmond MacCarthy, Osbert Sitwell and John Betjeman' (Christopher Sykes, *Evelyn Waugh: A Biography* (1975)). It may only be in people infected with the spirit of *Scrutiny* that this provokes a wry smile.

Leavis was insistently and indignantly aware of the personal aspects of what in public passes for an impartial critical judgement of contemporary work. The darker aspect of the amiable networks is their treatment of dissidents. When, in his teaching and in *Scrutiny*, he challenged current standards the academics and the conventional critics naturally fought back and naturally not by frontal counter-attack. It is difficult now to convey the quality of the hostility to *Scrutiny*; it is evidently not accessible historically to Francis Mulhern, whose *Moment of 'Scrutiny'* relies on contemporary published comment. The best that anyone associated with *Scrutiny* could look for among ordinary educated people in the 1930s was good-natured amusement at something *outré*, well-meant and rather ridiculous, but among the informed of the literary and academic world there was more formidable though guarded hostility. Tillyard was reported as saying privately that *Scrutiny* was 'dangerous'; but generally a policy of dignified inattention was preferred, with behind-the-scenes opposition to Leavis's advance in status.

In the early days, soon after Leavis's marriage, it was fatally easy for the right people to under-estimate him: what, twenty years later, could be seen as the achievement of *Scrutiny* was hardly more than a programme, boldly sketched out but more notable for its attack on things as they were than for what it had actually done. Support and admiration for Leavis had to be based on his few pieces of writing and sympathy with his opposition to the dull and second-rate entrenched in positions of influence. The negative aspect, the angry opposition to whatever is currently accepted as authoritative, was (and is) so familiar in short-lived journals and 'movements' that the confidence of the entrenched and embedded was understandable, given their impercipience of his quality. When, ill judging, the Leavises called their house 'The Criticastery', he was surprised at the hostility of the ridicule it provoked; he had supposed that the hint of irony and self-depreciation implied by the parallel with 'poetaster' would offset what 'Cambridge' saw simply as an arrogant gesture of setting up an alternative centre of critical judgement.

His insistence on staying in Cambridge and fighting the opposition, which he used to justify as a refusal to give up the quality of students and the methods of teaching that allowed him to do his best work, probably sprang from a courageously combative trait deeply engrained in him. He spoke admiringly of his father's reaction when, as a known 'pro-Boer', he was jeered at as 'Kruger' from a doorway group – he turned back and walked up to them, cowing them with: 'Did you want to speak to me?' It was in this spirit of open challenge that Leavis applied to the Home Secretary for permission to import *Ulysses* for teaching-purposes, instead of buying it under the counter as other dons did from reputable Cambridge book-sellers. In open controversy he was a formidable opponent, well able to control his anger and suspicion and making effective use of ironic courtesy. But the hidden influence of hostile cliques and coteries disturbed and preoccupied him. I have heard that he exclaimed: 'They say I have persecution delusions – I *have been* persecuted!' The two things are not mutually exclusive. It is of course quite unlikely that people conspired against him. There was no more need for that than there is for wolves to conspire before snarling and snapping at a sick member of the pack; an awareness of group sanction is enough. Although he was notably sane I thought from one or two letters I saw that he had a thin paranoid streak – as other sane people may have a depressive streak – which most of the time, but not in extremity, he could keep well under the control of his high intelligence and alert social wariness. Queenie Leavis's influence was not on the side of control, though she showed no sign of his special difficulty. Like any number of us she was avid for kudos and jealous when it was given to people less deserving than herself, but these ordinary characteristics were in her extraordinarily strong, producing an accumulated charge of hostility for which she was driven to find targets. With her at his elbow Leavis did well to keep his sense of persecution as nearly at arm's length as he did. The course of his life, as everyone knows, was littered with disciples who betrayed him and allies who let him down, sometimes very sincere well-wishers to whom the angry rejection brought pain and lasting distress. As a fringe member of his group, not working in English studies and not living in Cambridge, I found it hard to keep track of the changes that made enemies out of former friends (and sometimes reinstated them). I escaped any open breach; our active relations lapsed, but when there was occasion we were able to correspond in a friendly way to the end of his active life.

Leavis made no attempt to separate literary work, creative or critical, from the author's personality; not for him the polite fiction that feeble or offensive or meretricious writing might be the work of a pleasant chap whose feelings should if possible not be hurt. One of my students at L.S.E. in the 1930s, intelligent but in the common swim of the politically urgent and culturally abreast, came to me in genuine distress and quite earnestly begged me to withdraw from *Scrutiny*, showing me in the latest issue a scathing attack on someone or other, presumably the acquaintance of someone in her set: how *could* I associate myself with such things? I had no inclination to defend the violence of the particular attack and I knew it was not isolated, but neither had I any wish to leave such 'victims' in complacent self-satisfaction and protectively cushioned by their like. It was when feeble or objectionable work was widely over-valued that he made his attacks, desperately fierce with anxiety as he saw the basis of sound judgement being undermined. He could find no way – perhaps there is no way – of combating a man's inflated reputation without attacking the man and his work. Whatever personal idiosyncrasies exacerbated his sense of being surrounded by hostility he was essentially right in the conviction that standards of excellence were under continuous threat from the entrenchments of mediocrity.

Of course the fairly able, the medium good or unevenly good, are a vitally important part of any society and its culture. The most difficult part of their role is to recognise and give effective support to excellence beyond their reach while still maintaining their own self-respect. Their greatest temptation is to acquiesce in the pattern of mutual support – the timidities of criticism, the polite mendacities, the over-enthusiasm for slight achievement – by which they

assure each other of their excellence. Understandable and good-
natured as the process is, it blurs differences and erodes standards.
From time to time scathing voices denounce the pretentious or self-
complacent mediocre. Pope, Matthew Arnold, Leavis, each in his
own way fought against the denial of standards which left the
current mediocrities of the period comfortable in their over-
estimation. Each very soon needs his ephemeral targets footnoted
for identification, but though the names change the same figures re-
appear, the immortal dullards, the unabashed meretricious, in every
generation; they enjoy the big sales, the positions of influence, the
respect and acclaim. Leavis in his late years spoke of failure, seeing
the enemy still entrenched in its strong positions.

George Crabbe stated the recurrent problem:

> Our Pope, they say, once entertained the whim,
> Who feared not God should be afraid of him;
> But say they fear'd him, was it further said,
> That he reform'd the hearts he made afraid?
> Did Chartres mend? Ward, Waters, and a score
> Of flagrant felons, with his floggings sore?
> Was Cibber silenced?

Can he ever be silenced? We know what committees in the world
of arts and letters he serves on now. But Leavis never gave up. In
a letter of 1968 he spoke scornfully of the British teaching of
American literature that allowed *The Lost Generation* to be prescribed as a paper in an English course and added that British
academics who had spent a year in America must be intimidated
or suppressed if they couldn't be cleansed and educated. Who
feared not God . . .

Assailing the establishment and the current modes is nothing in
itself – there are always plenty of ephemeral satirists to do that.
It is the accompanying positive achievement of men like Leavis,
the demonstration of higher standards achieved, that makes a few
stand out as lasting landmarks. Leavis's critical writing is an enduring
store of reminders and demonstrations of a 'serious' approach to a
wide range of literature, 'serious' in the sense that he aimed constantly at exposing his whole personality and moral structure to
the work, and to the whole work in the complexity and subtlety

that its use of the English language brought about. That ideal, a meeting of the whole personality with the whole work, is beyond attainment of course, but Leavis came infinitely closer to it than the common run of literary journalists and academic literary critics. It is because his criticism was the morally serious work of a sensitive and educated person and a finely skilled reader of English that it remains worth returning to, whether for illumination or for challenge and fertile disagreement.

If he had been content simply to be a critic while he earned his living by university teaching his life would have been easier. At least as important in his eyes was his role as an educator in a wider sense. Nearly at the end of his life, in *The Living Principle*, he quotes as epigraphs Wittgenstein's exclamation 'Give up literary criticism!', Lawrence on the need to fight tooth and nail to defend the new shoots of life from being crushed out, and his own remark at York that 'nothing today is more important than to keep alive the idea of the university-function – the essential university-function and what goes with it: the idea of an educated public'. In the early days it was this aim that *Scrutiny* was meant to serve; and in those early days he and Queenie used to express velleities of founding something like Meiklejohn's Experimental College. After a holiday on the Norfolk coast she came back with fantasies, joking but wishful, of setting it up in a disused hotel at Weybourne; in those days she had more scorn and ambitious high spirits than bitterness. There were more serious plans for organised missionary endeavour through disciples among teachers of English in public schools and grammar schools. Though the idea of deliberate organisation quietly faded it was replaced by a much more realistic form of gradual influence, initially stemming from the collaboration with Denys Thompson, who had actual experience of teaching English for the school ages. It was in schools and in colleges for the training of teachers that Leavis's outlook on literature in its context of contemporary life had most direct, observable effect. Inevitably, however, influence of this kind is fairly soon absorbed, usually with modifications that make it progressively less like its source. How much his influence on teachers has contributed to the survival of his educated public is a matter for cautious, though not despondent, estimate.

Scrutiny was central to his enterprise of education. Its adverse comments on the current literary and cultural scene were one side of the effort to vindicate standards higher than those prevailing; Leavis was also hopefully alert to contemporary work that might, if with reservations, be called in aid, a feature of *Scrutiny* sometimes under-rated. But its main value for an educated public has been its positive contributions to English literary criticism, the part of Leavis's achievement that will survive longest. The achievement lay not only in his own writing but in the encouragement and guidance he gave to younger writers. He was always on the watch for con-tributors – John Speirs for instance – who would work in their own field, far apart from his, but would aim at the same standards of serious independence as his, well aware of established views but not blinkered by them. It was for this encouragement that I and many other contributors were immensely indebted to him.

We could write on anything in literature and its cultural context that we felt personally concerned with. The *Scrutiny* 'programme', if there was such a thing, was remarkably capacious, unlike that of any other journal of the time. On the one hand it was explicitly contemporary in its comments on education, advertising, literary journalism and so on. On the other hand the topics it handled might come from any part of English literature, from Langland onwards, anything that might be covered by a very wide university syllabus of English studies in their cultural setting; and in this respect it presupposed 'academic' interests in its readers. But it was not for academics speaking to each other about their specialisms; it still addressed a general, as well as an educated, public. Whatever the topic the contemporary aim was still pursued, though tacitly. The writer came to it from his experience in the present-day world, however venerated the work and however encrusted with accretions of criticism. Again, however, this contemporary quality was not expressed within the readymade frameworks, political, religious, philosophical, that offered themselves at the time. Those ways of thinking were certainly not excluded but they were not encouraged to take the place of the practised reader's grasp of a literary work in its minute particulars. Still less did the programme accept the constraints, rigid at any one moment though quickly superseded, of the intellectual fashions being worn at high tables and cultivated parties. The fact that the literary quality of a work remained Leavis's central concern baffled some of his otherwise sympathetic critics who wanted to tease out the abstract moral system that would validate the judgement of 'literary quality'. Leavis addressed (and by doing so hoped to create) a public of readers who, first, were skilled in the use of the language that had formed and been formed by English literature and, second, were 'moral' people bringing the values of any author into relation with the conditions of the society in which they were now living.

He looked for work that was serious in the sense that the contributor was writing because he personally needed to write – to solve a problem, clarify and define shades of feeling, justify an unconventional opinion – not because it was part of his role as an academic authority, nor a step in his career, nor something saleable in an existing market. The sort of thing he wanted might come to hand quite unpredictably. With the nucleus of reliable contributors dispersed by war, the issue for March 1941 was saved by an essay on Racine by R. C. Knight, whom Leavis could identify to me only as 'a Birmingham lecturer apparently', and by the unexpected reappearance of Traversi (waiting for call-up) with an essay on *Henry V*. He put out feelers and gave encouragement, but most essays sprang from a contributor's spontaneous wish to explore an interest of his own. Leavis did suggest that I should write on I. A. Richards, at a time when he was disappointed in hopes for Richards' personal support and knew that my admiration of Richards' early work was tempered by a sense of its limitations, but that was the nearest I came to producing an essay to order. Of course he suggested books for this or that reviewer; and he was too much inclined, for my liking, to indicate at the same time what he thought of the book himself; that tended to have a contrasuggestive effect on me and slightly complicated reviewing, but I seldom really disagreed with him.

Although in the 1930s Lionel Knights and Denys Thompson took a large and effective share in the editorial work the main burden of responsibility was inevitably Leavis's. Queenie typed his letters when a carbon was needed (and typed his reviews and essays) but most of his letters were hand-written, including long and careful letters to contributors and possible contributors and would-be contributors. If one had known only of the scathing controversialist, the half-truth, it would have been a surprise to find how anxious he was to be tactful and unwounding when he discouraged unwanted contributors. He was gentle towards people who were not as incisive or penetrating as he wanted but who yet did good work without inflating its importance. When I had suggested that we might ask Olaf Stapledon to review for us, Leavis replied that he fell into the difficult class of those he positively wanted to attach but who hadn't enough edge to appear often in *Scrutiny*, a 'difficult' class because they were modest and unpushing and so made him more uncomfortable about them. Those who were pushing and not modest he could of course deal with and talk about very differently. Every now and then the minor bothers that crop up in the running of any journal created further distracting demands. A reviewer made a slip that allowed the authors of a publication to protest indignantly, and I find that apart from Leavis's letters to the authors, to the reviewer (who was abroad) and to the other editors, he had sent me nine letters and a telegram before the episode was concluded.

There was recurrent harassment from money difficulties of a kind scarcely conceivable to the subsidised or grant-aided reviews of later days. In March 1941 he was writing that it looked as if we were likely to be down by at least £9 on each number, and this could hardly go on for long. He added that the British Council ought to subsidise us instead of asking us to send copies abroad at half price – he 'pointedly' made it *gratis* and intimated that, seeing our position, he thought the request odd. The only financial support I heard of was £80 from one private benefactor, £50 from another, and at last, in 1947, a grant of $2400 from the Rockefeller Foundation to be spread over three years – though by that time sales had increased and there was no difficulty about paying the printer and the distributor.

The greatest difficulty remained what it had always been, of finding contributions of the kind and quality he wanted. In the early 1940s the preoccupation of former contributors with war work (often in distant parts of the world) increased that difficulty. The resultant need to write for almost every number himself, though it produced much of his valuable work, was met only by intense effort in face of the slowness of his writing. Inarticulacy (as well as insomnia and indigestion) had been a symptom of his post-1919 condition, and though after a time he came to speak fluently and emphatically I imagine that by then he was often relying on what he had hammered out previously and privately. After his marginal notes and exclamations his thinking apparently went on through the process of writing, with the consequent breaks and interpolated qualifications as he disentangled the main line of argument without the over-simplifications that do violence to the reality of thinking. In March 1939, worrying about the June issue, he said he knew from experience that he could probably squeeze an article out of himself, though unwillingly, if he had to (on this occasion it was not necessary). 'Q' and Mellers, he added, dashed off essays while he was writing a paragraph – but he concluded that he had character anyway, else he couldn't stand up against it. In spite of his sometimes desperate need for material he was considerate and endlessly patient with contributors who had difficulty in writing or too little time free from other work. It was a remarkable achievement to produce his own fine criticism while he coped with *Scrutiny*. The whole formidably difficult undertaking was, in spite of some failures, carried through with a degree of success that his early detractors could never in their most anxious moments have anticipated.

His physical constitution, in spite of the post-war stress disorders, was immensely strong or he could certainly not have sustained such a heavy programme of work together with his domestic anxieties, especially during Queenie's courageous endurance of treatment, eventually successful, of breast cancer. He had always kept himself fit by physical activity, swimming, skating when there was a chance, and, almost to the end of his life, running. It was a part of his identity in which he took some pride (liking to remark, for instance, that being able to swim 50 yards under water was a help in reading Swinburne aloud), but he never allowed it to imply a reproach to the non-athletic like me. He was wonderingly tolerant of the inert relaxation I found in reading detective stories. No cheap literature was any relief or distraction to him; when he was making journeys to Norwich where Queenie was having treatment for radiation burns, he told me the only thing he could find to absorb him in the train was reading and re-pondering the Shakespeare sonnets. I think that as the earlier difficulty in talking receded he did find relaxation of a sort in expounding his views in informal conversation (with repetitive allusions to his enemies); there used to be a rapid jogging of his crossed leg while he listened to someone else with an effort of patience until an opening came for his emphatic intervention. But there was no talking for display. The aim was never to score off you or win a conversational point, but always, whether forcefully or persuasively, to convince.

Recollections of a distant past, like these of mine, include distortions, misinterpretations and factual errors; anyone who believes otherwise about his reminiscences is being beguiled by his good intentions. What is exempt from these hazards of recall is the residue at the end of a lifetime, the feelings left. For me they are gratitude – that above all – with deep respect and, in an uncertain way, regret. I am left half wishing he had been different enough not to have had to endure, and to cause, so much unhappiness; but half convinced that a different person could not have done the particular work he had to do in face of rampant cultural inflation and the debasement of literary currency by influential people and institutions.

Contributors

MICHAEL BLACK University Publisher, Cambridge University Press; wrote two articles on F. R. Leavis in *New Universities Quarterly*; author of *The Literature of Fidelity* and *Poetic Drama as Mirror of the Will*.

M. C. BRADBROOK Former Mistress of Girton College and Professor Emerita of English Literature, Cambridge; author of *Artist and Society in Elizabethan England, Women and Literature, 1779–1882* and *Dramatic Forms in the Age of Shakespeare*, etc.

NORA CROOK who is Jamaican, read English at Newnham College, taught in a Cambridge primary school and now lectures at the Cambridgeshire College of Arts and Technology.

BORIS FORD Formerly Education Secretary at the Cambridge University Press, Professor of Education at Sheffield and Sussex Universities; Emeritus Professor of Education, Bristol University; editor of the *Pelican Guide to English Literature* and *New Universities Quarterly*.

GWENDOLEN FREEMAN read English at Girton College; contributor to *The Guardian, Spectator, Times Literary Supplement* and other journals; author of *The Houses Behind, Children Never Tell* and *When You Are Old*.

D. W. HARDING A former editor of *Scrutiny* and (with Gordon Bottomley) of *The Collected Works of Isaac Rosenberg* (1937); Emeritus Professor of Psychology, London University; author of *The Impulse to Dominate, Social Psychology and Individual Values, Experience into Words* and *Words into Rhythm*.

JOHN HARVEY Director of English Studies at Emmanuel College, Cambridge; an editor of *The Cambridge Quarterly*; author of *The Plate Shop*. His novel, *Coup d'État*, comes out early next year.

DAVID HOLBROOK Director of English Studies at Downing College; author of *English for Maturity* and *English for the Rejected*; *Flesh Wounds* and *A Play of Passion*; *Selected Poems*; studies of Sylvia Plath, Dylan Thomas and Mahler; and of a number of books on the psychology of culture and literary criticism.

L. C. KNIGHTS Former Winterstoke Professor of English Literature at Bristol University and Emeritus King Edward VII Professor of English Literature at Cambridge; author of *English Literature and Society in the Age of Jonson*, *Explorations* (three series), *'Hamlet' and other Shakespearean Essays* and *Selected Essays in Criticism*.

SEBASTIAN MOORE Monk of Downside Abbey, Lecturer in Theology and Campus Chaplain at Marquette University of Wisconsin; former editor of *Downside Review*; author of *God is a New Language, No Exit, The Fire and the Rose are One, The Inner Loneliness* and other books.

RAYMOND O'MALLEY From 1959 University Lecturer in Education, Cambridge; from 1972 Director of English Studies at Selwyn College, retired; Fellow of Selwyn and Moderator of Cambridge O. L. Plain Texts Examination.

IAN PARSONS Joint Chairman of Chatto, Bodley Head and Jonathan Cape and a former President of the Publishers' Association; editor of *Men Who March Away* and other books.

MARY PITTER Began a career in architecture in 1945 and switched to teaching art and pottery in a secondary modern school in Staffordshire; taught at Moor Park preparatory school for boys, 1970–6.

MICHAEL TANNER Lecturer in Philosophy at Cambridge.

DENYS THOMPSON Teacher and then headmaster for thirty years; edited *The Use of English* (1939–69); author of *Culture and Environment* (with F. R. Leavis), studies of the press and advertising, and *The Uses of Poetry*; editor of *Change and Tradition in Rural England*.

FRANK WHITEHEAD Reader in English and Education, University of Sheffield, 1972–81; previously taught in grammar schools, Lecturer in English at London University Institute of

Education, and editor of *The Use of English*; author of *The Disappearing Dais.*

RAYMOND WILLIAMS   Professor of Drama at Cambridge; author of *Border Country, The Volunteers, Communications, The Long Revolution, Modern Tragedy, Cobbett* and other books.

Index

Index